Mahima

A Memoir

VIERA MASIH

iUniverse, Inc.
Bloomington

Mahima
A Memoir

iUniverse books may be ordered through booksellers or by contacting:

iUniverse
1663 Liberty Drive
Bloomington, IN 47403
www.iuniverse.com
1-800-Authors (1-800-288-4677)

ISBN: 978-1-4502-6949-0 (pbk)
ISBN: 978-1-4502-6950-6 (cloth)
ISBN: 978-1-4502-6951-3 (ebk)

Library of Congress Control Number: 2010916051

Printed in the United States of America

iUniverse rev. date: 11/23/2010

For
Joshua, my son
Rachel, my daughter
The blessings in my life

Contents

Acknowledgment

Many thanks to the Team at iUniverse for their interest in this manuscript and their meticulous care in the preparation of this book. The quality of the volume is due in no small part to their trademark attention to detail.

I would like to extent my sincere thanks to my friend Hemchand Gossai not only for his careful reading of the entire manuscript twice and his editorial advice, but in particular for his words of inspiration and motivation and his ongoing encouragement.

I am also grateful to my nephew Ashish Masih a graduate student at Utah State University who was singularly responsible for retrieving a number of lost files, and without whose commitment and advanced computer skills, this manuscript would have taken considerably longer to complete.

Finally, my deepest thanks and appreciation are for my children Joshua and Rachel who indeed are my joy and gifts of wonder in my life. They have supported me in every way even as they have continued shaping their own journeys. It is my hope that the rhythm of life as they have learned in their growing up years continues to shape and foster the quality of their lives in the future. And then there is my ever faithful companion Sammie, my sweet and loving dog who sat at, and often on my feet as I wrote.

I am eternally grateful.

A Note

This book is the true story of a girl named Mahima. Mahima's long journey was bracketed by her innocent childhood, romance of her youth and a sentimental yet tragic road during the adult phase of her life. Every crossroad of the journey of her life and the paths between them was shaped by many unforgettable and indelible moments. At times those paths elevated her to the summit of the highest mountain and at other times they brought her to the depth of the deepest valley. Sometimes the surroundings of her journey were like beautiful blooming and fragrant gardens and at other times fallen dry leaves caused by a storm and crushed under foot. At times she saw the glorious days of the bright and shimmering sunlight, and at other times she traveled through torrential storms. She journeyed through those paths, enjoyed them, faced them, shaped by them courageously or at times even surrendered to compromise. Such was the definition of her journey.

Prologue

This is my first book. From my early childhood I have had a passion for writing and painting. Painting the pictures of the divinely created gifts of nature, the beautiful, colorful glory of the birds and flowers, and then penning and transforming the paintings into the words and recording them in a little notebook, practical or abstract gave me an internal contentment.

Years ago, when I came to the United States to continue my formal education, I wrote long letters to my family members. Having a big family who wrote regularly and diligently, I felt fortunate to read and write constantly back and forth. My letters were written in Hindi—my native language, a beautiful and lyrical language. The world of technology took a steep turn for me and before long the letter writing gave way to phone conversations. This made it an easy and exciting way to communicate with all my family. The busyness with my studies, work and family also contributed much to this transition. I found it more gratifying to speak with them on the phone for two minutes instead of spending ten minutes in writing.

However seven years ago, that writer within me re-awakened. I also found a fear and challenge within me. I feared that if I didn't write in Hindi, I may lose the ability to communicate in my native tongue and also lose my fluency in Hindi. With that fear within me, I picked up my pen again and started writing in a note book, a little at a time, an episode here and an episode there. During that time of writing I found within me, a deep impulse to write a story, a book length story—in Hindi. How? I did not know at that time. Without lingering on the idea and with no further delays, I started connecting those little pieces in some kind of chronological style. Why was I doing it? I had no self-evident answer. I am not a writer by profession. But I have a story to tell and in my heart I knew that it must be told. And thus it was, in a period spanning two years, I crafted two hundred pages. I read those pages, and read them again and then again, until they became part of me. From that moment, I got a perdurable encouragement, not from a third party, but from within myself; an encouragement to the extent that I began translating my Hindi manuscript into English. I now had full confidence in myself. In the beginning phase of the translation, my confidence was fragile and often I was on the edge of losing hope. The lingering question in my head was, "Will I ever be able to finish my mission?" But I did not quit. The English translation of the book *Mahima* is not literally verbatim from the Hindi, but a very close rendering of my original work on *Mahima* in Hindi.

While writing this book, my emotions overpowered me on numerous occasions. I wept often with a recollection of pain and angst, but I laughed often with joy, writing about certain funny episodes. I also learned to wade through my emotions by pausing and then continue on writing. Most of my writing was done at day's end, after I came home from my full time job, in the calmness of the evenings, with my faithful companion, my dog Sammie resting on my feet under my computer desk. I also wrote in the early hours of the mornings with the singing of the birds and the coolness of the fresh sun rays peeping through the windows of my home office. At times, I was tired and fatigued and perhaps even bored while writing. In those moments, I paused thinking that if I am writing during my boredom, my readers may also get bored. So I took long pauses walking or swimming.

Whenever I read a novel, English or Hindi, I take a quick glance through the pages to find out if the language used by the author was easy to understand or not. I like to sense the touch of the author by feeling him or her close to me as if he or she is speaking with me in person. Keeping that in mind, I tried my best to narrate this story in simple comprehensible language reflecting the nature of the journey as well.

It is my hope that this book will be read in my ancestral home, India and my adopted home, the U.S; that is my heart felt desire. Perhaps those who read it may find courage and resonate with my story, and perhaps in a meaningful way my story will become their story, that I would see as nothing but a beautiful gift from our God generating and defining the path of love. I would be delighted to see the gift of our lives be filled with joy, happiness and true love, so all of us could see this world as a blooming garden spreading its fragrance in all the surroundings. Such beauty is not to be taken for granted or destroyed.

Love is a sacrifice. Why do we human beings not understand the power of love? In the Indian society we hear so many young girls and boys who accept their parent's selections of their future mates. Often those young people in love gave the sacrifice of their true love. Why did they do it? Why did they suffer from the brutal deep pain of it? Did they do it to preserve the traditional values dictated by their elders and culture or to sustain the parents' social status or were they forced to do it? These questions do not have universal answers. But we may answer these questions by asking a question. "Why can't we, the parents of our children, who have earned the right to be called mothers and fathers, for the happiness of our children, keep their love alive and respect their decisions, and for the sake of humanity sacrifice some of our human traditions, and the inherent brokenness hidden in them?"

Recently in a village of North India, a young girl and a young boy were murdered, because of who they were in their families, and their religion. They married against their parents' wishes, and the murderers were not the strangers, but were family members. One Hindu young boy was brutally beaten and thrown between the train tracks where the poor innocent young soul was crushed under the oncoming train. His sin—he loved a girl born within a different religion than his and he wrote her a love letter expressing his feelings to her.

My heart bleeds when I hear such stories. Not too long ago, a father killed his beautiful nineteen year old daughter stabbing her to death. Her sin—she married the man she loved who belonged to some other caste of the Hindu religion (perhaps—a low caste in the sight of the father). Not only in India, in the United States too—a father burnt his pregnant daughter, son-in-law and their three year old son—alive. The sin—his daughter married her husband against the father's wishes and the husband was born in a low caste family in the eyes of the father. These are some of the stories—the stories of the extreme brutality, stories of brokenness and hate; stories generated from human conventions to divide rather than unite; to construct barriers rather than demolish walls. Many of them must be challenged and stopped.

Mahima, the main character of this book and my childhood friend is also a victim of those cultural conventions and brutalities. She grew up with me, went to school and college with me and shared her life story with me.

Chapter 1
Early Childhood

$\mathcal{M}$ahima was born in a big family; a family of six sisters and one brother. She was the youngest; apple of her Pappa's eyes and Mamma's beloved. Perhaps, after giving birth to Mahima, her Pappa and Mamma lost the hope of another son and they gave up upon the idea of having more babies.

A long long time ago, her Mamma founded a small school. The school was located inside the military compound of the town. There were only a few students to begin with. By the time Mahima was ready to start her first grade, it was already a high school for girls only, one of the best in the city. She was barely five years old when she took her first step in her Mamma's school. She was excited to put on her new uniform which was tailored by her oldest sister, and the black buckled shoes with a pair of white high socks to her knees. Her hair was tied in two pig tails with two red ribbons, and such was the dress code. Her *takhti* (the wooden writing slab) was brand new and nicely polished with the clay. She had to carry her own black ink bottle and a pen made of a thick straw. All those new school supplies were enough to give her the thrill of a little school girl. She loved writing on the wooden *takhti* with her ink pen, erasing it and polishing it over and over again. She enjoyed sitting with the other girls of her age on a rugged rug spread in the classroom.

Mahima's older sisters also studied in the middle and high school wings of the same building. At the recess bell, they along with their friends came to pick her up from her classroom. Beautiful little Mahima was just like a toy for those friends of her older sisters. They loved to pick her up in their laps. They pinched her chubby cheeks, fed her with their own hands, played with her and spoiled her. She enjoyed being the focus of attention of those grown up girls. She hopped back to her classroom after the recess was over. She was a happy little girl, free as a bird, wrote on her *takhti*, fed by the older girls and adored by her teachers. At the closing bell, she ran to her Mamma's office, who was the head-mistress of the primary section, and both rode a rickshaw together after school to go home. After reaching home she threw her school bag somewhere, anywhere in the house and without changing her uniform or taking her shoes off, she ran to her favorite old Nani's house with her *takhti* in her hand. So was her daily routine. Nani was a lovely elderly lady, a neighbor, who lived just a few houses down from her house, and was happy to be Mahima's baby sitter in the times of need.

"Nani, Nani! Look what I wrote on my *takhti*."

"Let me see my *beta* (honey), what have you written on your *takhti* today." She jumped into her Nani's lap and Nani took no time wrapping her in her arms to see and admire what she had written on her *takhti*.

In the first and second grades Mahima was ranked number two in her class, which meant second position. When she was in her third grade her math teacher was her own Mamma, who always encouraged her to be number one. She was very frightened of her Mamma, when in her class and particularly so of her on the day of a quiz or an exam. One episode that took place in her third grade left an indelible mark on her. She was standing in a queue of girls, waiting for her class work to be graded by her Math teacher, her Mamma. Finally, it was her turn. She placed her assignment paper in front of her Mamma. Mamma looked at her just like she would look at any other student in her class and then looked at her class assignment. She picked up her red ink-pen to go through the math problems and check them. All of a sudden, she lifted her eyes from the paper and turned towards Mahima. For a moment her eyes were glued to Mahima's face and Mahima's heart was in Mahima's throat—choking her. What is to come? A million questions floated in her little brain in that moment.

"SLAP!" On her cheek."

"OUCHH!"

Mahima made a mistake. Instead of adding she subtracted. And that was a big mistake on her part; carelessness in reading the directions, sloppiness, said her mother.

Would Mahima make the same mistake again? Never! That was one and only one episode-a harsh, but a lesson worth learning. The school day ended and just like any other day, she and her Mamma rode their regular rickshaw home from school. Mamma's tightly wrapped arms around her all the way home sitting in that rickshaw conveyed that the perdurable love for her daughter cannot be forgotten. They arrived home. Mamma did not let Mahima go away from her sight. How much remorse her Mamma felt after slapping her little daughter, could not be forgotten either. Also, the deep pain within Mamma's heart was so transparent on her glorious face—unforgettable winsomeness. After that day Mahima could never dare to be sloppy any more. She repeatedly checked her school work and was extra-extra careful to read and follow the directions.

Mahima's Pappa was a homeopathic doctor. He also ran a typing and shorthand coaching institute along with his practice. His earnings added to Mamma's were enough to feed the family of nine and take care of their basic needs. All lived in a small three room house, seven children, Mamma and Pappa. Mamma cooked the meals for the whole platoon, and that was nothing but incredible. She was indefatigable. Every single morning, she was the first one to get up and began the day's routine. She cooked breakfast and fed everyone. She packed lunches for all. She worked hard all day long, came home tired from her teaching job, unwrapped her sari, threw it on the bed, changed into a comfortable gown and went straight to the kitchen. The kitchen was not well equipped with the modern gas or electric range, dishwater and running water. She burnt the coal to cook. The first thing on the burning coal before cooking dinner was to boil a kettle filled with water to prepare the evening tea. The tea was served with some homemade snacks prepared by her.

Mahima's older sisters helped Mamma with cleaning, washing the dishes, laundry and other household chores. Pappa's duties were to stop by at the market place every evening to pick up the daily supply of vegetables and meat on the way home from his clinic. Bhaiya (her brother) was also responsible for the outside house chores, but mostly he was occupied with playing *gulli-dandaa* (an authentic Indian game) and flying his homemade kite with the help of Mahima, who held the spool. One of the six sisters was assigned to light four lanterns and hang them in the four corners of the house before dusk. The house was not equipped with the electricity. There was no electric lines close by to get the supply of the electric power. After dinner, those lanterns were moved to the bedside tables and were used as the table lamps to read and study.

The sleeping arrangements of the household were flexible and adjustable depending upon the season and the weather conditions. In the months of winter, two sisters shared one bed. There were three beds for six sisters. Bhaiya was the lucky one to own his own cot, the stinky little cot with his dirty stinky socks hidden under the sheets. None of the sisters dared to even go close to his cot. He was given a tiny bedside table to keep his own lantern—just for him.

The routine before bedtime in the winter season was to snuggle in one of those beds under the warm blankets and eat peanuts. Bhaiya was only allowed, if he washed his feet with soap and water. There was no central heat in the house. The remaining burning coals from the cooking grill used for preparing the supper were good enough to keep the rooms warm for a couple of hours or at least one room out of the three. The older sisters studied in their beds, sitting up with their legs covered under the blankets and the upper part of the body including the heads covered in a shawl. They shared a lantern placed in between the two cots. The younger ones including Mahima slept under the blankets using the body heat of the other sister. They covered their bodies all the way to the top of their heads to protect them from the bright light dispersing from the lanterns and also to give warmth to their cold freezing noses. Bhaiya was the most studious one. He sat on his cot with his entire body wrapped in a warm wool blanket. The only visible part of his body was the pair of his two eyes, which stayed closed for the most of the studying time and his book wide open placed in front of him resting on his bent knees. After the night rest and in the early hours of the morning, everyone was required to fold their comforters and linens and stack them on one cot placed in the corner of the verandah.

Summer time in Mahima's household generated its own entertainment and enjoyment. Everyone slept in the big courtyard of the house; nine cots with nine mosquito nets, tied in the poles or onto the trees with long strings attached in every direction. Such summer entertainment reached its peek in the monsoon season. Mamma served as a weather forecaster and invariably when she saw a threatening cloud in the sky, she would quickly awaken everyone in the middle of the night to pull the cots under the covered verandah. Mahima's main playing partner was her Bhaiya with whom she thoroughly enjoyed playing, and it was with him that she regularly went kite flying.

The supply of fresh water came from the hand pump outside the house in the corner. Mahima enjoyed pumping the water into the buckets and her bhaiya was responsible for transferring the drinking water into the pots, and the laundry water into a big tub. House cleaning duties were shared by the sisters. Everyone laundered their own clothes and line dried them. The heavy clothes like sheets and Mamma's saris were professionally laundered. Other than the school uniform Mahima had two other outfits, the pair that she wore while the other was being washed and dried.

Chapter 2
KITE FLYING

*S*chools started late in the morning during the winter months, which meant less day light in the evening and longer nights. During those winter months, especially after dinner, in the dark, there was not much to do for the family besides staying in the beds, studying, reading, playing some board games and experiencing the coziness of the family. Spring and fall were a different story. The school hours were from seven in the morning until one o'clock in the afternoon, and then everybody enjoyed the hours of afternoon and evening inside the house. All seven children and Mamma came back from school a little after one o'clock every afternoon, almost at the same time. Pappa also took a lunch break and biked home from his dispensary to join the family. After lunch he refreshed himself by taking a short nap before going back to his work. Most of his typing and shorthand coaching was done in the afternoon hours and patients were seen in the mornings. Mamma and children stayed inside the house to avoid the excruciating heat and the unbearable heat waves during those peak months of summer. Mamma's rules were very clear and strict for all the children. To follow those rules, everyone had no choice but to stay inside the house and rest from two to four o'clock in the afternoon. Thus everyone took a short nap other than Mahima and her bhaiya. They closed their eyes and pretended as if they were with the crowd of seven and participating with them in napping. However they frequently opened their involuntarily closed eyes to check upon everybody's status and to make sure that Mamma and the rest were deep asleep.

"Hey Mahima! Get up." Bhaiya whispered in Mahima's ears,

She was ready as always. Her bhaiya sneaked out quietly, barefoot, walking on his toes, and then Mahima did the same to follow him. Both headed towards the hedges of the jasmine bushes by the gate of the house. Bhaiya carefully pulled his handmade kite hidden inside the protected hole in between the bushes and she was designated to pick up the hidden spool wrapped up in a strong string. Both ran away in an open field which was not too far from the house. Bhaiya strung the kite and both were ready to go.

"Ready! Mahima!"

She held the kite from two horizontal corners. With her arms stretched on both sides, she ran backwards to the other end of the field while bhaiya kept releasing the string from the spool. Both were ready for the fun.

"One…two…three." Bhaiya counted loudly from the other side of the field.

She threw the kite up in the air at three and bhaiya controlled it from the other end. He held the string in his left hand and moved his right hand back and forth to release the string and make the kite dance high in the sky. In no time, the kite stabilized and bhaiya gave the string of the flying kite in his sister's hands.

"Wow!"

Flying the kite used to be a heavenly experience for Mahima. Bhaiya enjoyed watching his sister flying the kite and he kept his eyes glued on it in case it took a dive. If it did, he immediately took the string from her hands, controlled and stabilized it, and again Mahima took over flying it. They had a solid two hours of enormous fun almost every afternoon.

"Hurry up Mahima!" It was almost 4 o'clock.

Bhaiya pulled the string with both of his fast moving hands back and forth to bring the kite down. The long string covered the big field within a few seconds and Mahima rolled the string over the spool as quick as she could with one handle of the spool sitting on her left elbow and her right hand fingers moving rapidly. They packed their equipments and ran back to the house and in no time they resumed their napping positions—napping!

Mahima's house was located just opposite to the boys' hostel. There was a public road in between. The boys living in that hostel were the engineering students from all over the country and were studying at the university located in the town. There was a big playground on the other side of the hostel, which was nicely maintained with the green soft grass and flowers to surround it. That was a perfect place for Mahima to run around and burn her extra energy. She was only eight years old at that time. The boys loved to play with her, chase her around the field, and treat her like a little baby doll. It was a perfect entertainment for them. They took her in their rooms, served her cookies, candies, toffees and other edible items. Little Mahima loved that special attention. She was fascinated to see their rooms, books, study tables, lamps and nicely made beds. Each of them had their own room decorated in different unique ways. In contrast, she did not even have a bed to be called her own, but it did not bother her. She loved to share her bed with one of her siblings. Her future fantasy began from that time of her journey. At that tender stage of her life she dreamt to be just like those boys, to attend a big college and study hard. A desire for achievement began incubating within her.

Chapter 3
Broken Bangle & Color box

*T*he years kept fleeting by and Mahima was already ten years old. Just like most other ten year olds, she was in fifth grade. She was a studious child and was maintaining the first position in her class. Not only in studies, but she loved to participate in the school sports also. At that tender age of ten, she also developed an interest in writing, painting and drawing. Her inveterate desire to study hard and to go to that university upon growing up just like those boys was still etched in her consciousness. Her teachers were also very pleased with her progress and so was her Mamma. She was remarkably ambitious and an extraordinary girl from her childhood.

Mahima was fond of wearing glass bangles. She loved the bright colors of the bangles and wore them on both of her wrists. She waited for the salesman to come to her neighborhood. She was always the first one to run after him, catch him and bring him in her courtyard. The bangle salesman felt lucky to be surrounded by many customers ranging from little girls to the older women. They made him happy by asking him to put the bangles on their wrists and provided him a good business.

It was prohibited and against the dress code to wear the bangles in her school, but she loved wearing them at home and other places. The jingling sound and the gorgeous bright colors of the glass bangles fascinated her and she wore a lot of them. She kept those bangles on her wrists until the last moment before leaving for school. That was a memorable morning when she was bathing before going to school. She realized that those bangles had to come off. Her other sister impatiently waited outside the bathroom door for her turn.

"Hurry up Mahima, we are getting late."

Mahima started pulling those bangles off of her soapy hands. She did not realize that there was one cracked bangle among many.

"Ouch! Oh, Maa!"

She cut the top of her right hand and a stream of bright red blood mixed with water started dripping from her hand, gushing towards the drain of the bathroom.

"Mamma! O... Mamma!"

"Mamma…Come here Mamma." She screamed in panic and tears started rolling down her cheek.

Mamma was also getting ready to go to school and was in the middle of wrapping her sari. She ran towards the bathroom holding the unwrapped part of the sari in her hands.

"What happened Mahima?"

"Look Mamma… look at my hand."

Her body was shaking, trembling and she was totally terrified. The blood was dripping non stop from her hand.

Mamma wrapped her in a towel, picked her up in her arms and brought her out of the bathroom. Everyone was traumatized after learning what just happened. Bhaiya grabbed a handkerchief from somewhere in the house and wrapped it tightly around her hand to stop the bleeding.

"Mahima, you are too young to wear these glass bangles. No more bangles from now on."

Bhaiya took advantage of the delicate situation to demonstrate his authority as a big brother and took no time to take off the rest of the bangles from both of her wrists. Her Pappa ran without delay to grab a rickshaw with the rickshaw wallah to take Mahima to the clinic. Mamma sat with Mahima in the rickshaw and bhaiya followed them on his bicycle.

"Don't cry. The doctor will take care of it." Mamma wrapped her arms tightly around her sobbing daughter.

They were at the clinic in no time. The nurse picked up Mahima and sat her on a high stool by the high table. The doctor took her right hand into his and gently took off the tightly tied bloody handkerchief. The blood was still dripping and a white bone under the skin was peeping through the three inch slit in it.

"Oh! Mahima! You slashed your hand really badly. How did you do that?"

Tears were flowing down her cheeks. Her sobbing was quite obvious conveying the message that she was in pain and agony.

"I am sure it is hurting."

"Yes, doctor." The words hardly came out of her mouth in between sobbing.

"Okay my dear. Do not worry. I will have to sew it with three stitches."

'Stitches? What stitches? Are those stitches going to be like sewing clothes?' Several questions roamed through her little head in a fraction of a second.

The nurse pulled a long wire from the side drawers that looked like a crochet-needle with a hook on one side and also a roll of thread. Mamma sat by her side holding her other hand tightly. She sent bhaiya to buy some oranges from the corner fruit shop while the doctor was threading his sewing needle. Each and every action taken by the doctor was being observed by Mahima very intently. She was absolutely convinced that the next several minutes of her life were not going to be fun but rather indelibly painful. So, the only alternative that remained for her was to capitulate herself in her doctor's hands.

The doctor poked the needle into her skin without even numbing it. Mamma tried her best to distract her. She turned her face away from the bloody site and kept stuffing her mouth with the slices of orange peeled and passed by her Bhaiya. Ah! How tortuous, unbearable, excruciating was the pain she had experienced that day.

"All done." The doctor announced after poking her three times and wrapped her hand with the bandage.

"What a brave girl! Now, wipe your tears and go home."

Those three stitches left a life long three inch scar on the top of her right hand, perhaps a reminder of the episode. Nonetheless, she did not develop a dislike against those colorful glass bangles. She preserved the same passion for them and wore them occasionally with great care.

Mahima loved painting, painting the pictures of the birds and the flowers. She was in her fifth grade when one of her bird paintings won the prize in the army art show. She also stood first in her class academics. Knowing her passion for painting, her parents rewarded her with a brand new color box.

That coloring box of twelve colors was a priceless gift for little Mahima. She packed her color box in her back pack and took it to the art class to show it to her friends. Her close friend Mala had a cheap book of colors that she used for her paintings. Mala had to get the color off from the color book by rubbing a wet brush soaked in water on it and then transfer that color onto the painting paper.

"I wish—I also had a color box like yours." Mala expressed her desires openly. Mala was under-privileged.

"Mala! Do you really like my color box?" After a thoughtful moment Mahima asked her.

Mala shook her head with her big wide open eyes focused on the color box.

"I really do like your coloring book Mala. Let us make an exchange." Mahima suggested.

"Really, Mahima?"

Mala was surprised. She could not refuse the offer. A bright shine reflecting in Mala's big eyes was so evident. How could Mahima forget that moment when she as a little girl sacrificed such a valuable gift to her best friend? The contentment and profound happiness Mahima felt deep in her heart by helping her friend could not be described in words. That contentment surpassed receiving that precious gift of a beautiful coloring box from her parents.

The trade was done and the exchange was made. It was not an even exchange, but an exchange filled with love, care and gratitude, which gave Mahima an absolute satisfaction, a precious and a perdurable memory for life. The story was not over as of yet. Mahima had to prepare herself to face the challenges at home. How would she convey the mystery behind losing the coloring box? The truth did not seem to work and the lie would not be good. She was well aware of the fact that there was no money tree growing in her house either. She would lie, a lie for a good reason, why not?

She reached home after the long day at school with a determined decision to lie. How? She had no idea. The first person to face was bhaiya, who was eagerly waiting for her to come home and see her coloring box.

"Hey Mahima! Let me see your new coloring box."

She was not expecting to face that question or any one that quickly. Though she was quite ready to deal with the situation, she remained silent for a few moments. The demand made her numb, motionless, and speechless. She played as if she had not heard him, tried to ignore his request and walked away from him.

"Come on Mahima. Let us paint something." Bhaiya was not in a mood to give up.

She had no option, but to stick to her plan of lying.

"Bhaiya! I don't know how, but I lost the color box somewhere in school." Very bravely—she lied.

Instantly, the news was delivered to Mamma-Pappa by bhaiya and within a few moments the whole household knew and shortly thereafter the neighbors too. Mahima was punished. She accepted the punishment more than willingly. She had to stand in the corner of the room facing the bare wall for fifteen minutes and never got another color box.

Chapter 4
Middle School

Summer break was over—the new session started. Mahima was in the middle school. Her classroom was in the wing away from her Mamma's. The only time spent with her Mamma was in a rickshaw back and forth. What a blessing for her! The very first day and the very first period after the morning prayers was the Hindi language class with Mrs. Singh, the great Hindi teacher. She entered in the classroom like a judge in the courtroom and all the girls stood up out of respect. Mrs. Singh placed her bag gently in her desk-drawer and at the same time, she pulled out a wooden ruler, a twelve inch long ruler—used in the Geometry class. She appeared like a boot camp instructor. There was not a trace of smile at her face. She placed the ruler on the right side of her body within her reach.

"Sit down." Her domineering voice made the whole room fearful and the girls trembled.

All sat instantly, simultaneously within less than a fraction of a second. The classroom established a pin drop silence, not even a breath was heard. Mrs. Singh stood up, picked up her ruler and banged it at the hard wooded table top.

The sound echoed throughout the whole room. The girls jerked, jumped and back on their seats. The innocent smile on their faces turned into horror. The beautiful, innocent eyes forgot to blink.

"Sit down." Mrs. Singh commanded again, though the girls were glued to their chairs.

Their eyes rolled around to see the others. They were still in great shock and motionless. The only moving part of their bodies were their eyes, focused on Mrs. Singh and moving as she was moving back and forth and row to row along the desks of the girls with a ruler in her right hand. After a few minutes, she delivered her first speech.

"Any mistake, carelessness, not turning in the assignments on time, distraction in the class will not be tolerated."

Mrs. Singh dictated her strict rules the very first day and the very first period of the school. She held her ruler tight in her fist and slapped it at her desk several times.

The first day, the very first hour in a new school was without any thrill or excitement. The girls were paranoid, helpless, numb and traumatized. For Mahima, this early morning experience was the worst nightmare, more than that of Mamma's Math class. One whole year with Mrs. Singh did not seem to be possible. One whole hour of each day with her seemed a nightmare. What could be done? That was the question roaming in each mind of those little girls.

Mahima and the girls had no option, but to cope with the pressure during the first period. Yes, the ruler was used on some girls periodically. Mahima saw and felt the pain it caused. She would care less about other classes, but Hindi work was timely and efficiently done by her. She sat in her class like an angel and was very lucky to escape the hard hit of the ruler by Mrs. Singh on her palm. By the end of that school year, Mahima was proficient in Hindi language. All the poems, history of several authors and poets were crammed by her and she could recite them verbatim. So, the year with Mrs. Singh was over.

Kavita and Mahima were best friends in middle school. They shared their time together and studied together as well. They also ate their lunch together during the recess. Kavita loved Mahima's *roti* (Indian bread) and dry potato curry packed in a lunch box, cooked by her Mamma. Mahima's favorite was Kavita's lunch box packed with butter and tomato sandwich. They were delighted to share each other's lunch.

"Mahima, does your Mamma make *roti* every morning?"

"Yes, she prepares breakfast and lunch for all of us."

How could Mahima's Mamma afford to purchase that expansive double-*roti* and the sticks of butter for a platoon of seven?

"My mother is asleep when I get dressed for the school in the mornings. The servant wakes me up. He gives me breakfast, prepares my lunch box and brings me to the school too."

Kavita had a small bicycle with a tiny luggage-carrier behind it to carry the school bag. She belonged to a rich family. She rode her bicycle to the school with her servant behind her on his own big bicycle. Her servant carried her school bag hanging on his shoulders every morning. Mahima did not have a bicycle and she used to walk two miles one way every day. Kavita's house was on the way to school.

"Mahima! Why don't you walk to my house and I will give you a ride to our school." Kavita made a generous offer and Mahima accepted it gladly.

Kavita and Mahima rode on that little bike with both the backpacks hanging on each side of the luggage carrier. One of them sat on the carrier and the other peddled. The kind servant stayed behind them and made sure that both the girls arrived safely at school.

Kavita's house was located in a huge compound. It was surrounded by numerous mango trees of various varieties. Mahima and Kavita played hide and seek in the garden and enjoyed the cool shadow and refreshing breeze sitting under the trees. Kavita took private sitar lessons and she also had a tutor to help her do all the homework and prepare her for the tests and exams. Mahima had none of the above. She wished that she could take sitar lessons too. Knowing that her parents could not afford that, she had to resist the temptation. She was allowed to sit with Kavita and her instructor during the lessons. Kavita sat on a nice *kaaleen* (expensive rug) holding her sitar in a perfect position. Her instructor sat on the other side of the *kaaleen* in a yoga position with his *tabla* (Indian drums). As soon as the melodious sound came out of the strings of the instrument, Mahima started wandering in a fantasy land, thinking and dreaming, perhaps one day, some day in the future, she would also play like Kavita. She loved to hold her friend's sitar and also tried to play some strings whenever she got a chance.

Chapter 5
ACADEMIC DREAMS

"*M*ahima! It is now time for you to learn some house work and help your sisters." According to Mamma, the training had to be started right away.

"Go and ask didi (her sister) to get you the broom and you sweep the floors."

"Alright Mamma, I will do it before long." She reluctantly obeyed Mamma.

She had no interest in any of the household chores. Her older sisters were there, why should she? Poor, sweet, old nani, who lived in the neighborhood and was dependent on others, she could not even walk without a stick. Most inviting was that nani always gave her toffees and sweet-*rotis* as her wages. *Who will do her house work?*

"Mamma, I will be right back. Let me go and see nani." Mamma was well aware of the fact that no one could stop Mahima from seeing her beloved nani.

She ran to nani's house, jumped into her laps. Nani waited anxiously for her every afternoon.

"Oh my little doll! Did you eat something after coming back from your school?" That used to be nani's concern every single afternoon.

"Go in the kitchen. There is a *meethi* (sweet) *roti* in the *katordaan* (roti keeper)."

That sweet-*roti* made by nani was way tastier than the *hot-jalebee* (Indian sweet) made by the expert *halwaii* (sweet maker) in the town.

She felt abundantly blessed by helping her nani, sweeping her floor, pumping water from the hand-pump and filling nani's pots for her daily needs. She also washed and dried nani's dirty dishes, arranged them in the utensils' cupboard. At times Mahima washed her clothes and also made her bed. In return nani gave her baskets full of love, toffees and *meethi roti*.

A long long time ago nani gifted a doll to Mahima's oldest sister. That doll lived for decades, but very much bruised. Mahima was the final owner of that doll. She kept it hidden through the year in her trunk under the clothes. Summer break was the only time the doll was pulled out from her trunk. The reason was to marry her. Poor doll, perhaps older than her oldest didi, wrinkled face, many-many bruises on her body, but was ready to be married again every summer. Her neighborhood friends, Asha and Rani, nani and Mahima were the assigned sewing mistresses of her wedding garments; a little petticoat, blouse, red sari with a beautiful shining gold-border. The hand-written invitation cards by Mahima, Asha and Rani used to be hand delivered to the guests every year in the summer. The time for the ceremony was usually in the afternoon, when the elders of the house were napping. Asha and Rani were the helping hands of Mahima for all the wedding preparation.

Under the guava tree, a colorful sari hung over four poles, with all four sides covered, decorated with the leaves was the temple place for the wedding. The bride sat in the middle, embellished in her wedding sari and jewelry. The reception meal was prepared by Asha and Rani, the best cooks. The main item was the fresh ripe guavas, cut into pieces and garnished with some spices. The beverage menu was also standard every year. The cold drink of lemonade made fresh using the hand picked lemons from the lemon tree in the corner of the two boundary walls of the house. The only thing missing in the whole ceremony was the groom. Nonetheless, Asha and Rani were the beloved in-laws of the bride. After the party, the bride typically went to her in-laws just for a day and returned to her home the following day to Mahima. And that was the tradition set for every summer, 'A wedding ceremony with no groom.'

As always, the time kept fleeting by. Mahima was emerging a beautiful young girl. She was still as innocent as ever. Her dressing style was still a frock, but a little longer than before, just below her knees. Mamma's and Pappa's rules were amended for her and became more strict. She was not allowed to visit the boys in the boy's hostel across the street. She was restricted regarding whom she could visit and who she could not in her own neighborhood. Along with the other active rules, she needed permission from her older siblings or Mamma or Pappa, if she desired to play with her friends. Also the time restrictions and curfews were to be obeyed strictly. She did not quite understand the reasoning behind all the changes of the rules, but she followed them without questioning. She was still a little chirping bird for her Pappa. Every evening, he picked up some sweets on his way home from his shop for everyone. Without wasting any time, as soon as her Pappa got off his bicycle, she ran to him and jumped into his lap, and her beloved Pappa treated her like a baby and fed her the sweets with his own hands.

After the afternoon snacks of sweets and tea, routinely Mamma went into the kitchen to get the supper ready for the whole platoon. Mahima's responsibility was to set up a little table with a chair for Pappa, who enjoyed being the first one to dine. He kept an eye on Mamma's progress in the kitchen and gave her his company. As soon as the first *roti* came out off the stove, he rushed to the hand pump to wash his hands, sat at the table to be served.

Mahima served the puffy *rotis* to him with *daal,* curried vegetables or meat. It gave her great joy and contentment to serve her Pappa.

At the age of fourteen she started high school. That was the year when Mahima had to appear for a board exam and study diligently. One significant development occurred a few years before. The municipality power line was stretched in the neighborhood she lived and her Pappa was the first one among all the neighbors to apply to get electricity in the house. After receiving the electric power the house shimmered with the electric bulbs—one in each room and two high wattage bulbs in the front and on the side of the house. No more burning the lanterns with oil and also no more studying in the dim light of the lanterns and candles. The sisters were relieved for instead of lighting the lanterns for all the four corners of the house, they just had to flip the electric switches.

Pappa's heartiest desire for Mahima was that she studied to be a doctor. To move into that direction, it was required for her to take some biology classes. To honor her Pappa's desire, she signed up for her classes and Biology was one of them. First day of classes, she entered the biology laboratory. At each of the tables in a tray filled with water, there was a dead frog stapled flat on its back—dead, ugly, slimy green frog. She could not tolerate that sight and also the unbearable stinky smell.

'Oh! My heavens! Can some one get me out of this room?' That was the only thought in her head. She felt light headed, nauseated and sick. She had no options other than staying in the lab for that whole period. Somehow or the other, she managed that hour, a very long hour.

After a long day at school, she came home with a major headache. She was under tremendous stress, very tired and uncertain. She decided to take a nap and sleep off her stress, which was not easy at all. The frogs were crawling all over her and in her bed and everywhere else, dead and alive on the floor, on the walls, on the ceiling, and every where. What a devastating nightmare? She had no intention of continuing that class filled with the dead, stinky frogs. At the same time, she did not want to break her Pappa's heart by giving him the bad news. Not taking that class meant no future of becoming a doctor. Her mind was swirling like a hurricane. A battle kept going on within her. *'Should she stay in that class or should she tell her Pappa the truth?'* She also trusted that if she would tell her Pappa the whole story with a reasonable explanation, Pappa would understand. *'Who will if he won't?'* Pappa came home from work in the evening. He was curious.

"How was your day beta?"

"Pappa, I did not like the biology class at all. I did not like to work with those dead stinky frogs and there were so many in the lab. I almost fainted." She declared boldly that she had no interest in biology.

"That is quite alright. So, would you like to change your subjects?"

"Yes."

So, that was the dream of becoming a doctor—ended before it started.

That was the year when Mahima noticed some physical changes in her body, nothing but her maturing process to a young woman. In those days the schools did not offer any education in the area of 'growing up' process. She was fortunate to have so many older sisters to educate her. Brief descriptions by one of her sisters about everything including the sufferings and cramps which occur during those changes were explained to her. She was basically left with surprises and fear, which were natural for a little girl during that time of transition.

She was prepared but really only in theory. She was sitting in her classroom on a little wooden chair with a book-desk in front of her. She had her school uniform on. A light blue frock, buckled shoes, and knee high pair of socks. She was working on her class project along with the other girls. All of a sudden, she felt wetness. She moved a little to the left and then to the right and noticed a big patch of blood soaked into the gathering of her frock. *'Oh! Maa!'* and she stayed glued to the chair, very still, did not move at all, her entire body felt paralyzed.

The bell rang and the next period started. It was time to move to the next classroom, but how, and how could she run like other girls? She decided not to. She stayed in that small chair with her head down, with droplets of tears dripping from her big eyes and landing on her open book in front of her. There was no one around and no one to help her. Luckily there was no class scheduled in that classroom. She decided to keep sitting there for as long as she could. After a few moments she heard someone walking into the room and she did not have the guts to lift her eyes up to see that who was the person. The Vice Principal of the school, Mrs. Kumar in her white *sari*, with big bloody red eyes and a mean look was standing right in front of her. The girls never stayed within her field of view and ran and hid like rats from a cat. It was very rare to see a smile on Mrs. Kumar's face. As a matter of fact, none of the girls ever saw a smile at her face. The same Mrs. Kumar stood in front of Mahima with a big smile on her face. Mahima was still shaking and weeping.

"Mahima! Get up and come with me." She offered Mahima her hand.

For an instance, Mahima was stunned looking at Mrs. Kumar. Quickly she wrapped her frock with one hand, gave the other one to Mrs. Kumar and followed her to the staff room.

'Is it real or a dream?' Mahima was still in a shock after seeing Mrs. Kumar's kindness and loving demeanor.

"Sit here and listen carefully." Mrs. Kumar spoke with Mahima in her usual commanding voice.

"Do not worry and stop crying. This happens to all the growing girls. This is part of nature."

After getting that initial support and counseling from Mrs. Kumar she seized the opportunity to talk more with her.

"Mala, Sangita, Anjalee… to all of them?" Mahima asked in her sobbing voice.

"Yes my dear, to all of them. You will be just fine. Now get up and change your frock." Mrs. Kumar got up, opened the hidden cupboard in the staff room and pulled a frock to hand it to her and the change of clothes too.

"Make sure, you tell about this to your mother at home."

Mrs. Kumar commanded and Mahima was sent home with one of the school servants in a rickshaw.

The last year of her High School was the year to prepare for the State's Board exams, which were scheduled to be held at the end of the session in March. She was determined to study hard as she had not forgotten the ambitions she created in her mind years and years ago to go to the university like those boys, who lived in the hostel across her house and met her in her childhood. The best time to study was at night, when the rest of her family members were asleep. At times, many, many times, during the power failure, she studied in a candle light or a lantern.

"Mahima dear, get some sleep." Mamma was always concerned in some way or the other.

"Mamma! She knows it, don't bother her." Pappa always supported Mahima. That became a routine conversation between her parents.

The Board exams were held in the month of March. After the exams there was a two month wait for the results to be announced. Those were the longest two months for her as her future was totally dependent on the results of the boards. She waited, but impatiently. The results of the Board exams were always published in a special section of the national newspaper. No one knew the final date of the results until a day or two before or sometimes after they were out. If the roll-number (student's identification number) was missing or unpublished, it meant that the student failed. Mahima kept chasing and bugging the news-paper-man, who delivered the daily newspaper to her Pappa. On the 23rd of May, it was announced in the whole town that the High School results will be published the following day—meant the 24th early morning.

The most exciting night in Mahima's life was the night of 23rd—a sleepless night. That was the night which would determine her future. It was very late at night and everyone in the house was fast asleep, a pin drop silence with the occasional loud snores by her Mamma. It seemed that Mahima was even unable to blink her eyes. She was well prepared to receive the newspaper with the high school results in it. She laid in her bed with a torch by her side, keeping in mind the unannounced power failure in the house and in the neighborhood. Her eyes were focused on the clock, which was ticking slowly, way slower than her heart rate. It was past 2am and there was no sign of the newspaper man. She picked up the torch and started rolling it in between her two palms. Each and every moment she faced was filled with anxiety, uncertainty and a variety of emotions. That early morning would decide her *kismet* and what the future holds for her.

"Mahima! Come on, the result is out." The newspaper man shouted from the other side of the boundary wall without even thinking that the other people in that tiny neighborhood were deep asleep.

Mahima raced towards the boundary wall of the house with the lit torch in her hand. In the dark, barefoot with a torch in one hand, she lifted her other hand all the way to the top of the wall to snatch the newspaper from his hands. In the meantime the whole neighborhood and the household woke up. Her hands were trembling, her heart felt like it moved into her throat. She flipped the pages quickly and in no time she found the name of her school printed in the deep layer of the newspaper. The next step was to find her role number; missing role number meant bad news. Her fingers sliding on the published role numbers and her eyes kept reading those numbers...

"2...5...4...1...A. This is my number. Yeah, this is my number." And she slid her fingers on that number several times to make sure that that was her number and the real number.

"I passed in first division." Mahima screamed on the top of her lungs with joy and happiness.

"Great job! " Pappa filled her in his arms and Mamma was filled with admiration.

By the time everyone could digest the good news it was already 4am. No one was in the mood to go back to sleep. Mahima was anxious to meet with her friends first thing in the morning and share the news. After seeing hers she also saw her friends' roll numbers in the paper. Mamma was in the mood to celebrate and could not wait. She went in the kitchen, made some *halvaa—poori*, a special breakfast prepared on special occasions and an early breakfast was served to the whole household.

Pappa could not resist going to the market early in the morning and bringing bags full of freshly made sweets to share with the neighbors as a tradition or rather to announce the success achieved by his youngest daughter. Mahima made a special bag of sweets for her nani and ran to her house as early as the first ray of the sun peeped into her yard.

"Nani, get up. Open your eyes. I passed in first division." She entered into her nani's room and woke her up by jumping on her bed.

Poor nani, half asleep-half awake, sat up in her bed rubbing her half opened eyes.

"Come on my love, my darling, come close to me." Soft spoken sweet nani invited her in her arms.

Along with her other friends she kept making frequent trips to her school office on her bike every day for a week. One week later the marks-sheets also arrived in the school office. Mahima stood in that long queue of girls, waited eagerly for her turn to receive her marks-sheet. Only one clerk was on duty to deliver the marks-sheets to a big herd of girls. She was extremely restless, unable to stand still, very impatient. Her hope was to get good marks. The marks had to be good as she passed in first division, but truly she wanted more than the first division. Why not? She studied day and night. She was thriving for some distinction, which was like passing the courses with honors.

The wait time was longer than the long line of girls. The line moved just a little by little, an inch by inch to get to the clerk. Finally her turn came. She eagerly took the sealed envelope from the clerk's hands, checked it out by signing the 'received' column in a big register sitting at his desk. Instead of opening the envelope containing her marks sheet she ran and sat on a bench under a tree in the corner of the field of the school. She looked around to confirm that no one was watching her and finally she opened the envelope.

"Wow!"

"Unbelievable!"

She got distinction in three subjects; Math, Science and English. She could not believe her eyes. She jumped on her bike and flew home to share the good news with every one in her family, but most of all, to her Pappa.

The next school year began. The story of her success did not end there. After a few days into the new session, the merit list from the State arrived in the school office. Mahima was pulled out of her classroom to the Principal's office. That was the first time in the history of the school that a student was awarded the National Merit Scholarship. She walked with the assistant to the principal's office and sat in front of her at the opposite side of her desk.

"Congratulations, Mahima!"

"The state rewards 500 students with a merit scholarship every year and you are number 39. I am proud of you. Go to the clerk's office, fill out the scholarship forms and bring them back to me."

Mahima was the happiest person that day. She was thrilled. The dreams seemed to be coming true. The reward of her hard work and determination and perhaps an incentive given to her by those boys living in the hostel played a big role for her achievements and her academic success. That was the scholarship which opened enormous paths for her future academic progress.

The next two years of her journey did not only seem to be long but very tedious and cumbersome too. She would be preparing for the Intermediate board exams and also at the same time for the entrance exam at the university of her dreams. She was a fighter. She was very much aware of the fact that getting into that university was not an easy task. She had to compete with several thousand students from all over India. Mahima's dream to become an architect meant that she had to clear the general entrance exam and after passing that exam she had to take another departmental exam for Architectural Engineering.

Her dreams to go to that university from her very early childhood were not unrealistic. Hard work pays off and she was a firm believer in that concept. She convinced herself by thinking that the other students appearing in the entrance exam were just like her. They were not from Mars or any other planet. So, with a hope and a positive attitude, she immersed herself into the books, and to keep herself fit she jogged for two miles in the morning and played badminton in the evening.

Her house was built during the British rule. An old brick and concrete house with the arch shaped roof. Three rooms meant three arches with approximately four feet of flat surface in between the two on the roof. That flat area was her day time open air study room; a perfect secluded place to study in peace, where no one could distract her. She loved studying there especially in the warmth of the winter sun. After coming back from her school in the afternoon, she climbed up a wooden ladder to go to her study room and stayed there until sunset or until the time of the night the words in her books became blurry. She took one tiny break with a cup of tea and some home made snacks. Following her studying until sunset, she rode her bike to play badminton on some lighted courts. She had dinner with her folks and continued on her studies afterward. She always kept one candle close to her in case of power outage. And that was her time table set during that time.

It was the month of March—the month for the test following her intense study. She took the intermediate board exam with full preparations. The results of those exams were expected to be announced at the end of May. Immediately after the intermediate boards, she took the entrance exam for the university in the month of April and those results were expected to be out in the beginning of May. The university session was to begin in early July.

There was a month between her entrance exams and before the results of those exams. One whole month, just waiting for the results was no fun at all, but at least she got a break from her books. That time was the beginning of a real life journey for her. She rode her bicycle every day, back and forth, several times to the main office of the university to see if the list of selected students was posted. Pappa's words kept echoing constantly in her mind, 'The labor of hard work pays off'. She was not built to escape from any hard work.

She knew that she prepared day and night to achieve her goal and she was confident of success. It was also obvious that the other students did the same. Several of them may have had professional coaching too; nonetheless a tiny streak of doubt was very natural.

Finally, the list of the selected students was displayed in front of the main office of the university. Mahima's eyes and fingers started racing on that list, as before when her high school result was posted in the newspaper. It was another miracle in her life. A feeling of joy ran into her body and mind, an absolute moment of happiness and satisfaction. She was one of the selected students.

The next hurdle to be crossed was the departmental exam at the university—an exam that lasted four hours with one ten minute break. The list of the selected students came out in two days after the exam and lo and behold, she did not miss that list either. It was well done and a done deal. She flew home again on her bicycle, threw the bicycle at the gate of her house and ran inside.

She reached home huffing and puffing. Drops of her perspiration were dripping from her forehead in that excruciating heat of summer. She could hardly speak. Entirely ecstatic, she was out of breath.

"I got admission in the department of Architectural engineering."

"Oh, Maa! Pappa! I am so happy… happy… happy."

The past eighteen years of Mahima's journey were filled with nothing but joy, happiness, and innocence and to top them all, a tender loving care by her parents and the older siblings. She had not experienced any failure. There was only success and more success at each step of the ladder she was climbing. Not only her, but no one knows what the future brings for us. She was very unaware of the fact that at any step of her journey, the road may take a steep turn.

She got accepted at the university, but the results of the Intermediate board exams were still pending. They were expected to be announced during the last week of May. In a few more weeks, her future fate was to be determined and she had nothing but high hopes and big dreams. She did not have much to do in those couple of weeks, except to dream going to a new university of her dreams and become an architect.

The time kept creeping and finally the day for the intermediate results to be published in the national news paper arrived. The same newspaper man who delivered her high school results delivered that one too. She kept flipping the pages, but was unable to find the name of her school. Also many consecutive role numbers were missing. Her heart vacillated between beating rapidly and skipping a beat. According to her Pappa; there must be some publishing or printing error. Missing roll numbers meant the failing roll numbers and how could so many girls with consecutive role numbers fail? Pappa had a point which made perfect sense. Mahima along with Pappa and Mamma had to face a sleepless night. She kept thinking what subject she failed. She couldn't think of any. The failing of one subject in the board exam meant failing all together and this also meant repeating the whole year.

It was a painful night for her. She spent all night crying and worrying about the unknown to come. Early morning, her friends, some alone and some with their parents came to her house to explore more fully the chaotic situation. They decided to meet the principal at her house. The principal was informed by some higher sources that the role numbers of the whole center, where sixty five girls from different schools took the board exam were missing with no apparent reasons.

The investigation through the school started immediately. In just a few days the reason of those missing role numbers was discovered. In the center, where several girls from several schools took the exams, a mass cheating occurred. A teacher from one of the schools gave the answer to a test question to some of her students and it was a wrong answer, which created an immediate suspicion to the board members of a mass cheating in that center, and the result was that the whole center was put on hold for further investigations, perhaps a long investigation.

The news shook the whole town. It was worse and tremulous for career oriented girls like Mahima, who were looking forward to begin their new professional academic journey. What a tremendous pressure on all those little girls. They were not impregnable at that age. That episode turned their lives upside down. Mahima stood numb, helpless. Her dreams for a future success, her dreams to become an architect, the dreams to go to one of the nationally reputed university, dreams to work hard to achieve the goal incubating in her since her childhood—all seemingly shattered. What if the matter would not be settled on time, before the opening of the university? Each and every moment was a challenge filled moment with unanswered questions and future uncertainty for her. Time was fleeting rapidly and the investigation was taking its own time. The end of the day results were nothing but frustrations for so many innocent girls tangled in that bizarre situation. Counseling session started, board meetings with the schools started—with no immediate solution.

The deadline to submit the mark sheets and the certificates at the university passed. Mahima got an extension for two weeks to turn in all the documents. That request was based upon those unforeseen circumstances and was accepted by the university after several attempts, but basically in that time she hoped for the best and preparing for the worst. Those two weeks passed also. She received a regret letter from the university that her admission was canceled. Her dreams were shattered—a huge, unbearable downfall in her life.

All sixty five girls were advised to repeat the final year of their intermediate school and start going to school without wasting any more time and take the boards again. That was the one and only one solution for them. It took six months for the board members to declare their judgment. The teacher, who made the girls cheat was fired, the girls who cheated were suspended for two years and the other girls, who were in that big hall of the center had to repeat the year.

Mahima--a fighter could not stay a fighter any more. She had no desire left within her to take the university entrance exam again next year. She had no other choice left but to repeat the whole year and take the intermediate board exam again. Somehow or the other she prepared herself without any motivations for the boards, passed them with a second division and started taking classes at a local community college in a hope to pursue a masters in science degree.

That time of her journey was a tedious one and the road was rocky. It was not an easy task for Mahima to accept the circumstances and move on. It was the hardest challenge to make an agreement with life at that stage; nonetheless, she finally capitulated and agreed upon taking a different path. Those dreams incubating in her mind for the last twelve years stayed in her memories like a catalog of several bad nightmares. The unforeseen ruthlessness and unfairness of life left an indelible mark on her young life. Unwillingly and reluctantly, she started her session at the community college.

Chapter 6
First Love

*T*he new college was coeducational. There were more boys than girls in the school. The dress code changed. The girls were required to wear conservative clothes, which meant, no frocks in college. It was a big change for Mahima and she had to adapt to that willingly or reluctantly. Her dress was *salvaar-kurtaa* with *dupatta* (a long shirt, loose pants and a scarf) and mostly she wore open toe shoes all around the year other than two months of winter. Her long hair was always in two braids tied in ribbons and hanging on both sides of her shoulders. Her routine was to ride her sister's old bicycle to the college, which was about two miles away from her house. Her books were always strapped on the carrier behind the seat.

There were sixty students in her section with only twelve girls among them. Perhaps, the field of science could not attract the girls. The college only offered the Bachelors degree in Science. Pappa and Mamma enforced and reinforced some strict rules on their youngest daughter. She had a set limit to talk or mingle with boys and was never to forget that she was born and raised in a Christian family. In that college of a small town in India, Mahima was the only Christian student. Not only that, there was not a single Christian professor on the campus either.

She was unique, jovial, friendly and ebullient. To top it all she was considered the most beautiful girl in her college and obviously the focus of the boys' eyes. They gazed upon her from different corners of the college campus. She realized that she was not only talented; she was a gorgeous young woman too. No wonder her Pappa and Mamma imposed those strict rules to be obeyed. The session started and the classes were in their full swing. Everybody knew everybody in the classrooms. The front row in the classroom was reserved for all twelve girls or they themselves reserved the row for them. The boys sat in the other rows behind them.

Among so many boys, Rohan looked very distinguished. He appeared to be very civilized, quiet, kind and calm and a bit shy. He was tall, dressed up in nice modest ironed dress shirt and dress pants. Suffice it to say, he was a very handsome young man, noticeable, especially by the girls. Mahima could not get her eyes off Rohan after the very first introduction with him. For days and days she observed that Rohan occupied the seat right behind her. He waited for her to take her seat and with no delay, before any other boy, he took the seat behind her. He gazed at her in a sneaky way and when their eyes met he always gave her a tiny smile and she did the same in return. In the corridors, outside the classroom, he never looked at any other girl, but always found Mahima in a crowd of girls around her and signaled her with a smile. This nonverbal communication kept going for days and days. His eyes were crystal clear and his body language was as transparent as could be.

The Math class ended. The professor handed the tutorial sheets to the students and left. The students picked up their notebooks and books and started dispersing one by one. Mahima started collecting her books slowly, taking her own sweet time, deliberately. Rohan had the same intentions. He stood behind her seat watched each and every action of hers. There was a resounding silence in the classroom. He started walking out of his row. The sharp silence was broken by the sound of his foot steps and he came and stood in front of her.

"Mahima!" Rohan whispered.

First time, the very first time Mahima heard her name from his mouth. The nervousness--she was trying to hide; her speedy heart rate—she tried to hold. She lifted her face and looked into his eyes. Those eyes with a smile conveyed an unmistakable message to her. They kept searching into each others' eyes, standing face to face, so close that they could feel each others' breath.

"So, Mahima, you play badminton, right?" He broke the silence.

"Yes." She gave him a brief reply and giggled at his approach. She looked at his face for a few moments.

"Do you also play badminton?"

"Yes, I do-- in the university club."

"Alas!" Mahima was amused. Playing in the university club meant that Rohan was a good badminton player.

"I would like you and me to play mixed doubles for the college intramural. Would you?"

"Sure!" How could she refuse!

"We will have to practice at the university club."

That was a tempting and irresistible offer that came unexpectedly. At least one of the dreams of playing at the university club of the university she had hoped to study in, seemed to become a reality. She shook her head up and down ten times in complete agreement.

That day was a very special day for her. That was the day when an unspoken communication turned into an exchange of a few words, the day when the first spark of love took place in their hearts. She was happy, jumping and hopping all around her house. It felt like a miracle. They will be practicing together, playing together and they will get to spend a lot of time together. Practicing badminton on the wooden floors of the university club was a privilege for her. She felt a sweet restlessness for the first time in her life. She was unable to focus on the college work, house work or anything.

"Mahima! Never forget that you are born in a Christian family."

Rohan was Hindu and she was a Christian girl. What if they became more than just friends? Question after question consumed her, but she did not care to answer them at that point.

Tomorrow was a whole day away. She could hardly wait.

"Would I see him tomorrow?"

"Would he find a way to talk to me?'

"Does he like me?"

After a long night, there came the next morning. She got ready to go to the college. Her clothes were well ironed and her hair was well done. She looked herself in the mirror several times, from several different angles. Before long she was on her bicycle and on the way to her college. The short journey was a journey filled with dreams and fantasies. She arrived at the entrance of the bicycle stands, got off her bicycle and hand wheeled it to her spot to put it on the stand. Unlike other mornings, Rohan was waiting for her by his bicycle. He was looking at her and smiling in her welcome. She placed her bicycle on the stand and locked it and took the books off from the carrier. Rohan did the same and walked close to her.

"Could you please wait for me in the classroom after the classes are over?"

"Sure." She accepted the offer and proceeded towards her classroom.

The day seemed to linger on for her as she waited for him until the end of the last lecture. Finally that moment came. All the students dispersed and departed and the classroom felt entirely like a ghost house. The old solid metal ceiling fan blowing the hot air with a synchronized clicking sound, punctuated the silence.

She stayed on her seat and kept writing something in her note book. Rohan was right behind her sitting and pretending to be reading his book. Both stayed motionless for a while. Perhaps, they were waiting on each other to start a conversation or maybe in those moments of silence they were having some unspoken conversation with each other. After a few moments he got up, collected his books, pulled himself out from the row behind and walked towards her. She kept pretending as if she had to write some important notes into her notebook. She could hear his steps coming towards her. He came and sat on the seat very next to her, very close. She lifted her eyes and looked at him. Once more, Rohan started the conversation.

"Hi Mahima!"

"Hello!"

Rohan's eyes were more conversant than his words.

"Yes, Rohan." She gave him a little boost.

"Okay, Mahima, I was thinking you and I should start our badminton practice this evening."

He completed his sentence after several pauses in between and she failed to control her giggles.

"I am sorry! Practice… and where?"

"At the university's wooden indoor courts."

"Don't you have to have a membership to play there?"

"Yes, I have it and we can go there any time." He confirmed.

"What time would you like to practice tonight?" She asked.

"How about seven in the evening, is that okay?"

"Sure, seven is perfectly fine."

This short and sweet conversation brought them a bit more close to each other. Both got out of the classroom. They walked together and they cared less if any one would see them together. The common interest in badminton was perhaps an excuse for them to start a friendship with each other. They walked towards the bicycle stand, holding their books in their hands, opened their bicycle locks, tucked their books in the carriers and walked slowly to the main gate holding their bicycles in their hands.

"Mahima, would you mind if I ride my bike with you up to the bridge?" So politely and humbly, he asked.

"Not at all."

They rode their bicycles from the main gate of the college to the famous bridge of the town. Neither of them said a word. It was a very quiet journey, full of contentment and the pleasure of togetherness. There were many-many rickshaws, *tongas* (horse buggies), trucks, pedestrians, cows on the road, very crowded, but nothing could bother them. They kept peddling slowly, feeling each others' closeness, talking heart to heart and engulfed in each other. The bridge was half way from their homes to the college. After that bridge, there was a split of the road to their houses in different directions.

The end line of their short journey arrived in no time. They crossed the bridge together and got off their bikes to share a few words with each other. After a few moments of quietness Rohan spoke.

"Mahima!" He tried his best to convey his feelings in words. She anxiously awaited and kept gazing at his face.

"I wish that this bridge was not there." He made it obvious that he did not want to split that journey to go onto two different paths.

Mahima was unable to control herself. She started giggling loudly without caring about the crowd who were watching her. People walking by were turning their heads and gazing upon her to be sure they had seen right. No one could understand the real reason behind her loud giggles. Rohan gave her a big smile and laughed, lifted his leg from behind the bicycle and sat on the seat. He held the handle in one hand, reached to Mahima and pinched her nose softly.

"You silly girl, seven o'clock this evening." And he peddled away.

"Very well, but don't be late, otherwise I will run away." She screamed and took off on her bicycle.

Chapter 7
BADMINTON COURTS

"*I* wish this bridge was not there."

"Do not forget that you were born in a Christian family."

Those two statements were echoing in her mind. She was falling in love—which she had no control over. Mahima's Mamma and Pappa would sacrifice anything and everything for their youngest daughter. She had absolute confidence in them. As elders they had better knowledge of the world, the cultures, the society and how the traditions played a very important role, especially in the area of relationships and marriages. They were well aware of how very rare it was for a Hindu family to accept a Christian girl and that was the reason they warned Mahima not only once, but several times. As Mahima was growing into a young, beautiful woman and studying with young men, that kind of warning and caution was well understood. Also she was the only Christian girl in her whole college with so many pupils. Mahima kept thinking that the small bridge over that canal was easy to cross, but how will she be able to cross the bridge of religion, which is built by the people and their ruthless traditions. Also, without any doubts—is built very strong.

The clock was ticking and so was her heart. There were only a few hours left until seven o'clock. That was her very first meeting with Rohan away from the college, the very first badminton practice with him too. She also had to finish her college assignments before six. She had one more hurdle to face and that was her Mamma. How and what was she going to tell Mamma? She prepared herself. It was just a badminton practice and there was nothing wrong with it, but a practice with a male classmate—that might create a suspicion. She decided to tell her the truth, but half truth. In case Mamma asks about with who was she having practice? She decided that would make some instant reply.

It was six in the evening and her Mamma opened the kitchen gates. Mahima closed her books, collected all the study material and placed them at the corner of the table. Like a thief, she entered into the kitchen.

"Mamma, let me knead the dough today." Very lovingly, she came behind her dear Mamma, wrapped her arms around her neck and offered some help. Mamma turned around and looked at her face with an obvious expression of surprise. At the same time she looked confused as well. She did not say a word, but wondered silently, *'Is this the same Mahima, who always procrastinated doing the household chores? She always made excuses that she had to study. What's wrong with her today?'* Mamma took a good look at her, gently unwrapped her arms and smiled.

Mahima rushed to the hand-pump, pumped some water in a small bucket and ran back into the kitchen. She grabbed a cup and measured the flour from the canister, transferred it in a mixing bowl and started kneading it for *rotis,* rapidly.

"You look in a big rush Mahima. Do you have to go somewhere?" Mamma got curious.

"Yes, Maa, I have a badminton practice at seven o'clock at the university courts." Her hands started moving at full speed kneading the flour.

"I got it now."

"Isn't seven a bit late?" Sweetest Mamma did not ask any details.

"Na, Mamma. Don't worry. The courts are indoor and safe. I will ride my bike and be back after an hour of practice."

'Oh, Thank God she did not ask with whom?' And Mahima took a deep breath and finished kneading.

She washed her hands and ran inside to change into her uniform of white sports skirt, a polo style white shirt with collar, tennis shoes and rushed out before Mamma could get a chance to ask any more questions.

"Beta, roti is ready, come and eat quickly."

"Maa, I am not hungry. I will eat later." She hung her racket on the carrier and peddled away with a million of questions on her mind; *'What if Rohan is not there?'* and *'what if I arrived before him?'* And many many more…

She saw Rohan from a distance, standing by the roadside close to the main gate to the courts holding his bicycle. He also wore a white shirt and shorts.

"Hi Mahima!"

"Hello! I hope—I am not too late."

"Not at all. Let us go inside."

They walked towards the cycle stand holding their bicycles in their hands. Just like at the college stand, they placed both the bikes and locked them, pulled their badminton rackets out of the carriers and proceeded towards the courts. The three wooden indoor courts were taken by the other students, who were also practicing and having a good time. Mahima and Rohan sat on the bench, observed the other players and waited. The courts belonged to the university, the University of her Childhood Dreams, where Mahima was determined to study even though those dreams were shattered a year ago, the memories stayed fresh. She was not completely healed as of then. She only heard about the goodness of those wooden courts through her friends and others, but never did get a chance to play on them or even to go inside. How lovely would it be—if she was a student in that university?

Sitting at the bench with Rohan by her side, she was consumed by the bad memories of the previous year. That episode changed her and her life totally in a different direction. Rohan had no idea about the injustice occurred with her a year ago. The hard work of two years went down the drain and left her like a helpless child. It would have been much better if she was not selected and admitted to that university. She had a heart felt desire to become an architect. How tediously and full of desires did she climb that ladder step by step all the way up to the top, up to her goal, and how harshly and cruelly she was pushed down from that height. The thought of that episode still made her perspire and tremble. It gave her an unbearable pain. Such a confusing and horrifying maze of a journey was that period of her life.

"Where are you? Mahima!" Rohan woke her up.

"Let us go practice. The middle court is empty now."

Both got up and started their first practice together. It was entirely a unique experience for her to play on the wood and she loved it. They practiced for an hour and came out sweaty. It was dusk and the street lights were turned on. The road from the courts to Mahima's house was quiet and lonely with the dense mango trees on both the sides creating a scary and ghostly feeling.

"Will you be alright riding back home alone?"

"Yes, I will be fine." She showed courage.

"I will come with you. I will drop you at your home and then I will take the back road to mine." He insisted.

Mahima and Rohan loved being each others mixed doubles partner. Every night after the practice both rode their bikes together, talked and laughed, and shared their precious moments. Rohan dropped her at the gate of her house. They were young, carefree and engulfed in each other, forgetting the nefarious, narrowly restrictive human traditions and rules.

That night they walked out of the courts after their routine practice. Rohan came close to Mahima and took her hand in his.

"Come; let us sit for a while."

He pulled her close to him and they walked inside the walls of the open squash courts. They sat on the floor of the court with their backs resting against the wall and legs stretched. Again there was a pin drop silence for minutes, which always scared Mahima.

"I have to give you some news." Rohan spoke.

It was a cold night. Mahima was shivering, perhaps out of nervousness. There was a dim light coming from an adjacent lamp pole. They could barely see each other. She gazed deep into his eyes and waited for the news he was about to deliver.

"I told you that I took the university engineering entrance. Guess what... I am in." He was very happy.

"Great! Rohan! This certainly is a great news."

Rohan studied hard for the exam and he was ambitious too. His desire was to be an engineer. The news was great and along with its goodness it brought some mixed emotions for both of them. Rohan and Mahima were to study in different colleges, but both the colleges were located in the same town.

"Does it mean that you will leave this college?" She was anxious.

"Yes, Mahima, but I will keep visiting you."

She felt disturbed. Not even a year ago, she lost the golden opportunity to study at the same university where Rohan was about to. The memory was still fresh in her mind.

"Rohan, I have never told you this before." She was heavy hearted.

"What's that?"

She shared her story with Rohan, about the episode took place not too long ago, about her shattered dreams to be an architect, and he heard her with great tender care. They sat together on the floor of the courts, relaxing their heads against the wall for a long time, holding each other's hands.

Rohan would become an engineer in four years and Mahima would also finish her college by that time. Would he really come to see her in the college? Was he really in love with her? Who will play badminton with her? All those questions were roaming in her mind.

"Don't worry. I am still with you in the college for the next three months." He took both her hands into his and kissed them.

"We have to prepare for the finals... practice for the tournaments. You--the girls' champion, me--the boys' champion, and both of us the mixed doubles' champions. How does it sound?" And they laughed.

'And after three months who will play badminton with me? Who will be my mixed-doubles partner? Will you find some other partner at the university? Who will talk with me? Who will ride bike with me? Will you really come to see me? What if you don't?'

Chapter 8
Exchanged Vows

*T*hree months passed in a blink of an eye. Rohan had gone to study engineering at the university. The culture, the society and the traditions would not allow Rohan to come to the college, just to see her. Mahima was well aware of those bitter realities, but she was in denial and failed to accept them. Though it did not seem to be possible at that time; her eyes always wandered to see Rohan. At the bicycle stand, in the field, perhaps at the main gate, or any where else, she sought to find Rohan. Maybe, he was busy in his studies or maybe his parents established certain restrictions on him—maybe not. Her thoughts wandered day and night.

She lost her interest in badminton and spent most of the time studying, participated in their sports and college functions. She kept herself busy as much as she could. At times she speculated, perhaps--his parents discovered his friendship with a Christian girl. Speculation after speculation went through her mind. Though both knew the power of those religious barriers, nonetheless, there was a hope, always a hope, a tiny streak of hope.

The second year of college was nearing its end. The preparations of the annual college function were in full swing. After the classes, all the participants had to stay for the rehearsals. The name of the play selected for the stage performance during the annual function was *"Meri Pyaree Beebee"* meant 'My beloved Wife'. Mahima was given the role of a confused husband. The characters in the play were only girls, boys were not involved. It was a chaotic day at the college during the night of the performance. Every one was running like chickens with chopped off heads. The stage was all decorated. The acting crew was all made up and ready to go. The whole auditorium was full with guests. Mahima took her position on the stage and the curtain opened. *'Oh Lord! Please have mercy upon me'.* She was nervous.

The crowd in front of her made her more nervous. Seeing a mass of people in the audience, students, boys and girls, parents, professors, she almost lost it. She was lucky as in the first scene the main role was acted by the maid of the house--a very talkative maid. Mahima's role as a husband was to observe the maid, throw some angry expressions and walk back and forth across the stage to show a husband's restlessness. It was done pretty well and the curtain closed.

After the first scene there was a solo before the next scene to reset the stage. Two students sat on each side of the split curtains, holding the strings in their hands and ready to open the curtains. One… two… three, and the curtains opened. The second scene began. Mahima's character, lounging on the sofa in the living room, was immersed in reading a book, holding a cup of tea in the other hand.

The loud ringer of the telephone in the corner of that stage interrupted the husband. He jumped out of the couch, spilled the tea all over the floor, and ran to pick up the phone in a rage of anger knowing that the bugging wife was calling from some market place.

"Hello…" The husband answered the phone.

After that big stretched hello, Mahima heard a loud laughter in the audience followed by 'Oh Mahima darling, at least turn the phone around."

Someone shouted loudly and the laughter among the audience turned into a roaring sound of thunder within a fraction of a second. The poor husband became so nervous talking to his wife on the phone with the mouth piece on his ears that without paying much attention to the audience he kept talking without fixing it.

The days following the annual function brought nothing but torment for Mahima. She was teased by the boys everywhere, in the corridors, outside and inside of the classrooms. *'Oh Mahima darling, at least turn the phone around.'* became a slogan and haunted her for days and days.

The days passed by but Rohan did not come to see her. She kept waiting for him. She trusted that Rohan will come and they will meet again. Where and how? She did not know and could not find the answer to the question.

She finished the undergraduate work and earned her bachelor's degree. Her future plans were to go for her Master's in the upcoming session at the same university where Rohan was studying engineering. She applied and was accepted and that was the year she moved out of her house to stay in the girls' hostel. She became busy again—spending all day in her classes and in the library. She resumed playing badminton which was her passion and physical exercise too. She played badminton every evening for at least one hour in the courts or at times in the hostel with other girls. After dinner, every night she walked to the library to study in the quietness of it. That was the same university she dreamed about a long-long time ago. If not an architect, she would be a future scientist and that was perfectly fine for her. The university campus was very big and was spread with different departments, several boys' hostels and one girls' hostel. Mahima did not know where Rohan lived and it was not easy for her to find his whereabouts. She also was a bit upset as he did not keep his promise to come back to see her. So, why should she even try to find him? She had mixed feelings of anger and love for him.

The top floor of the library was the quietest area. Having small carrels surrounded by wood walls, two walls on two sides, one in the front, a study desk and a chair in the middle and another mirror image adjacent to it made a perfect setting for studying. Mahima was studying in one of her favorite carrels. She heard someone came and sat in the adjacent carrel. Without paying any attention, she continued her studies and kept herself focused making her notes. In a few minutes, she heard a whisper.

"Mahima!"

She turned her face to the right and looked.

"Rohan!" She almost screamed.

The same Rohan, the same Rohan with the same smile on his shiny face was sitting by her side. She could not believe herself for a second, '*Is it a dream or real?*'

"Oh. My! You... Rohan." She whispered in the midst of that quietness. He gently pulled his chair close to her and confessed,

"Mahima, I am sorry! I could not come to see you—I will tell you later."

A brief confession took place and immediately after that he got up and disappeared. She kept gazing at him. His actions left her stunned, speechless. She stayed in her carrel, unable to focus on her books any more. She was disappointed. Alas! After about a year--she saw him and he did not even sit with her for two minutes. Why? Will he or will he not meet her again? Questions with no answers kept storming her brain. Then, a few minutes later, he returned again and left a folded paper at her desk and disappeared again. She could not quite understand his mysterious actions.

She picked up the folded piece of paper and stuck it in her purse without even opening it. She had no intentions of staying in the library any longer. She rushed, collected her books and note books, almost ran down steps, got out of the library and rushed towards her hostel. As always, she had to beg the gate keeper of her hostel to unlock the main door and also as always he took his own sweet time to find the keys. As soon as he unlocked the door, she entered inside the gate and started running. She pulled her room keys from her purse, unlocked and then locked it from inside. She turned on the light switch on the right side of the door and took the letter out of her purse.

"I am sorry Mahima. I did not have courage to go to your college to see you, as you know that I was not a student there any more. A lot of times, I passed by your house hoping to see you, but no luck. I am sure you understand."

Yes. She could understand—she could understand that a boy and a girl, one Hindu and one Christian could not meet. It was totally against the rules and traditions made by the social hypocrites. She felt helpless. She could do nothing.

Knowing the rules yet they were unable to resist seeing each other. They forgot all about that year of separation and started seeing each other more frequently, almost every day. After the day's hard work and studies, they went to the top floor of the library, which became their meeting place. Not many students studied on that floor, which was in their favor. Mahima and Rohan sat at the corner table behind the book shelves and they talked about their day's progress or just enjoyed being with each other. When they were together, they did not care about those unfair worldly rules, did not even care if anyone saw them together. They were just two brave young students in love. Away from each other, they were always frightened thinking—*would they ever be able to break the strong wall made by the society, religious hypocrites, those who evidently had no concept and heart for humanity.*

Every night at the closing hour of the library, both walked to the bicycle-stand together. Rohan picked his bicycle, walked with Mahima to the gate of the girls' hostel and then departed. That became their daily routine.

Once more they started playing badminton together. Being the university students, they were allowed to use the indoor courts at any time, day or night without worrying about the membership dues. They became the mixed doubles partners for the upcoming intramural tournaments, which required intensive practices and work outs. Both of them managed their time to study together in the library and go for the practices in the evenings. Rohan skipped rope and Mahima swam laps for 30 minutes every early morning to stay in shape. All day of classes, evening practices, and assignments in the library after dinner made life very busy for them. They were confident that the journey up to the semi-finals was achievable, but after that, the final championship did not seem to be an easy task. They were somewhat anxious, but worked hard to compete with the opponents, who were the state champions, a big challenge for them.

The day of the big tournament arrived before long. Mahima was prepared and so was Rohan. The day of the finals was a day of commotions, a chaos in the girls' hostel as well as in the boys. The mixed doubles opponent girl lived in the same girls' hostel. The two parties of girls were cheering for their favorite player. The posters of supporters for both were displaying all over, in and out, in the cafeteria, in the club room and everywhere. Mahima rested all day. She took a long bath before going to the courts and put on her uniform, tennis shoes and tied her long hair in two tight braids and pinned them up. She was escorted by her supporters to the badminton courts.

She entered through the main gate. It was different, different than what she experienced in her old college playing days with Rohan. She was greeted by a big crowd of other students--her fans. Up until that day she was unaware that she had a multitude of fans, a big group of her supporters to cheer her, to inspire her. She proceeded further and looked at the right side. The stand was completely full with bicycles, scooters and motorcycles. There were also some cars parked on the street side.

She, along with her supporters stepped into the main door going to the wooden courts and turned her head to look around—remarkable. Other than the middle court the hall was filled with chairs and the spectators were all over. She took no time in finding her way to the locker room, splashed some water on her face and dried her face. Then she took a final look at herself in the mirror, grabbed her racket and walked towards the side of the center court. Rohan was there with his racket in his hands to join her. Both of them entered in the court from one side and the other pair from the other side. All four were introduced to the spectators by the announcer. They waved their hands and walked around the courts. Rohan's parents sat in the very front row. How could she miss seeing them? Her parents were unable to come. The coin was tossed by the referee.

"No need to be frightened. Focus and play tactfully." He came close to her standing in the middle of the left side of the court and whispered in her ears.

All four took their positions and the match started; there was absolute silence in the hall. The only sound echoing in the hall was the click-click sound of the shuttle cock hitting the rackets and the clapping of the viewers. It was a very challenging battle. In the end, they lost the championship and were runners-up, but really it did not seem to matter to either of them.

The badminton season was over and they had no practices for a while. It was time for both of them to spend more time in the library and pay more attention to their studies.

"Oh, I need a break. Let us go somewhere." Mahima proposed after spending a rough, boring day with the books.

"I am also very tired and not much studying left for me either."

They collected their books and notebooks and exited the library. He peddled his bike to his home and she walked towards her hostel. At the scheduled time, she came out of the hostel and as always, Rohan waited for her at the gate. He picked up his bike and both began their walk to some unknown destination.

"Would you like to sit on the carrier?" He sat on the seat of his bicycle.

"How? What if I don't fit and fall?"

"Come on, you will not fall. Sit and hold me."

She tied her *dupatta* (scarf) in a knot behind her back and sat on the book-carrier with both legs on one side. He peddled with her sitting behind him. She wrapped her right arm around his waist and held the luggage carrier tight with her left hand. They rode on the mud roads in between the fields of a little village. After a mile long mud road they entered in the army compound of the town, which was a well maintained, clean, quiet and bright area with very nice roads and with little traffic. The beautiful, tall eucalyptus trees along both sides of the road were spreading their aroma into the fresh air, into the environment. Rohan kept peddling his bicycle slowly and Mahima sat tight with her arms wrapped around his waste and her fingers locked in the front of his belly.

They reached the campus of the primary school where she learned writing her alphabet and the numbers on her *takhti*. Her mamma was still the principal of the primary section. In the middle of the three wings of the school building, there were mango trees, a drinking water fountain and some stone-benches for the pupil to sit and eat their lunches during recess. Rohan placed his bicycle by a mango tree and both sat on the stone bench. There were no lights in or outside the school. The glistening moon in the sky was dispersing its cool rays throughout the school field, rays penetrating through the dense leaves of those mango trees. The moon light reflecting upon their faces was enough for them to see each other. They kept looking into each others' eyes. Deep down in Mahima's heart was a big fear of the difference of their family religions.

"Do your parents know that we see each other?" She broke the silence.

"Yes, and they saw you on the day of our tournament. They were there to see the match."

"Oh! Do you know, I also saw them that day? They sat in the very front row." She responded quickly.

"Really? How did you know, which one were my parents in that crowd?"

"I recognized them at the first sight. How couldn't I? Don't you look just like your mummy? Do you know how nervous I got after seeing them sitting in the front row? I did not reflect my feelings on you."

Rohan could not control himself. He laughed loudly.

"Okay, now tell me, what did they ask about me and what did you tell them?"

"I told them everything about you. Whatever they asked, I told."

Her anxiety mounted.

"Tell me Rohan! What all they asked? Tell me word for word."

"They asked how we met. When? Where? All of it."

"Did you tell them everything?"

"Oh, Yes."

"When you reach home late, do they suspect?"

"Perhaps, as they usually ask about you."

Her Mamma and Pappa were also aware of their friendship. They kept reminding her that it was not easy for a Christian girl or boy to be accepted by a Hindu family.

"May I ask you something, Rohan?" She had a bundle full of questions for him.

"Certainly."

Mahima gathered all the courage in the world and asked; "Do they know that I am Christian?"

"No, but I will tell them soon."

"Do you think they may object?"

"No Mahima, they are very broad-minded."

"My Mamma and Pappa too." She concluded happily.

That was a happy day for her. Rohan gave her a promising assurance. Her face blossomed like a fresh flower and she felt free like a bird. She moved close to Rohan, looked into his eyes and surrendered herself in his arms. That was the day when both could see a special spark in each others' eyes, an abundance of hope and a multitude of dreams. They sat on that bench for a long time holding each other.

She knew that all her parents wanted were her happiness and that was why they kept warning her about the traditions defined by the different religions and the walls between them. Perhaps they were over-cautious and overly concerned for their youngest daughter as she was their only child who was studying in a big university with boys. Rohan proved them wrong that day and convinced her that his parents were broad minded and did not believe in the callowness of those religious differences.

"Oh my goodness, it is already eleven. The time to be inside the hostel is no later than nine."

The matron lived right behind the girls' hostel in the staff quarters. She kept a good and close eye on the girls. Her round making time every night was at ten sharp, to check on the girls and make sure that all the girls were inside and in their rooms. After that it was the gate-keepers responsibility to lock the main gate.

They got up and rushed back. Rohan peddled a bit faster than usual and Mahima sat on the carrier. They reached the hostel gate in no time. It was totally dark outside the hostel. The two electric lamps on the two pillars of the main gate were enough to brighten the main entrance, where the gate keeper, like a security guard sat on duty. He was wrapped in a heavy blanket, curled up in a straw chair and snoring. An empty cup of consumed tea and a few cigarette butts were lying by his side. The main door was locked in a heavy big brass metal lock hanging in the middle of it.

"Chawkidarji! Wake up." Rohan shook the gatekeeper's shoulders gently, whispered in his ears and tried to wake him up, and that was not an easy task.

Chawkidarji opened his eyes slowly, rubbed them in an effort to open them as wide as he could to recognize the people standing in front of him. He looked at Rohan and then at Mahima with his half shut and half opened eyes.

"Chawkidarji, please open the door please!" Mahima requested and pulled his hands out of the blankets.

He took his hand back inside the blanket and pulled the key ring from his pockets and finally he stood up.

"Mahima! How come you are so late?" And then he was wide awake.

"Oh Chawkidarji! We had a lot of college work and we were studying in the library."

Poor Chawkidarji was accustomed to listening to similar stories every night from the girls. He had no intentions to argue and did not want waste any of his sleeping time. He opened the door and let Mahima in.

"Thank you Chawkidarji"

And they departed.

Rohan and Mahima were inseparable. They studied together, played together, went to the movies and other places together. The only time they were away from each other was during their classes and bed time. They had no worry about what may the future bring for them. All they knew was that they were there for each other and made for each other. Knowing the traditions and the customs, they tried to keep their meetings secret, away from the eyes of the acquaintances.

The sports season was over and the tedious preparations for the finals were in full swing. Both were ready to take a break from the books. They planned a weekend day trip to a hill station named Mussoorie, a small beautiful town built on the top of the mountains, which was about a two hour bus ride from the town they lived in. The plans could not be finalized before her Mamma's permission, which was mandatory in particular for an out of town trip.

Every Friday evening after her classes she typically went to her house to spend some time with her family. When she reached home on that Friday evening, her Mamma was in the kitchen preparing dinner. As always Pappa was number one to be served. Pappa took his position to eat. He sat in his chair and his little dining table placed in front of him. Mahima took the privilege to serve her Pappa nice and fresh puffy *rotis* with curry prepared by her Mamma. After the other household members were fed, she took a delight in accompanying her Mamma for dinner. She and Mamma sat, ate together and talked about several topics that occurred during the past week. She knew that her dear Mamma never said 'no' to her for any reasonable request, but a streak of guilt within her kept bugging her; the guilt of lying. She did not have courage to tell her Mamma that she was planning the out of town trip with Rohan. Though it was just a day trip, but it was with Rohan, which meant that very likely, the answer could be a big 'No'.

"Mamma!" She was afraid.

"What is it Beta?" As if Mamma could read her body language.

"Mamma! We--some girls from my hostel are planning to go to Mussoorie for a day." She lied.

"That's fine. Why are you so nervous?" Mamma was the sweetest of all.

"When are you planning to go?"

"We will take the early bus on Sunday morning, spend the day there, and return before late night."

"Do you have enough money or you need some?"

How could she refuse such an offer? Mamma gave her some more money. She finished her dinner quickly, gave a big hug to Mamma and good-night kiss to Pappa, picked her bicycle and back to the hostel.

Next day Mahima and Rohan met in the library.

"I have asked Mamma and I have her permission to go to Mussoorie. What about your parents?" She was dying to give the good news to him.

"They don't ask much."

"So, how about taking the early bus at seven tomorrow morning?" Rohan asked.

"Fantastic, I will be at the bus stop a bit before."

A multitude of emotions; blissfulness, anxiety, fearfulness kept running into her blood all night long. She had to cope with a sleepless night in the waiting for a new morning. Early in the morning, she left her bed and rushed to the girls' bathroom at the end of the hall. She turned the water geyser on to heat up the water to bathe, and meanwhile made a morning cup of tea in the electric kettle she always kept on a shelf in her room. She took no time to get ready to be at the bus stop by 7am. She picked her pocket book and walked out of her hostel and across the front road to catch a rickshaw. There was only one rickshaw puller, who was not quite ready to start his work day that early in the morning. He was bundled up in his woolen blanket and he was in his deep sleep.

"Hi. Rickshaw-wallah!" Mahima shook him and woke him up.

"Can you please take me to the bus stop?" She asked humbly.

The rickshaw wallah was very happy to see her smiling face first thing in the morning and was more than happy to get his first job that early. He was also a tiny bit mad to lose his sleep. He took his arms out of the warm blanket, rubbed his eyes and woke himself up with lighting a *beedi* (cigarette) from his pocket. He stuck that *beedi* in between his lips joyfully. Mahima jumped into his rickshaw and the journey to the bus stop began.

Rohan from his house and Mahima from her hostel made it on time to the bus stop to catch the seven o' clock bus. As soon as the bus driver opened the door they jumped and occupied the two seats in the extreme back row. One by one, other passengers entered and took their seats. They were gazing at Mahima and Rohan as if they have never seen a young girl and boy together; they gazed at them as if they were eloping. Looking at those peoples' facial expressions and the obvious body language, Rohan and Mahima failed to control their laughter and loud giggles. They did not care. They were free and carefree. So what if they were seen together? They wanted to leave that fear of people back in their town and enjoy their togetherness and the beauty of a new town. The bus made a number of stops in several villages on the way and finally reached the foot hills of the beautiful mountain range.

Mussoorie in India is an exotic hill station built on a very high elevation. Tourists from all over the world enjoy their vacations there. The city is built in the first range of Himalayas. It is known as "The Queen of Hills". Snow covered white mountain peaks, heavenly view of the glistening valley below and the coolness of the long mountain range make the place a fairy land. There is some history behind this hill station. In 1925, this place was famous as a vacation city for the English people only and was only available to the English. In the middle of the city--there is a natural pathway called "Camel's Back Road", the name fits perfectly—with its ups and downs. Kampty Falls is a very beautiful picnic spot with a garden and a lake. The highest peak of the city is called Gun-Hill. The only way to travel there is via cable cars and they operate non stop.

Mahima and Rohan were enjoying the outside view of this heaven on earth—especially for them it was. The road in between the mountains was steep and narrow, with no side walls at several spots. It seemed risky but was worth it. The deep valleys were decorated with creeks, rivers, dense trees and fog. It was a perfect view of an amazing creation. Sitting in the back of the bus, they were nervous and frightened. *What if the brakes of the bus failed and the bus rolled over into the valley?* And that's what was going through their minds.

After a steep ride up in the mountains, finally the bus made it to the bus stop. All the passengers got off the bus and so did Mahima and Rohan. It was cold just like the winter weather in the plain area and the valley. They were determined to go on the highest mountain of the town and the only way to reach there was via cable cars hanging on the thick cables, one going up and the other coming down to balance the strain on the cables. There was a long line to purchase the tickets to ride the cable car to the highest peak. After a long wait they got the tickets and were able to get into the car. The car was tightly packed. Only a few people could get the seats, the rest had to stay standing. Both stood by the window close to each other in that crowd.

"Rohan!" "

"Yeah!"

"So many people in this car and the car is hanging on those cables. What if the cables break?"

The view from the windows of the car was heavenly, though the ride was scary. One could see the deep valleys with millions of beautiful trees and wide spread jungles. Perhaps, there was some wild life too.

"What will happen if there is a power failure? We will stay hung in the air… forever." Poor Rohan kept watching her pale frightened face and kept smiling.

The cable car reached the top and every one had to get off the car while it was still moving. Just like other people, they jumped out. It was much cooler at the top. They were glad that they brought their sweaters with them. There were gift shops, food stalls, and a lot of fun stuff. The place was filled with a number of honeymooners, who were getting ready for their pictures taken in those traditional mountaineer's costumes by the professional photographers.

"I am so cold." Mahima was shivering and her teeth were clattering.

"Let us find a hot chai stall." Rohan took off his muffler and wrapped it around her neck.

They walked along the foot path and found a place to sit. The view of the whole mountain range was spread miles and miles with a distant horizon, scattered white clouds and spots of dense fog. The view was miraculously breath taking. The beauty of God's creation was adding to the pleasure of their togetherness. No one was around them. The only sound they could hear was the sound from the waves of the cool breeze.

"This is really a heaven… so beautiful." That was her first time on the mountains.

"Yes Mahima, This is my first time too."

"Rohan, both of us are only twenty…"

She could not complete her sentence. A fountain of tears flooded her eyes streaming down her cheek. She tried her best to control them and also her best to convey her feelings, her heartfelt concerns. He felt her pain. He got up and sat on his knees in front of her, wiped her tears, held her face and gently lifted it up. She innocently looked into his eyes.

"Rohan! How much do you love me?"

Her innocence, even in asking that question she knew that Rohan loved her from the depth of his heart.

"Very much."

She wrapped her arms around him and immersed in him—sobbing.

"I always have this deep rooted fear inside of me; the fear of traditions, our different religions, the line drawn between our religions."

"Yes, Mahima, I understand. Both of us are very young. After I finish my engineering in two years, we will talk to our parents and tell them about us."

He consoled her, took her face in his hands, kissed her on her forehead and then on one eye and then on the other. He looked deep into her eyes and said.

"Your eyes are so beautiful… never let the tears of sorrow blur the beauty of your eyes."

They took the last six o'clock cable car. Mamma's orders to be at home before ten were to be remembered and honored. They got off the cable car, ran towards the bus-stop, and caught the last bus to their home town. That became a memorable day for both with some exchanged vows, a dream of a future with each other.

Chapter 9
GRADUATE SCHOOL

Two years drifted away in no time. Mahima finished her Masters degree and Rohan completed his engineering. He continued for his Masters in engineering and she started as a Research Assistant at the same university. She was offered a handsome fellowship to work on a grant and also to use that work towards her doctorate degree. She lived at her home with her Mamma and Pappa, not in the girls' hostel any more.

It was her privilege to get an office of her own at her work place, where she could work on her research project and study as well with no outside distraction. A further transition occurred when her girlish clothes were retired and she started wearing saris to work, just like other young women. As ever she was still in love with the glass bangles, matching with her sari, and a number of them on each of her wrists. Those were not prohibited any more. Rohan's Master's degree program began as anticipated. Mahima did not have to go to the main library as she used the one in her own department. He kept visiting her in her office to chat and to have a cup of *chai*—prepared by the office *chai*-corner.

Two more years passed by but Rohan could not gather the courage to talk to his parents as he had promised. All of Mahima's sisters were married at that time and she was the lucky one left to spend time with Mamma, Pappa, Bhaiya and Bhaabi. Match making process for the youngest daughter became the family's priority. Knowing that they will not be able to proceed in that area of match making without her consent, Mamma decided to have an open talk with her.

"Mahima, dear, come on here."

Mamma invited her for a conference in her room. It did not require a genius to guess the topic and the agenda of the upcoming meeting.

"Beta! How is Rohan?" Mamma knew about him and her. She was well aware of the fact that they loved each other. At the same time she also knew that it was next to impossible for a Hindu family to accept a Christian girl in their family.

"He is doing very well, Mamma." She tried to keep it very brief.

"Do you still see each other?" Mamma was in the mood to find all the details.

"Yes, Maa."

"Listen, Mahima! I think it is time for him to talk to his parents." Mamma came to the point without hesitation.

"Do his parents know that both of you see each other?" She continued.

"Yes, Maa. Rohan also told me that they are broad minded."

"Beta, don't you think that he should discuss everything with them openly?

"Yes, Maa. Next time when I see him, I will talk to him."

Rohan was not only from a Hindu family, but belonged to the Brahmin caste, the very pinnacle of the caste system. Strict rules of separation were implemented upon them and they were prohibited from seeing each other. In a fraction of a moment, the dreams of seven years were crushed in a million pieces. Their whole world was turned upside down.

Mahima's life took a sharp turn at that intersection of her journey. She surrendered and accepted with a broken heart that she was not strong enough to fight the battle with the society. She knew the delicacy and purity of her relationship with Rohan. There was no way on this earth she could ruin it or cause any damage to it. She was very young and had a whole future ahead of her. She decided to go for higher education and dedicated her life to the research project, she was working on. She prepared a proposal for her own research work and submitted it to her supervisor. After looking at the proposal, her supervisor advised her to apply abroad for higher education. Mahima acknowledged the advice and without any delay she started applying for admissions to universities in the United States of America. She was fortunate to be accepted at one of the universities in the United States, Saint Louis University, which had a very good program in her field of interest.

For the three months she had not seen Rohan. It was sometime in the middle of the summer, very early in the morning, she was working in her office. As always, her office door was shut. Rohan knocked, opened the door and peeped.

"Please come in." Many many thoughts ran through her mind at that moment and she was surprised.

He stepped inside and closed the office door, walked and sat on the chair across her office desk. She kept gazing at him as if she was in a dream.

"How are you Mahima?"

"I am well, and you?"

"Doing well too."

And then there was a long pause.

"I hope everything is well with you. You really gave me a big surprise today." She was still in a shock.

Both sat facing each other like two absolute strangers. *Why did Rohan come to see me? Perhaps, he broke all those rules, restrictions and laws imposed upon him. Maybe he was trying to extract the possible out of the impossible.*

"Everything is well. I am very busy these days and working on my thesis."

"It means, only a little time of hard work is left."

Both were struggling hard to control their emotions. After a few moments of silence Mahima spoke.

"Rohan! I have to give you some news."

"What's that?"

"I have been accepted at Saint Louis University in the US and also offered a Research Fellowship."

"Oh, Wow!" The news was a big surprise to him.

"Yes, the session starts just in two months at the beginning of September, and I have only two months to work on my visa papers and ticket."

They chatted for a while about their future plans. If Rohan had asked her to stay and not leave the country once and just once, she would have stayed without hesitation just to be with him and had continued her research in India.

In those days it was not an easy task to obtain a visa for the United States, especially a student's visa. A number of students she knew who wanted to pursue their studies in the US who applied for visas were rejected. The fear of rejection did not bother her a bit. She had a hope and a strong faith within her. She prepared her visa papers and did not leave any supporting document behind. With no delays whatsoever, and with all her documents along with acceptance letters in her hands, she boarded an early morning bus to New Delhi. A solid five hours bus ride meant plenty of time to prepare for the interview with the U.S. Consulate. She had no fear, no worries. Whatever will happen—acceptance or rejection, she prepared herself to accept it willingly. She knew in her heart that whatever will happen will happen for a reason, of course she was hoping for a good one, one in her favor.

The five hour journey on the bus was a journey for her to reflect, to think over and over again—the purpose of her life, all good things happening in her life, a promise for a good career in her future, her academic success, and beyond all else, her relationship with Rohan. How would she be able to forget Rohan and the time spent with him; the sweet time of her youth with him, and her first innocent love. It seemed to be just impossible even to spend a moment without him in her thought. The bus was running at full speed and her thoughts were racing in her mind. Her heart was like a big battle ground. She had a constant fight with God. She felt like she was lost in a maze. She was hurt. She was grieved. She was angry at the whole world, the people who destroyed a love-a true and innocent love?

Pappa's words spoken a long time ago kept echoing in her thoughts and those words were said in the distant past before she met Rohan. What a bitter reality! What an unbearable burden she was carrying on her shoulders at this young and tender age! It seemed just impossible for her to live in the same town but away from Rohan. She wanted to run away, far, far away from Rohan and the thoughts of Rohan. She felt desperate to get her visa stamped in her passport and leave the town forever.

The bus entered into the main gate of the Interstate bus stop at New Delhi. She got off the bus and caught a three wheeler to the US embassy, which was quite a distance from the bus stop. She could not enter inside the main gate of the embassy as the long line of the applicants was extended all the way to the main busy road of New Delhi. She found the last person in the line and stood behind him. Her tired body, swollen eyes and blurry vision were not able to see a foot ahead of her future. She kept moving forward step by step, slowly and patiently. She had hope, a positive attitude and she waited for her turn to come.

Her application was checked and accepted at the window. After submitting the application, she was at least able to enter into the waiting room and sit under a ceiling fan. She sat there for hours looking at the people going in and returning after being interviewed. She tried her best to read the expressions on their faces reflecting their success or failure or perhaps disappointment. She waited there for a long time for her name to be called. The anxiety kept turning into panic and the nervousness was beyond her control. She was very thirsty. The drinks inside the embassy were beyond her affordability. There were no drinking water fountains inside either, though she could see a few outside in the courtyard of the embassy. She decided to wait and remain thirsty as she had no intentions to miss her turn.

Finally her name was called. She proceeded towards the window of the counselor. She was frightened deep inside, but confident and a belief in herself. She hoped not to have any problems communicating with an American counselor as she had acquainted herself with American English by listening to the radio station 'The Voice of America' every day, very early in the morning right after midnight. She also read the Bible in English and some English novels to improve her English as a spoken and written language. She arrived at her designated window. The gentleman sitting behind the window greeted her with a sweet smile and she reciprocated. She also took the initiative to introduce herself.

"So, your plans are to pursue your higher education abroad."

"Yes Sir!"

With no further questions he congratulated her and she was asked to pick up her passport with the stamped student visa in two hours.

With no problems whatsoever her student visa was awarded. Immediately, she stepped outside of the embassy to find something affordable to eat and drink and kill two hours. She picked up her passport on time and immediately ran to the road in front of the embassy to catch a three wheeler to the bus stop and made it on time to catch the non-stop bus to her town. One day of travel back and forth to New Delhi was a little piece of her life journey, but it turned everything around for her in a new direction.

Just one more, perhaps the one very last hurdle was to be crossed before the beginning of her new journey and that was 'the money'. Where would her travel money come from? Alas! That was a tough one. She had some money in her savings, just enough to purchase some necessities to take along with her. How would she be able to buy the one way ticket to the United States of America? Her Mamma and Pappa never possessed a treasure. There was no way on this earth they could help her even with a little. Her siblings—all married—there was no way she could ask them.

She collected all the papers; admission, acceptance, fellowship, passport with visa stamped along with all the other supporting documents and arrived at the local branch of the State Bank of India. There was nothing to be ashamed about. She was loaning the money, for a good cause, not begging for it. Persuaded by all those positive thoughts, she went straight into the office of the branch manager, which was located at the other corner of the university's main building. The generous manager made her approach a real simple one and honored her request after hearing her story and confirming it from her supporting documents. He called his assistant and ordered some tea and snacks for her. What a treat! She filled out a loan application while sitting in his office, with his help. She was required to buy a life insurance as collateral to receive a travel loan. She signed the insurance papers to pay it off on the basis of some monthly payments. Miraculously, the loan was approved instantly and the check in the amount of one way ticket was granted within a couple of days. She traveled back to New Delhi and purchased a one way ticket to the USA. The going abroad process was moving along very smoothly and in a timely manner. Much had to be done in a very short period of time. She had to shop for some of the necessities to take along with her and also had to complete her office work and turn it over to someone else.

Early in the morning as was her custom she arrived at her office and routinely ordered a cup of tea from the corner tea stall. As she was sipping the chai and organizing the scattered papers in her office, Rohan knocked and entered into her office. Mahima stood up and ran towards him. Once more, the two shattered hearts failed to control their emotions and embraced. Rohan's swollen eyes and unshaven face spoke volumes in reflecting his inner feelings. He looked helpless as if he hadn't slept in ages. He wanted to say something but could not. She could not control her emotions, panting in his arms helplessly, wiped her tears and sat back in her chair. Rohan sat in front of her.

"Let me order some chai." She called the assistant and ordered two cups of chai.

"My flight is confirmed for the 30th. Would you come to say goodbye to me at the airport?" She tried her best to be funny knowing that he would not be able to.

"I will certainly come to see you here in your office on the last day of your work." He assured her and left.

The day of her departure was nearing with all the preparations and busyness. On the last day at work, she knew that Rohan will come to say goodbye to her. She brought her tennis racket along with her. Some time ago both played tennis at the staff club of the university. She eagerly waited for him sitting in her office. She was helpless, heartbroken and prepared herself not to express any emotions to him. Perhaps that was the day—she would see him for the last time. Perhaps—last time in her life.

She was determined to prove to Rohan that she was truly happy. The truth was that after the years of togetherness with Rohan, the pain of that separation was unbearable. She had never felt that excruciating pain in her life before. The more she tried to hide that pain, the more she failed. She sat in her office in quietness of the morning. The past memories overpowered her, tears kept flowing non-stop. What was her kismet, or so called fate? She did not have any clue or any answer to her question? Why couldn't she get an answer from somewhere, anywhere? All she could see was Rohan. He was everywhere, in the fragments of her body, in her soul, and everywhere. How would she be able to live without him in any part of this world, close or far away? Would she ever see him in this life again? She was totally bewildered.

In the midst of her thoughts he knocked at the office door, walked inside and sat in front of her. He sat there motionless and speechless for a while. Again, there was an absolute silence in the office other than the clicking of the clock hanging on the wall. Both of them felt lifeless, hopeless. After a few minutes of such sadness Mahima got up. She took her tennis racket sitting in the corner of the room, held it gently on her two palms and offered it to him.

"You can keep it." And she broke into tears.

He lifted the racket gently from her hands and placed it at the table. He also pulled a silver necklace with a pendant of a beautiful yellow stone hanging with an absolute gorgeous sparkle. She turned around and he hooked the necklace around her neck. He was in tears, a stream of tears flooded from his eyes. Both of them were looking at each other hoping and waiting for some miracle to happen. They wrapped their arms around each other, perhaps for the last time and separated.

Chapter 10
First Flight

30^{t} h of August was the day when Mahima took the first step of her new journey on a new road in a new direction. Mamma and Pappa's youngest daughter was going to America, alone, for a good cause, to make her future, to start a new life. Mamma was heavyhearted but stayed strong. If it was only her decision, she would have never let her daughter go so far away from home and by all means would have found a match for her in India. Just like any other Indian mother that was her desire too. On the other hand Mahima's Pappa was her biggest supporter. He had no fear sending his daughter alone to a far away land. He had confidence in her and he knew that she was persistent and would survive. He was proud of her that she had availed a golden opportunity to make her career and by all means should take advantage of it. His heart was melting with the trauma of separation, but he stood firm in all his strength and did not let Mahima weaken in any aspect.

She looked into her past, and she could see nothing but Rohan. Looking into her future, ahead of her, she was frightened. Fear of uncertainty, unknown country, unknown people, different and unknown culture and on the top of every thing, graduate school in USA did not appear to be a piece of cake either. She was also convinced that she was fortunate to such a great opportunity. Yet, she was not completely healed by the shattered dreams of becoming an architect a few years ago. That episode of her life left an unhealed scar on her heart and she saw the new road abroad as the replacement of the old lost one. She was determined to avail the opportunity and move on in her life and progress. Her heart was sore and achy, still in a hope, in a fantasy world or perhaps in a hope of a miracle. What if Rohan had come back and asked her to stay— she would have stayed. In reality, she may never see him again, never for the rest of her life. None—not a single family member could feel that deep pain within her other than her Mamma.

The whole house was filled with the family members who traveled from the different cities and gathered in her house to give her a send off. Every family member was religiously performing their duties assigned by Mamma. Some were stuffing her suitcase with food and others with her clothes and also some decorative items to take along—a big chaotic environment was created in her house.

"Mahima! What if you don't find the Indian food there? What will you eat?"

That question made perfect sense.

"Mahima! We brought some sweets and snacks from the famous shop of our town. I will put the box in your suitcase." Her oldest sister announced.

"Don't forget the herbal shampoo. You may not get the same brand over there."

"I packed the home made mango pickle tightly. Make sure—you transfer it in a glass jar and add some mustard oil in it as soon as you reach there." Bhaabi added her instructions with the other women of the house. She was the focus of attention by every family member along with some loving neighbors and friends.

Her brother-in-law arrived in a big van with a driver. The van barely fitted through the bushy gate of the house and the driver parked it in the front courtyard. No one in the neighborhood, family or in the town had the privilege of seeing such a big van in their life time. It was like a big toy for the youngsters of the neighborhood. In no time the courtyard was filled with the young kids and the van was surrounded by them. Mahima's young nieces and nephews were thrilled to be a part of aunty-Mahima's send off occasion and also to ride in a big van with her to the airport. Bhaabi prepared *aaloo-poori* (fried potatoes with fried bread) to take along and packed them in a big basket with other food and drinks exclusively for a long five hours trip to the airport.

"Beta Jaya, make some chai and fill in the thermos. It will be a waste of time to stop at the tea stalls on the way." That was Mamma's order for Mahima's oldest sister.

The van was all packed with Mahima's suitcase, lunch baskets, fruit baskets and children.

"Mahima make sure your passport and ticket are in a safe place."

"Yes Maa, I have them in my pocket book."

The departure time arrived. Pappa called every one. He volunteered to house sit and was not the member of the traveling crew. All the sisters with their families, Bhaiya-Bhaabi gathered together around Pappa. Everyone held hands and formed a big circle—for a prayer time. Pappa prayed to God to protect Mahima, to guide her, and also for the journey mercies. That was the family tradition for any send off.

Pappa finished the prayer and called Mahima. He wrapped her around his strong arms, gave her his blessings, a kiss on her forehead and said goodbye.

Youngest to oldest entered into the van, children on the laps. The driver squeezed himself barely in front of the steering wheel. Mahima was leaving town. The town, in which she was born, grew up from day one of her life, and made a number of friends from young to old. The oldest of all of her friends was her favorite Nani, who was the most loving and caring person in her life, and was not only her baby sitter, but the best friend too. That day was the day for her to look forward to an unknown destiny and preserve the memories of a time gone by. That day was a day filled with mixed emotions of happiness and sadness, hope and doubts, tears and laughter. The driver started the engine. The wheels of the van started rolling to a new road ahead. She kept looking back through the rear window, waving goodbye to her Pappa. The van sped up and soon it was on one of the best Indian highways with a maximum speed of about 40 miles an hour, which was a perfect speed based upon the condition of the road and the traffic on it. After covering half of the distance on the bumpy highway, the driver and the others were ready for a break.

"Mamma, let us eat." All were hungry and worried for Mahima as if she would never get to eat *aaloo-poori* again in her life.

"Beta! Never be lazy to cook, and don't eat too much of the outside food."

Mamma had a whole book full of instructions for her youngest child. Mahima kept getting the showers of instructions all the way to the airport. The van entered into the city of New Delhi. The city was inaugurated as the capital of India in the year 1933. It overlays the site of seven ancient cities and hence includes many historic monuments. Some of them were visible while traveling on the city roads. The road to the airport was all lit up with street lights, array of beautiful trees and flowers. No one on that van had seen such a sight before. That was the first time for every thing for Mahima and all. That was the first time for her to fly. Before that day she never saw a plane so near to her. As the van drove along all the eyes were in the sky fascinated by seeing the planes taking off and landing.

"I heard when the plane starts taking off, it makes a thundering noise and the passengers sitting inside have to insert some cotton balls in their ears." Jaya didi suggested.

"Oh, Jaya didi! Where do you get all these weird stories from?" Everyone giggled.

"Mahima aunty! You sit by the window and when the plane goes in the air, we will wave and you watch us. Be careful and don't open the window." The young nephew gave his wise advice too.

It was just like a big family reunion on the airport grounds. Every one was having a good time—eating, laughing, talking, making jokes. Soon it was time for her to go inside the airport. A strange silence blanketed the fun and laughter. The happy faces looked faded and reflected the trauma of separation. Some were crying and others were controlled. Mamma surrendered to her emotions.

"Beta! Make sure to drop a letter soon. Don't delay." Mamma gave her last instruction in the minimum words she could speak and wrapped Mahima in her arms.

Maa, Mahima's Maa, before whom her life was an open book. The same Mamma, who uplifted Mahima in her down time, held her hands in her tough times, supported her, wiped her tears and always strengthened her hopes, was herself in tears.

She entered into the main gate and the others stayed in the viewing area behind the glass windows. Everyone's eyes were glued upon her, watching her moving forward in slow steps. Jaya didi was head of the crew, tiptoeing to gain some height kept waving to say goodbye to her little baby sister. Perhaps she was not sure, if she would see her youngest sister again or not. Mahima also kept waving for as long as she could see them, and soon all were dispersed in the crowd.

She stood in a long queue for her security check. She was extremely nervous not having that experience before in her life, but at least trying her best not to express her nervousness. She decided to imitate the other passengers, watching, observing and following them. The interior of the airport was packed with many-many people of many-many different nationalities. Who were all these people? Where did they come from and where were they going? On the top of all these questions in her mind, the most frightening was her Jaya didi's theory of the thundering noise. No matter what, but that theory made some sense.

Finally, she arrived at the gate of departure. All the passengers boarding the Pan American flight were sitting on the benches in front of the gate. Some were reading while others were dozing off. Overall it was a very calm and quiet environment. No chaos like at the train stations or the bus stops or even outside the airport building. That was the first time she ever felt a pin drop silence in a big crowd. She grabbed a seat on the closest bench. She did not feel like reading. It was past midnight. She was very tired, but her excitement kept her wide awake. She kept observing the passengers while waiting patiently for the boarding announcements.

In a few minutes of waiting, the boarding announcements were made and the passengers formed another queue. Mahima followed others. She showed her passport and the boarding ticket and was welcomed by the captain and the other crew members at the gate. What a different world she was entering into! She reached inside the plane. She requested a window seat and with no problems whatsoever she found her seat—and yes, it was a window seat. The gentleman sitting by her helped her put her carry on bag in the overhead compartment. She got situated in her assigned seat and observed the same passenger next to her fastening his seat belt. She fastened hers too the same way. Shortly thereafter the air hostess offered a tray with some drinks with a big smile on her face, 'water or orange juice'. She immediately picked up a glass of orange juice, thanked her and gulped it down her throat. She was thirsty.

It was an early morning flight. She could see nothing outside other than a deep darkness. No one on the flight was in the mood to talk. It made sense as all were strangers. She also closed her eyes to relax. Rohan… Rohan… Rohan. All she could see with her eyes closed was Rohan, and a crystal clear picture of him. He consumed her, in her spirits, in her thoughts and everywhere. The more she tried not to think about him, the more clearly she could see him. How different her world would be if they were together. Mahima would not have thought to go abroad. But that did not happen. The cruel reality paralyzed them and their dreams. Both knew that their love would indelibly remain with them until they take the last breath on this earth and no one in this whole world would be able to change that fact as that is the true definition of the first love.

The aircraft detached from the gate and started moving slowly. She opened her eyes wide and looked outside of the window. Other than an array of the runway lights stretched to a good distance there was nothing visible outside but the darkness. The engine made a loud noise and yes it was loud, not loud enough to insert any cotton balls into the ears. She looked around to confirm that no one was inserting the cotton balls in their ears. The plane was already on the runway. It stopped at the take off point. The engine made a loud thundering noise and immediately it picked up a very fast speed, faster and faster, and then the wheels lost contact on the ground and they rolled into the jet. In no time the big jumbo aircraft was flying in the air at a height over thirty thousand feet. Mahima's heart beat was racing with the speed of the big aircraft. She wished, really wished that if there was a chain like those found in the Indian trains to pull to stop the plane, she would have pulled it, got off the plane and would have run back to her folks—but that was not a possibility.

The aircraft was flying high in the sky. She kept looking out of her window, but found nothing underneath and a dark sky with a million of stars above the plane. The distance between her and Rohan seemed infinite, and kept increasing moment by moment. He was within her as her soul and she failed to detach him from her. After the food was served by the hostesses, the lights inside the plane were also turned off. She pulled the shutter of her window down. Everyone around her fell asleep, but she could not.

After flying several hours, the sun rays started peeping through the window. All the passengers were given a nice, warm hand towel to wipe their faces to freshen up for breakfast. Breakfast was served with a choice of chai or coffee. She requested chai as she was accustomed; a cup of morning tea served by her Pappa the very first thing every morning. The air-hostess offered her some lukewarm water, one tea bag, and a small packet of sugar. She was not sure, how to make a nice and strong cup of tea with all the ingredients given to her. She looked around and dipped that tea bag into the cup of water and squeezed it good with her fingers to extract all the flavor of tea from it, opened the sugar packet, stirred into the colored water and drank it. Obviously, how could she have served with that strong Indian ginger-chai on the plane?

The captain of the aircraft made the announcement in the preparations of landing, just two hours left to land at the airport in London. She felt anxious, excited, sad and happy at the same time. She tried her best to control her emotions, though with some interest prodded herself into spending those two hours reading a Hindi novel '*Kati-Patang*' by Gulshan Nanda, which she carried in her pocket book.

The plane started circling around the city of London—an enjoyable and beautiful early morning aerial view. Her head was turned towards the window and she did not want to miss any moment of the viewing. The air hostesses took their seats and fastened their seat belts also in preparation of the landing. The passengers were tightly fastened in their seats. Once again an absolute silence was established in the plane with over three hundred people. In a few moments the wheels of the plane touched the runway of the grounds of London. The passengers applauded to honor the captain and for his smooth and safe landing, or perhaps to release the stress of fear in them built during a long flight.

All the passengers disembarked from the plane and were given a break for two hours to stretch and roam around before boarding the same aircraft. Mahima followed the rest. She had no intentions of getting lost at the airport. She entered into some shops like other passengers. All she could say was—Wow! She had never seen those kinds of shops before in her life. There was no money in her pocketbook to shop, but she observed the shoppers and the cashiers and did do some window shopping. It was entirely a new world for her, a drastic change in the civilization and culture. All the items were marked with the prices on them, there was no room to negotiate, and no one was bargaining. She was astonished to see a hassle-free style of shopping.

Two hours at the airport fleeted by quickly, seven more left to reach—it appeared to be to New York, and another two to her destination. One by one, the passengers started re-boarding the plane. The past eight hours of her flying experience gave her enough confidence to be somewhat independent. She sat back on her seat and fastened the seat belt without even looking at her neighbor. The plane took off and just like before the air hostesses brought the cart full of drinks and food. She did not hesitate to request the hostess to give her two tea bags instead of one to make a strong cup of tea for herself. She had her meals, a nice cup of tea and spent the rest of her time in reading her novel along with some well deserved relaxation in between. At that point she was convinced that she had no other options but to keep moving forward and focus on her present in a hope for a good future. She made herself determined to stay strong in her will as she was aware of the fact that she had to start a new life alone in a new world, a new world which she only saw in the world maps.

After about seven hours of flying, the captain made an announcement informing the passengers that the destination was very close. The crew members started preparations for landing at JFK airport in New York. The plane kept on circling in the sky waiting for the green signal from the control tower to land. It was a bright and sunny day in New York with a couple of white clouds hanging here and there in the bright blue sky. She sat at the window seat again with her head turned to the left gazing outside and did not want to miss any glimpse of the new world she was about to enter any moment.

The tall sky scrappers, the Statue of Liberty standing firm in the middle of a huge pond of water, long and tall bridges over the rivers, the ships and the boats floating in the ocean and the bays, the cars racing on the highways. *Wow! What a dreamland, and a good one.* Her eyes refused to blink. The whole scenario was an absolute fascination for her. She was a bit nervous too, which was normal and natural. *What if she got lost in that place? What if she missed her next flight? How would she cope with the language and the people?* She was overwhelmed by many lingering questions in her head.

The captain announced the clearance for landing. The plane started dipping down little by little and kept flying just above the deep waters of the Atlantic for a long time. That was a very scary feeling for her flying so close to the water. Another 'what if' began puzzling her mind and that 'what if' was the most fearsome. *What if the plane fell in those deep waters of the deep ocean?* Once more the wheels touched the grounds of the United States of America. The passengers applauded again with the joy of reaching their destination safely.

Chapter 11
CULTURAL SHOCK

*I*t was a long journey and she could not sleep even for a moment. She had just two remaining hours to reach her final destination. She went through the customs clearance at the New York airport, as that was her port of entry. The next project was a bit more tedious. She had to transfer her suitcase to the domestic flight and catch her plane from the domestic side of the airport. Having done this, the second part was to go to the other terminal. The only way to do that was by the airport bus for which the bus fare was required. Mahima had no recognition or knowledge of the US coins. She got into the bus.

"How much?" She asked the driver.

"Quarters-nickels-dimes…" Something of that sort he replied.

Those three words by the driver were way beyond her comprehension. She was only familiar with the dollars and cents, not with specific names of the coins. She pulled all the change from her pocket book in her hand, opened her palm full of coins and placed it in front of the driver. He picked the exact amount of the bus fare money from her palm, fed it into the machine and gave her a nice smile. Overall, that was a very happy ending of her first experience in a New Land.

The next connecting flight to St. Louis was about to depart in a few minutes. To get to the gate of departure of that flight, she had to make it before the end of those few minutes. She grabbed her boarding pass and ran to the gate. She was very lucky to make it to the gate just a few seconds before the gate would close. She was the last one to board that flight. Huffing and puffing, she made it to her seat, placed her hand bag in the cabinet, fastened her seat belts, rested her head back on the seat and closed her eyes. She was at the point of total exhaustion and did not know when she fell into a deep sleep. She had no memory of that domestic flight. She woke up after the wheels of the plane touched the ground. That was the end of her long journey, and in a real way the beginning of a new one.

Mohan was a research scholar at the same university where Mahima was about to begin her new career. He was requested by her supervisor in India to pick her up from the airport. She got out of the plane with other people.

"Mahima…" Mohan called her name and walked towards her.

"I am Mohan." She had never met Mohan before.

"Mahima." She introduced herself and shook hands with him.

"How was your journey?" He asked as he helped her to carry her bag.

"Long, but it was fine."

What a relief for her after meeting with Mohan. They proceeded towards the carousel to collect her luggage; a single suitcase. Both stood there watching the other passengers picking up their luggage and leaving. Mahima's suitcase was no where to be found.

"My goodness!" She was clueless of the system. She thought, her suitcase was lost and gone. She was worried about the packed items of different foods, clothes, and gifts—all gone.

"Perhaps—because of the lack of transition time in two flights at JFK, the suitcase did not get transferred on time." Mohan guessed.

"There is nothing to worry about. Let us file a baggage claim and they will bring your suitcase home." Mohan consoled her, understanding her panicky situation.

She was left stunned. Yet this seemed to be a perfect system. Mohan carried her hand bag and she had her pocket book hanging on her shoulders. They walked out of the airport terminal and proceeded to the parking lot. He had a tiny two door cute green car. While the plane was landing, she saw so many cars, big and small, in several different colors on the roads racing in high speeds and she thought that it was a wonderful chance to be in one of them. He opened the passenger side door for her and entered from the other side and started the engine.

"Please Mahima, put your seat belt on." He requested.

That request was a surprise for her. She never fastened the seat belt while traveling in India, but she liked the idea. It made perfect sense to her as all the cars on the highways were running in a high speed. Their car also entered on the highway, a bright and well lit highway with the lamp posts every few yards in the middle of the divider spreading bright light in the darkness of the night. Mohan's car was cruising on the smooth road in high speed along with the others. Up until that day she was only familiar with two varieties of cars; fiat and ambassador. She was totally astonished to see several varieties of cars running smoothly on the highway just a few feet apart from each other and no one was honking.

Mohan's residence was about a forty minute drive from the airport. He had an apartment on the fifth floor of a tall building. They went through a moderate security check at the entrance of the building, and then walked to the elevator. The very first time in her life when she got the opportunity to ride in an elevator was in New Delhi. That was when she went to pick up her ticket from a travel agency and a guard operated the elevator by using a lever, and he made a stop at each and every floor of the building. Mohan pushed number five. The doors closed and it opened again on the fifth floor. They got out of the elevator and Mohan's apartment was just a few steps away. What a difference in life style she observed during the very first few hours in the country. He unlocked the door to his apartment and they entered inside. She smelled the aroma of some Indian food and spices. She could not believe that Mohan's wife prepared an Indian meal for her. She felt special. That welcome took away most of her tiredness of a long and weary journey. Lisa, Mohan's wife was American and Mahima did not expect anything Indian, especially Indian home cooked food. Lisa was awake and in the kitchen at that late hour of the night. She came out of her kitchen wiping hers hands on a towel, shook hands with Mahima and welcomed her. Lisa communicated in Hindi. It was a total shock for Mahima listening to an American, who was born and raised in the States, spoke Hindi. Lisa sensed her surprised facial expressions, very reflective of her wonder as to how come Lisa could speak such good Hindi.

"Yes Mahima, I can speak, read and write Hindi." Lisa herself volunteered.

"You speak excellent Hindi. Did Mohan teach you?"

"I went to college in India."

"Oh, Wow!"

"I will set the table, why don't you go and freshen up." And Lisa went back to her kitchen again.

Mahima was much relieved after meeting and talking to Lisa. The life seemed to be getting better and better moment by moment at every step in a new land for her. Mohan gave her a tour of their apartment. He opened his son's room gently and introduced their five year old, who was sound asleep in his bed.

"You will have to speak English with him." Mohan joked.

She took a shower and put some clean clothes on. That was very refreshing for her and she forgot all about her weariness. The dinner table was all set outside the kitchen in a little dining area. Green beans cooked with potatoes, *daal* (special lentil), chicken-curry, *raita* (a dish with yogurt mixed with grated fresh cucumbers) and to top them all, the freshly made puffy *rotis* (Indian flat bread). Every single item at the table was a delight and especially so since they were cooked by Lisa. Mahima ate like she had never eaten before as if there was no tomorrow. After dinner, she was served with a nice hot cup of strong chai, which she had missed for the last two days of her traveling.

Lisa and Mohan had all the arrangements for Mahima to stay with them for the time being. They pulled a folding bed out of a closet in their living room and dressed it up nicely. They departed to their bed-room and she slept like a baby in that comfortable bed. She did not even know, when in the middle of the night the phone rang and Mohan picked up her suitcase from the main entrance of the building. After a good night sleep she woke up into the first morning in a new land, which brought nothing but hope and a new promise for her future journey. Mohan and Lisa suggested that she stays with them for at least a week to get settled and to get acquainted with the new people, place and culture, and in that process they promised to help her. Mahima was left with no words but to thank them from the bottom of her heart. The fact of the matter was that it would have been impossible without them and their support.

After breakfast she walked to the department with Mohan. That was the first day of the beginning of her new academic career. Mohan was kind enough to introduce her to all the other graduate students, professors and also her research supervisor, a very nice gentleman in his 50's. He also showed her the carrel which was made ready for her with a desk, a chair, and a desk phone.

"Let us walk to the main office and get you registered for the classes as you know the classes will begin tomorrow."

Mohan offered extensive help to Mahima. He advised her not to sign for too many classes, because along with her classes she was required to devote a good amount of time in the research project for which she received funding.

Even before her arrival, Mohan and Lisa had spent time finding a suitable and affordable room for her. After a long day at the department and the University, they took her to show her new home. The house had an attic room with a slanted roof on the top floor with two other adjacent rooms on the same level rented to other students. There was only one bathroom for all three to share. That room was supposed to be her residing place for several uncertain numbers of years. In her room there was a small fridge, a cooking range with oven and a little sink to wash the dirty dishes. It was all furnished with a twin size bed, study table with a chair and a phone outlet if she needed it. There were two small windows; one that opened facing the street had a great view of the street, cars parked on both sides and several trees. The window on the other side was like a prison window with no view whatsoever.

"Do you like the room Mahima?" Lisa asked.

"Fabulous."

Ninety dollars per month rent; that was as good as one could hope for. She had nothing to complain about. All the other rooms in the house were also rented to other students, which gave it an environment of real student life. The lowest level was occupied by the landlord.

"It is only five blocks from the campus, an easy walking distance." Mohan added to Mahima's comments. She was happy with her new place. She had no other choice but to adapt to a different style of living. Lisa's and Mohan's presence and support were extraordinary.

The second day at the department was very productive. She walked to the department with Mohan and after reaching the department she was on her own, independent. She sat in her carrel, organized her desk and the initiation of her little carrel was done by writing letters to Mamma, Pappa and Rohan. Then in the late morning she had to attend her first class, which was held in the same building. She was a bit nervous. There were not that many students taking that class. The Professor delivered his lecture and she took notes, the little she could understand. Basically the whole lecture flew over her head, beyond her comprehension. The American English sounded like a foreign language to her. Perhaps, she was jet lagged and tired and could not focus, but nonetheless she had great anxiety as to what would happen if she failed her classes.

One week passed by quickly with Mohan and Lisa and their help. It was time for her to move out from their place, start a new life on her own in her little room and learn to be independent. Lisa helped her purchase some household stuff like bed-sheets, towels, some cooking utensils and obviously some groceries. She also showed her some of the nearby stores that were within walking distance.

Chapter 12
INDEPENDENT LIVING

*T*hen came the weekend when she had to begin her independent living, alone, all by herself in a small bedroom apartment. She got up early in the morning and decided to do some house work. Mamma wasn't there to help and neither were her sisters. No one was there to hear her excuses, so the only alternative left was to do it herself. The landlord stored one vacuum cleaner on each floor for the students to keep their rooms as well as the house clean. She vacuumed her room, dusted it thoroughly, cleaned the fridge, oven and the sink, hung two small curtains in those two windows, and made her bed nice and tidy. She also fixed her closet, hung her Indian garments on the hangers and arranged the two pairs of shoes she brought along with her. She looked up at the clock and it was only 10 AM. All her household chores were completed. There was no one to talk with, no milk man ringing the bicycle bell, no newspaper man, no house cleaning lady knocking at the door, no neighbors playing the loud music or worship songs--nothing. '*What a boring, lifeless world it is.*' She murmured.

She pulled the chair by the window and sat. She had no TV to watch, no radio to listen to, and no books to entertain her. All she had were the textbooks. She peeped through the window and all she could see were the parked cars by the road side, not even a single soul on that street. Perhaps every body was tired working five days of the week and they were relaxing inside their houses. The quietness of the environment was screaming in her ears—'*what is next?*' That was one of the unanswered lingering questions in her head.

The little enclosed, tightness of the box shaped room with just two little holes enough to peek through made her claustrophobic. She could barely get a breath of fresh hot air to breathe. There was no ceiling fan or the table fan. She wished she had brought a hand fan from back home. She could not tolerate the environment. She picked up her books and headed towards the department hoping to see some students to chat with, spend some time with the text books and also get acquainted with the research project she was assigned to do. The ten minutes walk was not sufficient to predict or throw any light on the road of her future journey. She walked through the departmental parking lot which was absolutely vacant. Not a single car or scooter or bicycle was parked in it.

She entered into the building and walked in the hallway. Not a single soul was visible in the hallways or in the rooms. The whole building was like a ghost house. Only the echoing sound of the flip-flopping produced by her Indian sandals could be heard. The offices were locked. The students' research room with her carrel in it was also locked. She unlocked it, entered inside and sat on her spot in absolute silence. She had never observed that kind of pin drop silence even in the library in India. She tried to study and make some notes but simply could not concentrate. The sound of flipping the pages of her books began to terrify her. She could not stay in her carrel for long and walked back to her one room apartment. *"Dear God! Why did you bring me here?"* She threw her books and the pocket book on the floor and stretched in her bed. *'How am I going to live in this country?'*

Lonely—so very lonely was she. The department and her tiny dinky room were the definition of her world, detached from the outside world. She got the telephone connection just a few days after she moved in, but no one with whom to talk. Phoning India was not possible as none of her relatives had a phone in their houses.

'My Dear Lord! Please give me some money from somewhere, anywhere, so I can buy a return ticket and go back home." That was her prayer from the depth of her heart for days in the beginning of her new life.

She had no idea how people who do not own the cars commute in the city. It became mandatory for her to find out about the public transportation services provided in the city and that had to be done before the upcoming weekend. Using the local transportation for going here and there in the city would at least give her a mobility and opportunity to be able to familiarize her with the city in which she had to spend unknown number of years. The idea of spending forty eight hours over the weekend in that room alone seemed to be a killer in itself and unbearable. Spending a minute was like spending a year for her in that tiny dinky room. The excruciating heat and humidity were like the last straw. It was way more unbearable than even the summer heat waves in India. The window fan suggested by Lisa did not help either. It only threw the hot humid air all over and made the room more suffocating. There was no central air conditioning or window air conditioning unit in the entire house.

A frequent good soak in the tub filled with cold water became the pleasant option for staying cool. The bathroom shared with three other people did not have a shower in it. She enjoyed the soak, changed into fresh clothes and got out of the house as soon as she could. Where was she heading? She did not know. She kept walking and walking on the side walk of a major road. By the time she came back to her apartment, it was about the time of sunset and it started getting dark. Saturday slipped by and became history.

"Tomorrow is Sunday. What am I going to do?"

She did not have her tennis racket or tennis balls; otherwise she could have planned to spend some time at the practice wall located on campus. She was worried about the next day, dead tired after a long walk, and still a little jet lagged. She fell asleep.

It was Sunday, the other boring day of the weekend. She had to face it and make the best out of it. She never sat at home, idle, even in India. How could she now? She decided to take another walk but in the other direction, with a motivation to survey more of the neighborhood areas and the places around it. She began her road journey. Not too far from her apartment, she saw a church, people parking their cars in the parking lot and entering into the church building.

"It looks like the morning service is about to start." She talked to herself.

"I don't know any of these people. I don't know if they are friendly or not. Should I go inside or shouldn't I?" She kept walking and debating within herself.

She had her Indian dress on, a long *kurta* (top), a *salvaar* (loose pants), *dupatta* wrapped in her neck (Indian scarf), and a pair of open toes sandals. Her long hair was divided into two braids with two hair bands tied in the end to keep them together. She was not sure if her outfit was appropriate to go inside the church and attend the services.

"God does not care for your outer beauty. He looks inside of you. So don't be shy, take your first step. go in and join other people."

Mahima's inner soul, her doughty character encouraged her. She followed it and her valiant attitude forced her to turn towards the church entrance. She was a bit nervous, but tried not to reflect it. She smiled and said hello to the people and they reciprocated but paid more attention to her clothes than to her. Overall they were hospitable. She went inside and sat in the pew. Looked around, shook hands and introduced herself to some. The services started with the opening prayer and singing of the hymns. She thoroughly enjoyed the service and the sermon. It was a great pleasure for her to meet with so many people and she was totally surprised to experience their friendliness with her. So, something good happened on that very first morning of the first Sunday in a new place. Something to look forward to, and an incentive to be there on Sundays.

Two months passed in the U.S. She was still communicating with Rohan through letters. He was also accepted abroad for his further studies and that was the message she received in his last letter.

Mahima started getting accustomed to a different life style. She learned to adapt to the new culture. She discovered the neighborhood streets to go for walks and also the bus routes to some stores and to the Malls. During that time she discovered a beautiful park not too far from her apartment, just about at a ten minute bus ride. She jogged, walked and did spend some weekend hours in that park. She also enjoyed watching people on their skate boards, flying kites, boating in the lake, and many other outdoor activities. And by all means spending some time in that park was a better way to refresh herself than staying in the tiny dinky hot room of hers.

Sunday morning was set for the church. The very first step to the church was tedious, but she became comfortable after that. In a short period of time she mastered the American English and she could comprehend the church sermons and the school lectures quite clearly.

Two hundred dollars brought from India were long gone in the first month's rent of ninety dollars and the rest in the other expenses which included the stationary for her classes. Her finances began to settle down. The monthly fellowship of four hundred and eighty dollars was plenty to pay her rent, tuition installment, books, phone bill and the groceries. She could also afford some money to buy some new clothes. She wore her Indian clothes along with a couple of western outfits she brought along with her from India. Her western outfits consisting of two bell-bottoms and tops sewn by her tailor in India were outdated in US. Just like any other young woman she desired to look like other students and dress like them. She went to the departmental store and bought two pairs of jeans and a couple of blouses, and also a pair of tennis shoes to go along.

She was required to meet with the Foreign Students' Adviser to give him her progress report—academic as well as in general. She scheduled an appointment with him. The adviser was a nice Asian man, very familiar with the challenges foreign students face in a country other than their own native country. He asked Mahima about her religious beliefs knowing that in general most of the Indians are being recognized as Hindus.

"I am a christian and I also found a church very close to my apartment. I have been going there every Sunday."

"Excellent! I know of an International Students' Organization. Would you like to check it out?"

"Certainly." Mahima got excited as she wanted to socialize and make friends outside the department also.

"I will give you the phone number of the gentleman who leads that group. It is a big group of many internationals. Most of them are students and they gather every Friday night for a prayer meeting and food."

Chapter 13
MEETING INTERNATIONAL STUDENTS

*T*alking to the counselor brought further hope in her life. She looked forward to meeting new people, to get together with them and make some new friends. Also, she thought that that would be an excellent opportunity to learn about the new cultures of the different parts of the world. A prayer meeting with food with a small group of the people of her own age group sounded like an excellent idea. It reminded her of the family prayers every night at her home before bed time and she drifted into reminiscing and dreaming about her past.

"Sonu, Mahima, everyone, prayer time…" Pappa called the whole gang. All sat around him in the beds or on the chairs.

"Whose turn for the scripture reading?"

That was a tradition in her house. One of her siblings read a chapter or two from the Bible. Pappa interpreted the text in the form of a short sermon. The other sibling said the night time prayer, a prayer of thanksgiving, a prayer for the relatives and a prayer for the needs of each and every family member. After that the 'Lord's Prayer' was said by everyone before retiring for the night.

Mark, the gentleman who led the Friday night Bible study was also from India. Mahima spoke with him on the telephone. The added advantage to her was that he spoke fluent Hindi. She was amused to learn that there were some folks from her country living in the States, who spoke the same language as she did. Mark arrived promptly on Friday evening to pick up Mahima from her apartment. He drove a big long van, which he used to transport students. After picking her up he drove to the other campus of the other university to pick more students and soon all landed at the front drive way of his house. He introduced Mahima and other students to his wife and daughter. In a short while, a number of other internationals gathered together. Some were from Jordan, a few from Afghanistan and India. Some of them were married and some were single—young men and women. Overall it was a lively environment at his house, very informal and comfortable.

Mark's wife was busy in her kitchen, cooking for the whole platoon of young people. The students brought a dish of their own country. They were friendly, warm, and talkative and were using the universal common language of English to communicate, but with various accents. A streak of hope, a promise of survival in a distinctly different culture enlightened her mind. She felt good meeting with the people of her own age group, matching hobbies and the students basically in the same boat with her.

All gathered in a big living room. Some sat on the rug and others on the couches and chairs. Mark distributed the print out of several hymns and they sang together, clapping hands and having a good time. After the singing Mark led the Bible study. He quoted some verses, interpreted them to be simply comprehended by all. The last part of the meeting was for quiet open prayer time. Several of the people offered their prayers and Mark ended the meeting with a closing prayer.

The final and the best part of the meeting was the home cooked food for all those hungry students. They enjoyed a broad variety of the international food prepared by Mark's wife and the guest students and the meeting was concluded.

Mahima kept looking forward to going to the meetings on Fridays. Mark's family became good friends with her and based upon her work load, she started spending the weekends with them. She joined them in trips for shopping, parks, tourist places, apple picking, and many other places. She also went to church with them on some Sunday mornings. They dropped her off to her apartment on Sunday afternoons. Mark's family was another blessing for Mahima during that crucial time of loneliness.

Three months passed by. She accepted the fact that she had no other choice but to stay in the United States of America, study and finish her master's degree. She stopped dreaming about returning to India any time soon. The bitterest truth she had to accept willingly or unwillingly was that she and Rohan could never meet.

Her high school and college girl friends in India were all married and with their husbands. She also fantasized just like any other young woman that one day a handsome Raja (a prince) will come and take her hands into his forever. She had no idea where and when that Raja will come. Mamma had been giving hints after hints to Mahima about a young man, who with his family lived not too far from their house in India. From the very childhood, Mahima did not favor arranged marriages and basically despised them. According to her, two people should know each other well before they take their marriage vows. To her, marriage should be a serious commitment and the foundation of it should be love. No strategies or business deals should come in between the sacred bond of marriage. She was the youngest of six sisters and a brother and had seen the drama of bride selection for years and years of her life.

A long-long time ago, when Mahima was very young and innocent, her parents were in the process of searching for a groom for her oldest sister, Jaya didi. Jaya didi was beautiful, slim and trim girl and well educated. She had big dark brown eyes, beautiful long black hair--always tied in two braids with little curls hanging behind her both ears. That special day, the naturally gorgeous, simple girl was forced to wear a nice silk sari and make up. She looked like an angelic figure, a heavenly beauty. The prospective groom's parents arrived at their house. They were given a warm welcome and were treated with respect and dignity by her parents. Mahima's eyes were trying to find the boy, perhaps the one who might be her future brother-in-law.

"Mamma! Where is the boy, the one for Jaya didi?" She asked innocently, softly and curiously.

"He did not come. If his parents like your Jaya didi, only then he will come." Mamma explained, but Mahima's little mind was unable to grasp that explanation.

"Such a beautiful didi. Why wouldn't they like her? You wait and see, Mamma, the boy will come running to see Jaya didi."

Mamma gave her a big smile in return.

The whole household was running back and forth, in and out to be in service to the parents of the boy. The appetizers with the soft drinks ordered from the market place were served immediately upon their arrival. The gourmet lunch with a couple of expensive meat and fish dishes was cooked especially for them. After lunch sweet dishes with pastries and other delicacies were ordered from the best bakery in the town. Since they traveled a long distance to negotiate and discover a bride, arrangements for an after lunch nap were to be made just for them. After their nap, it was the evening tea time, and the tea was served with some more snacks.

They thoroughly enjoyed the services offered to them by the girl's parents, Mahima's Mamma and Pappa. In the evening came the time for the parents to make a decision. Both sets of parents had an hour private meeting in a closed room. After that meeting a respectful send off was given to them.

"Mamma please tell us when is the boy coming to see didi?" Little nine year old Mahima who could hardly wait, and was not in a mood to quit, was extremely eager to know all about the elder's meeting.

Mamma seemed to be anxious. She had no answers for little Mahima. The boy never came to see didi because Pappa and Mamma were unable to fulfill the demands made by the boy's parents. Maa-Paa did not have a treasure hidden underground or elsewhere to put the boy on a motorcycle with thousands and thousands of cash in his pockets. Why were they asking so many things with such a beautiful didi? The whole ordeal was way beyond Mahima's understanding. As the youngest child in the family she saw that kind of drama many, many times. On one occasion, some folks came to see her older sister for a match for their son but the bidding went on the younger one. In any event, some how or the other all the five sisters were married before she came to the U.S. All those marriages were arranged by the elders of the house. Before finding the suitable matches for those five sisters, one at a time, her Mamma and Pappa had to endure the trauma of rejection several times.

According to Mahima, the arranged marriage deals were akin to the deals made in the meat and vegetable market. Shop for the price, negotiate, make an offer and pick the best one and use it. After five sisters, it was now her turn to go on the market. She had a hatred developed in her mind for forcing two unknown young people into a marriage which is defined as a sacred institution. She was determined to find her own Raja herself. She refused her Mamma's proposal for that neighborhood boy and wrote her a letter making an excuse that she had to focus on her studies before anything.

Chapter 14
MEETING VIVEK

*T*he winter season began. Mahima had a full quota of classes and research work. The days were fleeting with hardly any spare moment for her. On the weekends she enjoyed getting together with other students and friends. At times she went to the movies or just for a little outing. She started getting accustomed to her new life style.

On one Saturday the potluck dinner was at her friend Neela's place, a friend from the Bible study group. All the friends prepared one dish and took it along. Mahima also made some vegetable *pakodas* (nuggets) with green chutney (sauce). Neela lived about five miles from her. Mahima took a local bus and arrived at her place. Neela had a one bedroom small apartment and it was filled with at least twenty people. Most of the people were from the Bible study group. Some were sitting on the couch and others on the carpet. Everyone was talking, joking, singing, eating, watching television and having a lot of fun. Before long it was almost midnight. Mahima missed the last bus and she had no way to go home.

"I will take you home, I have a car." Vivek volunteered to give her a ride.

"Are you sure? Wouldn't it be an inconvenience for you?" She appreciated the offer.

"Not at all."

Vivek also participated in the Friday Bible study and Mahima met him several times before on Fridays. Neela and Vivek belonged to the same university and were good friends. It was after midnight, the streets were quiet with no traffic other than a car or two here and there, and they were on the road to Mahima's house.

"What part of India are you from?"

"I am from a small city in the state called Uttaraanchal, about five hours from New Delhi." Mahima answered.

"I am from Punjab, your neighbor. My hometown is also very small."

"Do you miss home?" Mahima was a bit curious.

"I have been away from my home for so long that I am so accustomed to living away from my family."

"I still miss my family in India. At times, I still think that I shouldn't have come to this country but rather stayed in India with my family and continued my studies there."

"How long have you been here?" Vivek continued the conversation.

"A bit over three months."

"I have been here for the last two months only."

"But…didn't you just say that you have been away from home for a long time?"

"Yes, four years in England. After finishing my Ph.D. from there I came here on a Post-Doctoral Fellowship."

"Oh, get it."

"I would not have bothered you and should have slept at Neela's apartment, but tomorrow early morning at eight, I have to go to my department."

"That's alright Mahima. I don't go to bed till late anyways. So what is you major?"

"Geophysic, and yours?"

"Biology."

"Now and then, I have to go to the department on the weekends too, just for a couple of hours, to check some machines."

"I see. I also go to my lab on Saturdays and Sundays just for a while."

"Really?"

After a few minutes of pause Vivek asked her,

"So, what made you come here?"

"Wow! That is a long story."

She took a deep breath and continued.

"Would you really like to hear it?"

"Yes, tell me. I am ready." Vivek was curious.

"Okay, Vivek, I will give you an abstract." And she continued.

"After my Master's degree in Physics in India, I was offered a Research Fellowship in Seismology. I am sure you know the subject studying earthquakes, before and after shocks, calculating the epicenter, means the focus of their origination and all that. I applied here at the university to continue my research, got accepted and came."

"Very interesting." Vivek admired.

"The house on the left, that's where I live. See, that little window on the top floor. That is my room." She pointed towards the third floor of the house.

Vivek parked his car by the road side and both walked to the entrance door. They climbed up the steps of the historical house.

"Thanks a million—Vivek." She entered inside and he drove off.

Mahima had never experienced a winter like that before. The snow falls, freezing rain and cold wind chills were unbearable. The best part about the winters was a long six week winter break. The worse part was the semester exams before the winter break, which meant she had to prepare herself for extra hard work. By that time, she had made quite a few friends and Vivek was among her closest friends. All her friends kept in touch with each other by socializing over the weekends and talking with each other on the phone in the middle of the week.

"Are you very busy preparing for your exams?" Vivek phoned her.

"Yes, I am very frightened also. These are my first exams in this country. What if I fail?"

"Come on Mahima, you won't. Would you like to take a little break from studying?"

"Sure, what would you like to do?"

"I was thinking of going shopping. I would like you to come with me, if you can spare couple of hours."

Mahima and Vivek became good friends in a short period of time. He came practically every weekend to take her to the stores for groceries and other shopping. She did not have to walk to the grocery store anymore, carry the heavy bags of groceries and walk five blocks with them. After her finals, they started meeting frequently and also started trusting each other to discuss some concerns and issues.

"Christmas is around the corner and my first Christmas in this country, so far away from my family."

"I know, isn't it hard on all of us to stay away from our families, especially during the holidays and the festivals." He could empathize with her as both were in the same boat.

There were a few moments of silence in their conversation.

"So, tell me, how did you celebrate Christmas in India?" Vivek sensed her emotions.

"On Christmas Eve we used to make many goodies; cake, *gujiyaa* (an authentic Indian snack) and so much more. We went to the late night Christmas-eve services, carol singing, and had a lot of fun. After all of that, into the early morning of the Christmas day, we ate those home made goodies."

She took a deep breath and continued.

"All of us got new clothes stitched for us. Pappa always bought a new sari for Mamma of his choice especially for Christmas. We wore those new clothes to the church on Christmas day. The family friends visited us and we visited them, exchanged our goodies. It used to be a nice and festive environment in the neighborhood." She was engulfed into her past memories with her family and friends.

"We will celebrate Christmas here too." Vivek made an announcement.

Christmas season in the US was on its peak. The road side lamp-poles, trees, buildings were decorated with wreaths and lights, and so were the malls, shopping centers, churches, and the buildings. Mahima was thrilled to see such a pomp and show for the first time in her life. Christmas was ten days away, but five weeks winter break had already started after the exams. She had to go to her department every single day just for a couple of hours to collect the data from the running seismographs in her department.

Vivek and Mahima continued phoning and seeing each other over the break. The Friday Bible study was on a hiatus during that time. He picked up Mahima every Sunday to accompany her to the church. It was a surprise for her to learn that being a Hindu Vivek kept his interests in Christianity and did not hesitate to go to the church or the Bible study. She was hesitant to ask him any religion related personal question.

"Today, after the church services, we will go shopping and get a Christmas tree and some decoration."

For some reason he tried his best to keep Mahima happy. Perhaps, he felt her need of the family togetherness, which she so surely missed during that festive time. After the church services, they were on the way to the mall. She kept thinking about Vivek and his religious faith. She was keen to learn more about him. Though it was not an easy task to talk about, but she decided to start the conversation.

"Vivek, you are from a Hindu family, right?"

"Yes."

"You go to the Bible study and also to the church with me. How is that?"

"I like to learn more about the Christian faith. I was attending the church services in England also, very regularly."

"Wow! It is so good to know." She was surprised.

And it was really a surprise for her to learn about Vivek's interest in Christianity. She had never met any one in her life back home, who was so enthusiastic in learning about different religions. She was the only Christian student at her college and graduate school. None of the faculty was Christian either. While pursuing her graduate program in India, she was the only girl in the midst of eleven boys. Never ever did anyone show any interest in going to the Church. Those eleven boys were aware even before the classes started that the twelfth student in their section was a girl and to top it all, a Christian girl. They found that out when they saw the list of selected students posted in the main office of the university. They were thrilled, excited. They speculated that Mahima's character was similar to the manner Christian characters were depicted in the Bollywood movies; as the night club dancer and/or an outgoing kind of girl. Their fantasies of going with her to the clubs, dances and bars fell apart the very first day of school they met her. Seeing her in Indian simple outfit with two braids hanging on both sides of her head amused them and crushed their dreams. The poor boys were forced to go with her to the campus coffee shop instead of those clubs.

"Mahima dear, you disappointed us all." All eleven sat around the table at the coffee shop. They confessed with disappointment and laughter teasing her. She was always the focus of attention for all. Nonetheless, they were interested to learn more about Christianity from her Pappa and took advantage of her house being in the same town. Her house became a recreation place for them away from their own homes in other states. They socialized, enjoyed the freshly prepared meals and chai and more than any thing else, her Pappa's company and teachings.

Vivek drove and Mahima sat in the passenger's seat reflecting on her past. Their frequent meetings started generating some special feelings for each other. She wanted to keep that relationship with Vivek as a friendship between two close friends and nothing beyond. She was still not over with her relationship with Rohan and had a deep fear down in her heart about the society and the boundary line drawn between the religions. It was not an easy task for Rohan to cross that line and it would not be an easy task for Vivek either. Her heart trembled thinking about the past episode of separation.

They arrived at the store. The mall was decorated throughout with colorful Christmas trees, decorations and lights. Christmas music was playing in all the stores and the shoppers were in good spirits spending their money buying the seasonal merchandise. What a beautiful pomp and show! There were decorated Christmas trees everywhere; some with white lights and snow flakes and others with rainbow colors and several ornaments hanging on them. The music, colors, the shimmers and the spirit of the festivity left her truly speechless. She again reminisced about her years growing up.

At her house in India, there were three guava trees and one of them was particularly small. That guava tree was the famous Christmas tree in the neighborhood. Nicely decorated with crepe papers of different colors, lighted with the small bulbs wrapped in colored shiny papers and some home made ornaments looked unique and reflected the seasonal sentiments of Christmas. It was an attraction to all the children and people of the neighborhood. Her Bhaiya was responsible for all the electrical work to decorate the natural tree and the house. He climbed on the top of the house to make a cross with two tube lights.

"Where are you Mahima?" Vivek woke her up from her dreams.

"I was just thinking, how we decorated our house in India, different from the way it is here."

"Let us find a Christmas tree for your apartment." Vivek suggested, pointing towards a small tree.

"Perfect, this one will be just perfect for my room."

They picked a perfect size tree for Mahima's room. It was nicely packed in a box. Vivek picked up the box and placed it in the shopping cart with some packages of Christmas lights and decorations. She was happy as if she had just conquered the world, excited about going home with all the shopping, decorating her room with a Christmas tree, decorating the Christmas tree with Vivek.

The tree was assembled and decorated. Her room shimmered with lights and wreaths. They cooked dinner together and enjoyed it together. He left after dinner with a promise to come back the following day to take photos of the tree and with the tree.

Vivek went out of his way to help her and to keep her happy. Perhaps he liked her as his good friend. He was also lonely like her, away from his family just like her, and trying to make friends like her. It was obvious at that point that both enjoyed talking to each other and looked forward to spending time together. She thought of him as a very good friend, but for some weird reason, he stayed in her thoughts while he was away. She missed him while he was not with her and waited for their next meeting. Was he trying to get close to her? Maybe—he was. Perhaps he liked her as his girl friend and had a soft corner for her in his heart or maybe he was simply helping her.

Their friendship grew rapidly. Once more, she had feelings for a boy who was Hindu. All of it was way beyond her control. Her determination to maintain only a good friendship with Vivek kept fading. He called her frequently and so did she. She looked forward for the day to be over so she could go home and talk to him in the evening. They spoke at length telling each other stories. Also, both looked forward for the weekends so they could spend more time together.

"It is Friday. Would you like to come for dinner?" She phoned him.

"Yes-yes, sure. What time will you be back at home?" He replied promptly. He waited eagerly for her dinner invitations as he loved spicy Indian food.

"Around six. Is that okay?"

"Superb! I will finish my work early. I will bring my camera."

Photography was his passion. She could hardly wait until evening. She came back very early from her department, cooked, took a bath. She was all ready in her Indian clothes to welcome him and also for her pictures to be taken by him. She dressed into her favorite plain chiffon blue sari with matching printed blouse she brought with her from India. Her long black hair was rolled in her favorite French style with side curls hanging on both sides over her ears. A very light make up with a light lipstick added to her a luminous glow. A delicate pair of pearl earrings and a gold necklace with a pearl pendant defined her sophistication.

She was not sure if she dressed up for her or for him or perhaps to take photos in front of the decorated Christmas tree. She did not even remember the last time she beautified herself in this country. Perhaps, Vivek would admire her seeing her in a sari. Those thoughts created a sweet turbulence in her heart. He came on time. She peeked through her window. She waited for the knock at her door. She opened it. He stood ineffable, right in front of her for a few moments, gazing at her.

"Look at you...You look lovely!"

She smiled and stood shy.

"Something special today?"

"Oh, No! Ever since I came from India I did not get a chance to wear a sari, and also today is the photo taking day, isn't it." She justified the sari and hid the reality.

He just smiled, shut the door behind him and came inside.

"What did you cook? Smells good."

"Would you like to eat or have a cup of chai first?"

"Let us have a cup of tea, if you are not too hungry."

She made some chai. Both sat in front of each other and sipped their chai; a refreshing cup of tea to take away the day's tiredness. Then they took some photos in front of the tree, some of her and of him and some together with the timer on in his camera.

"Now, tell me the truth; the real reason for dressing up today." Perhaps, he sensed the reality.

"Nothing Vivek... Just to take photos and I was just in a mood to wear my favorite sari." She explained, covered her face with her hands and started giggling.

"Really? So, I am also in a mood, in a mood for a night out to take you out to a nice restaurant." He expressed his desires. She accepted the offer, preserved her cooked meal for the following day in the fridge.

That was her first time she went out with Vivek as for fine dining. She was happy and excited, but nervous, an indescribable restlessness was within her. She got up, looked herself in the mirror and was ready to walk out with him. They exchanged unspoken feelings, a mutual attraction between both, a self defined liking for each other. Vivek was handsome and she was beautiful too. Both were educated and mature people, but the hurdle of religion was again the big one. The difference of religion played a big role in her separation with Rohan, which changed their paths completely and rocked the definition of true love. Why was that such a big factor? She or any one else had not discovered any explanation.

As much as she did not want to dwell upon her past with Rohan, a pinch of hope was within her that one day she will find him, but the reality was no where close to her hope. There was an ongoing tension within her.

"Mahima! You will never find Rohan again. Forget him and move on." And that inner voice never told her how? How could she forget her first love?

"Mahima! Mahima! Come back." Vivek woke her up waving his hands in front of her face.

"I am ready to go, are you?" She peeped through the window.

"It is very cold outside. Take some warm clothing."

She opened her closet, pulled a Cashmere shawl gifted by her Jaya didi as a sendoff present and she wrapped it around her shoulders.

"Ready?" He picked up his coat and they walked out.

There was only one nice and elegant Indian restaurant in the town. They entered and were escorted inside. The candles in the middle of beautiful flower arrangement at each table were shimmering and the dim lights on the walls above the wall hangings were reflecting the classical beauty of the Mugal paintings. Classical melodious instrumental music in the background was creating a perfect cultural environment. Both sat at the table facing each other. The gently diffused candle light enhanced the beauty of her shy twinkling eyes and the glow in her face. She could not convince herself anymore that Vivek was nothing more than a best friend. The truth was that she was in love with him. He kept gazing at her as if he had never seen her before.

"Are you on a vow of silence today?" Vivek broke the silence and she smiled.

"I have never asked you before."

"What's that?" She replied.

"Do you drink wine?"

"I had some in the department parties."

"Would you like a glass of wine before dinner?"

"Sure."

That was the night they realized that they were in love with each other and also they were not bold enough to express their feelings. The dinner was over and it was time to go back home. On the way back to her apartment they continued talking about the plans for the holidays.

"So, Mahima, you told me that you made a lot of goodies back home the night before Christmas."

"Yes!"

"Why don't we make some goodies here too?"

"That sounds good, but only two more days left for Christmas. When are we going to get the time to shop for the supplies to make them?"

"Do you have to go to your department tomorrow?" He asked.

"No, not until after the Christmas day."

"Okay. So tomorrow afternoon we can go shopping, then we will eat the dinner you cooked today, and after that we will make goodies all night long. Good deal?"

"Deal." Mahima instantly accepted the spontaneous plans eagerly and gladly. She was not an expert cook. She had observed her Mamma and the older sisters cooking and making Christmas goodies, and undoubtedly she helped them.

Both of them sat together, made a shopping list and went to the market to purchase the ingredients. They made some sweets along with saltines and samosas. Rolling the dough for samosas into a thin crust was a tedious project. They worked all night long and in the end when they got tired they rolled the left over dough into a giant crust to make a giant samosa, wrote 'Merry Christmas' on top of it with some twisted dough. He took a number of photos of her; kneading the flour, rolling the dough, filling the crust with the potato-stuffing and deep frying them.

On Christmas Eve both went to church and attended the services. Early morning on Christmas day Vivek came over again for breakfast and to open the Christmas gifts; a nice woolen coat for her and a winter jacket for him. The most needed necessities for the first winter in the States.

Chapter 15
A BLIND LOVE

*T*he month of January brought a lot of snow and bitter cold. Mahima had never seen snow in her life before. Her favorite spot in the winter season was to sit by the window on the top of a small table against a pillow resting on the side wall, wrapped in a blanket with a hot cup of ginger-chai in her hands. She sat there for hours and hours of the day and enjoyed the beauty of the pure white and fluffy snow, snow covered trees, glistening icicles; the miraculously created winter wonder land—simply amazed her.

It was essential for her to make one trip to her department on certain assigned days to take care of some instrumentation. Rain or sun or snow, she had to walk to her department. The 'Made in India' leather shoes gave up the very first time she walked in inches of deep snow. She decided to buy a pair of snow boots, which made a world of difference in walking and keeping her feet warm. She loved walking on the snow covered foot paths. After finishing her assignments she went on long walks in the snow, slipping and sliding, getting up and keep going. The snow covered roads, the snow covered parks, the freezing rain; all astounded her; the first time for everything.

How badly just a few months ago she had wanted to buy a return ticket to go back home, her home in India, and in no time, in the last few months, she fell in love with this country. Perhaps a country of her future home--a future dream. Undoubtedly, her friendship with Vivek was her incentive to stay. They shared common interests and enjoyed each others company. His passion for driving in the snow was hers too, but she had no car of her own. They loved going for long drives in the snowy winter season. They drove anywhere-- away to the park, to the frozen lakes, the snowy mountains, to the churches with snow covered towers or just to play in the snow and take pictures. They loved to drive the car on the frozen lakes, speed it up and push the brakes. That remained a fun game all winter long. All one could hear was the echoing of their laughter mixed with the squeaking noise of the car wheels.

The winter break fleeted away quickly. Her second semester began with a full load of research and classes. Both talked with each other only on their phones in the evenings after finishing the day's assignments. After her dinner and chat with Vivek, she made it a routine to go to the university library to study. She was determined to work hard for five days and leave nothing for the weekend.

The clear words spoken by her father a long time ago, 'A Hindu family will never accept a Christian girl' still echoed in her thoughts. She tried to ignore them. She was convinced that Vivek was in love with her and she was in love with him. What if the relationship did progress? Would she have allowed it to grow? The fact of the matter was that it was not in her control. She wanted to talk to Vivek clearly about his and his family's views regarding their relationship, but the question was 'how?'

She was afraid. She did not want to repeat the past. She knew her culture and the roles played by the elders and parents arranging the marriages of their children. *'How would his parents react after learning about their son's friendship with a Christian girl?'* She had no answer to all those questions incubating inside her. Their traditional views, pressure from the community, demands, expectations... she had no clue. *'Would they respect their son's decisions of independently choosing his life partner or would they not? If not—would he be brave enough to face them and tell them that he was old enough to make his own decisions in choosing his life partner?'* The best thing for Mahima was to discuss all her concerns openly with Vivek before their relationship took a serious turn.

Mahima's parents had an absolute trust in their daughter. Their happiness was in her happiness; nonetheless at the same time they alerted her to be careful. They had that faith in her that she would only make a thoughtful decision in that aspect of her life. Mahima was totally against the concept of arranged and forced marriages and her parents were well aware of her determination. Even so their groom search for their daughter was very active in India as well as in the U.S. Just like other parents, they felt the burden of the last daughter on their shoulders.

The cold winter season was about to be over and the beauty of spring season was almost around the corner. Those were the days to look forward to. The day light saving time began and everybody enjoyed the long evening hours. Mahima was deeply involved in a research paper to be published in a scientific journal and she spent most of her time in her carrel and in the library. Vivek called her.

"Thank God it is Friday and soon it will be the weekend."

"What is the plan, Vivek?"

"When will you get home?" He sounded ready for the weekend.

"I would like to finish the first draft of this paper before the weekend starts. Anyhow—not much left. Are you finished?"

"Yeah."

"I should be home by five."

"I will be there to pick you up. It is so nice outside. How about doing some outdoors this evening?"

"Sounds like a good plan." She agreed.

"We can get a food basket and have a little picnic in the park and go for a walk."

"Superb!"

Once again, she had those mixed feelings of fear and hope within her, which she could not control. Also, it was out of her hands to control the developing situation. She kept looking forward to being with him. How could she deny such a tempting offer? She wrapped up her paper work and came home early, got ready and sat at her favorite spot by the window just like always waiting for him and talking to herself.

"Mahima—give it a deep thought before you take any step."

"How?" She did not know. The more she tried to keep a distance from him, the more she failed.

"What if you get hurt again? Are you really in love with him? Step back and think. He is in love with you and you know that you don't want to hurt him either."

She saw his car making a turn on her street. She got up, grabbed her keys and pocket book and ran down stairs to the main entrance, unlocked the main door and to his car.

"Hello Vivek! How are you?"

"Doing great!" He looked very joyful.

"Wow! You look like in a super duper mood." She forgot the rest of the world after seeing him.

"Madam! The chauffeur waits for the order. Where to?"

"I haven't eaten any thing since this morning, worked hard on my paper. So, my dear chauffeur, could you turn your wheels towards some restaurant before I faint."

They grabbed a food basket of fried chicken, bread rolls, salad and coke, and drove to the park. Both were starving. They sat on a bench under a tree and gobbled up the food from the basket. After finishing dinner and disposing off the garbage it was time to relax a bit. Again, there developed a strange silence between them. The same silence Mahima always feared and tried to avoid.

"So, you really came back early from your lab this afternoon?" She was very good in breaking that kind of silence.

"Yes, I came back before lunch and did not feel like going back."

"I also don't have to go to work tomorrow or on Sunday. My brain deserves a complete rest."

That was one of the biggest parks in the country. It was beautified with miles and miles of greenery, dense trees, colorful patches of flowers, a vast variety of shrubs and well maintained and manicured grass. In the middle of it, there was a man made lake surrounded by a foot path—a nice towpath for the bicyclist and walkers. They were on that foot path, strolling and gazing at the beauty of the nature, the geese landing in their homeland after a day long trip from somewhere, the birds chirping and trying to find a perfect tree branch for the night rest. The dusk covered park snatched some light from the glowing moon and scattered it here and there. Intentionally or unintentionally, accidentally or incidentally, now and then his arm brushed against hers in an attempt to hold hands. After several attempts, it happened. They walked and walked in the quietness of the surroundings holding each others' hands. While roaming in the park they saw a sign saying 'Jewel Box'. They got curious to discover the whereabouts and what it contained within it. The jewel box was a huge green house filled with several varieties of flowers, shrubs, little several ponds of fish swimming in them and the tropical birds flying. The fragrance of the blooming flowers was intoxicating. They decided to stay inside the jewel box and sat on a big stone placed in one corner.

"How are your classes coming along?"

"All are well—but one." She replied.

"This professor is a pain in the behind. Mahima took the opportunity to complain about a professor she had to take one class with.

"I signed up for the course because I have to take it. I went to his office to get his approval and you know what he told me?"

"What?" Vivek got curious.

"He said that I will fail his class."

"Are you serious? How could he say that?"

"I was shocked too. I stood in front of him--speechless."

"What happened then?"

"Then he pulled his eye glasses down and gazed at me with his naked eyes as if he had never seen an Indian girl in his whole life. Finally he signed it, but very reluctantly."

"How absurd!"

"Yes, he is something. I walked out of his office in tears and walked straight to my chairman's office, told him the whole story. He laughed and told me not to be disappointed as that professor was known for his eccentric behavior."

She kept going non-stop telling all about that professor to Vivek and he kept listening.

"Well, that course is a prerequisite. So I have no other option but to cope with him and take his crap. You know—what he teaches in the class?"

"What, Mahima?"

"The history of the other scientists, their family history, who is married and who is not, number of children they have, all this but the subject, and on top of it, he would always pick on me to answer his questions."

"Oh! Now I got it. I have a feeling that the professor has a crush on you."

"Yeah…Yeah. Should I ask him what is there on his mind?" She joked.

"Why not, why not?"

"If you say so; next time I will ask him in front of the whole class."

"So, how and what are you going to ask him dear Mahima?"

"I will ask, if he is looking for a baby sitter for his grand-kids. I am available—but my rates are a bit higher."

And they laughed and laughed.

"I can hardly wait for this class to be over. Everyday, I go to his class and I come out with my head exploding."

"He really sounds like a psychopathic person." Vivek empathized with her.

"What are your plans after finishing your Masters?"

"Good question! Sometimes I think I should keep going on and get a Ph.D. That may take extra two-three years or maybe I should try to find a job after my Masters. I am not sure yet."

"What are your plans?" She asked him.

"I have one year of post doctoral fellowship and my supervisor promised to sponsor me."

"Wow! That is great. So you intend to stay here." Neither of them had any plans to go back and settle in India.

They were engulfed in a long conversation and forgot the time. It was late at night and almost closing time for the 'Jewel Box'. They got up and walked towards the car. Neither of them had any clue where the car was parked in that huge park. After walking for over an hour, the car was found. He dropped her at her apartment and left for his.

Lying in her bed, tucked under the sheets, she could not go to sleep. The painful ending of her first love kept haunting her. She was confused. She was restless. She got up, fixed her closet, folded some of her clothes lying on the floor and washed her face in the kitchen sink. People say that a glass of warm milk helps you sleep. She opened the fridge, filled a glass with milk, warmed it up, drank it and went back under the covers on her bed. The fear of unknown dominated her thoughts. Staying away from Vivek seemed next to impossible and the thought of coming closer to him scared her to death.

Once more, the fear of society, religion, traditions overpowered her. "What if?" That unanswered question still lingered with her. She was helpless. Vivek left for his home, and she hardly could wait to see him again. Other than the time spent at their universities, they were together. They shopped, went to the movies, bible study, church and everywhere else. Their weekends were filled with joy and fun. Either he picked her up and took her to his apartment or came to hers. They sat together and talked for hours and hours. They cooked together, had their tea time together. Both respected the boundaries of their relationship.

Vivek was a great cook and *gobhi ka paratha* (cauliflower stuffed bread) was his expertise. He prepared brunch every Saturday morning. He arrived at her place early in the morning and she was assigned to grate the cauliflower. Other than that she was not allowed to do any more work in the kitchen. They sat across the tiny table and enjoyed their brunch. That became a routine every Saturday morning and also gave them a boost for the rest of the weekend.

"You make the best *paratha*, Vivek dear."

He loved the admiration by her and she loved to see the reflection of achievement on his face and a sparkling smile. The weekend brunch was always followed by long drives to the parks, the amusement parks and other outdoor activities. Boating in the lakes and bicycling were their favorite activities. Six Flags was only about an hour drive from their place and taking advantage of the season pass, using them almost every Saturday of the season was a worthwhile adventure for both. Sunday morning was reserved for the church and to the temple after the services. She loved accompanying him to the temple and enjoying the free lunches offered by the temple every Sunday.

The second semester was about to end and the summer break was around the corner. Meeting Vivek changed her whole definition of this world. She was not lonely any more. He was her incentive and her true friend. They began dreaming about their future—a future together. It was impossible for them to stay away from each other. Nothing was hidden. Their circle of friends knew about their relationship and treated them as they were a couple.

During the summer break, Vivek had very light duties in his lab and Mahima did not have a heavy load of studies either, as she did not take any classes. She had a full time research fellowship, which meant that her project work had to be done at the department and no assignments were to be done at home.

Some moments of one's life, some events, and some moments of those events bring sunshine and joy even on rainy days. One can never forget those moments of life. Mahima's past journey was also filled with some of those memorable moments. On a beautiful Saturday morning they made plans to go for a long bike-ride. The plans were made after brunch at Vivek's apartment. He had his own bicycle, but she did not. Two people—one bicycle. The situation was complicated.

"How can both of us ride one bicycle?' She asked.

"Just wait and see, I will find the other bike."

Vivek opened the closed door of his roommate's room and got out holding a bike—his roommate's bike.

"Oh my heavens! Sneaky you. What if he finds out?" She giggled and giggled.

"Don't you worry about it, I will handle it" He was in a joyful mood.

"And we shall go for a long bike ride."

They took both the bicycles and began their journey—a journey filled with fun. They headed on their bikes to 'The Arch of Saint Louis', which was just ten miles away from his house. The Arch located in Saint Louis is known for its architectural marvel; a gigantic structure in the shape of an Arch and was built in 1968. It is a miraculously strong structure built by several metals used as the building blocks. One can go all the way to the top via two special elevators on both the sides and enjoy a spectacular view to the east and west of the city.

They rode through the towpath of the famous Forest Park, where others were enjoying the day, riding on their bikes, jogging, walking and some were there simply to be. They took several breaks—to eat, to relax, and to enjoy their time together and finally arrived at the destination. The bicycles were tied together to the bicycle stand and locked. The next step was to walk to the gigantic structure, under which there was a big hall, gift shops and a movie theater to show the movie on how the arch was built. They decided to learn a little history and bought two tickets to watch the movie. A short twenty minutes movie also gave them a time of relaxation after a long and tiring bike ride.

Then they purchased the tickets to go all the way up to the top to enjoy the view of the city from that vantage point. The 'no pain-no gain' theory was proving itself to be true. After facing the long lines to purchase the tickets they waited in the long lines to enter into the elevators. The wait was worth the while. The special elevators were like a giant wheel with four seats inside of the basket like chamber and there were about ten chambers at each of the two bases of the arch. She had seen the arch from a distance, but never got a chance to go all the way up before. It took about ten minutes in those elevators to reach to the top.

There were two sides of viewing areas, facing east and west. Some people were leaning upon those transparent slanted windows to enjoy the view and others were waiting for their turns. Finally, Mahima and Vivek got a viewing spot. Looking down from those little windows was like looking down from a plane; a gorgeous view of the creation. One of the world's largest rivers looked like a creek and the floating boats and the cargo-ships looked like hand made paper boats. The cars driving seventy miles an hour on the highways looked like the toy cars and the people looked like little crawling bugs. They enjoyed their time on the top of the arch.

They were ready for a coffee break. Coffee with some snacks at the lower level refreshed them and they were all energized to enjoy the rest of the day. A walk along the river, talking with each other, about the friends, life here compared to life in India and what not. The time drifted away. It was already dusk and they had to return home soon to put the roommate's bicycle back at the same spot they picked it from and obviously before the roommate's return to his room. They picked up both the bicycles from the stand to begin their journey back home.

"Oh! My heavens. Vivek! Look there is no air in the back tire." She almost screamed.

"My goodness… I will be darn."

"Wow! Wow!! Wow!!! What's going to happen now?" She got off the bicycle.

Luckily some other people with a pump came to help them, but unluckily were not unable to blow any air in the tube.

"What are we going to do now?" She tried to hide her nervousness in her giggles.

"We are caught red handed today. If we are late, we are in a big trouble with your roommate." And she kept giggling holding her tummy.

"You stay here by the bicycle and keep laughing. I am going home." He picked up his bike and took off.

"Good bye! Mahima! You can walk home. I will see you later."

He started peddling his bike faster and faster and she ran after him, huffing and puffing, perspiring. She was tired, out of breath, sat on the grass, and screamed from the top of her lungs.

"Go. Go. Go. Keep going. I am sitting here… and not going to move."

Vivek kept going. He made a whole circle of the area and rode back to Mahima. She was sitting on the grass. He threw down his bicycle, ran to her and lifted her up in his arms.

"What are you doing Vivek… please leave me."

She tickled him, but he held her tight in his arms and ran all the way to the punctured bicycle.

"Let us do one thing." He was totally out of breath.

"Say it, say it, what is your brilliant idea Mr. Vivek Kumar."

"The brilliant brain has a brilliant idea. If we are caught, we are caught."

He locked the punctured bicycle in the stand. She stood close to him and watched him doing whatever he was doing and could not figure out what he was up to. Then, he sat on his bicycle seat holding the right handle.

"Come on Mahima, sit in the front."

Mahima stood stunned for a moment.

"Come on now, we will ride together on my bicycle."

And she was speechless. He took her hand gently and pulled her towards him close to the front bar of the bike.

"Vivek! Ten miles! How are you going to carry me on your bike?"

"Don't worry, I promise, when I am tired, we will take a break."

He convinced her. She sat on the bar with both legs on one side holding the handle bar tightly in both of her hands. He held the handles with both hands with her in between his arms and the journey of a life time memory began. On the up hills, they walked with the bike in his hands, the down hills were nothing but fun. When he got tired carrying her in the front, she got off the bicycle and pushed the bike from behind with him on it or she was a rider and he was a pusher. After journeying through the side walks of the busy roads, they reached to their favorite place, the Forest Park. The park was calm and quiet with very few people. There were not that many cars on the inner roads of the park.

He kept peddling with her in between his arms with each movement of his outstretched arms brushing against her, with her long wavy hair flying in the air, distracting his vision and disturbing his thoughts. He sensed the language of her heart. He freed one of his hands and rolled his fingers into her hair to fix it—and she let him. Before hiding, the sun was peeping through the dense leaves of the trees in the forest and dispersing its last glory of the rays. In a few moments it vanished and the darkness did not take too long to cover the entire park under her wings. Both on one bike were absolutely silent; the sweet silence that speaks louder than a thousand words.

"I love you… Mahima." He whispered in her ears.

And they expressed their feelings to each other verbally and loudly. The narrow pathway with the hanging branches of the trees and bushes help them hide away from the sight of the whole world. Her heart was beating at its fastest. The wheels of the bike were rolling slowly and she gently turned her face towards his. And they kissed. The very first time they expressed their feelings to each other in a physical way and that short journey became a long story of love. The stolen bicycle had a sweet life long memory linked with it. The bike-journey ended at Vivek's apartment. They did not know the whereabouts of his roommate. With no delays whatsoever they jumped into his car to bring the punctured bike back and in no time the bike was placed in the roommate's room at the same spot and in the undisturbed position. There were no traces left behind. Perhaps—to this day, the roommate has no clue how his bicycle got punctured and how that broken piece of junk became a precious moment in Mahima and Vivek's lives. So ended the summer break.

Chapter 16
RELIGIOUS BARRICADES

One Saturday in October, Vivek and Mahima were at home. Vivek seemed anxious. He was particularly quiet and somewhat restless as if he had to share something with Mahima—something not good.

"I got a letter from my father from India." He sounded puzzled.

"I hope all is well at your house."

He seemed to be upset and disturbed. His actions suggested something was intensely bothering him. Obviously all was not well.

"Vivek, you are scaring me. I hope, you are not hiding anything from me."

"No… No… Mahima." He held her hand and sat close to her with his other arm around her shoulder.

"Mahima, Promise me that you will not fear."

Her anxiety was acute.

"Do you love me?" He wanted an assurance.

"Yes, yes Vivek, you know it, why are you asking?"

He took a deep breath and began his story.

"When I was in India, my father… through his friend found a girl for me."

Those words made Mahima totally numb. A thousand thoughts in a fraction of a second crossed her mind. *'How come, Vivek has never mentioned that before? Her parents were also looking for a match for her. So what? All the parents do. Why was that such a serious issue to him?'*

That is the Indian traditional way to find a match for their children and force them into the institution of marriage—the most holy institution of marriage, at times without even getting their childrens' consent. Her parents were also approached by some other parents for their son, but she had told her parents very forthrightly that she would never like to be forced into marriage.

"So what; my parents were also talking to this boy's parents who lived in the same town, and I told them not to worry about me."

"What happened then?" He expressed his desire to know more.

"Nothing, they keep on writing to me about that local match all the time, but they also know that they cannot force me into it"

She was still stunned and confused.

"Have you met the girl when you were in India?"

"Yes, just one time, once, just once, that also in front of the family members. Now they have already exchanged the words and finalized it."

Mahima was unable to comprehend. How could that happen so suddenly?

"What do you think now?" She asked knowing the cultural aspect of the matter.

"Next month, in the end of November..." He took a long pause.

"They are working on the date of the marriage."

She kept listening. She had nothing left to say.

"They want me to make my flight reservations."

That created an absolute silence in the room. She broke into tears. He pulled her close to him and held her tight in his arms.

"Mahima! Don't give up. I am very much broken since last night. My father is a very strict man. He rules the whole family."

He continued...

"Please don't be afraid, Mahima. I thought that I will make some excuse and won't go."

Mahima was in a total shock and traumatized. Deep within her, she was mad at herself. Why did she ignore her father's advice? Was she blind or was she overconfident in herself? Or perhaps, she estimated that their love will overpower all those human traditions and customs as the old adage, 'love conquers'. She was quite knowledgeable regarding the traditions and culture of her country and the division of castes as she was born and raised there. The same traditions which snatched her away from Rohan, left her alone with an unbearable heartache surrounded her like a dense, dark cloud. The month of November was just a month away. Vivek had no courage to tell his father that how could he marry someone else when he loved Mahima.

The days passed by quickly. Vivek did not go to India in November. He did not tell his father the real reason. His father accepted the request and moved the wedding date from November to the following January. How would he convey the message to his father before it was too late—no one knew. He repeatedly kept telling her,

"Mahima, somehow or the other, do not let me go."

Aside from the reality and everything else, Mahima had a faith in her and a trust in him. She was convinced that he had to have some unspoken reason to ask her to stop him from going to India. The panic within him had grown. How could she stop him from going? She was optimistic and believed that his father could not be that stubborn. Mahima wanted him to go to his father and tell him about her and him. As an elder and a father, his father would never be in favor to destroy the love that existed between his son and the girl his son loved. His father was a human being with a heart beating in him. He could not stay stubborn— and that was her faith. All parents find their happiness in their children's happiness, why wouldn't his father?

There were only two months left. Whatever had to be done had to be done soon. For some reason, Vivek feared his father. He was even afraid of phoning him. All he told Mahima was that the best decision would be not to go. He had no courage to convey the real message to his father.

The month of December arrived and so did the second Christmas. There were no plans for Christmas shopping, no decorated Christmas tree and no desire to celebrate the season like they did a year ago. There was a catholic church in a remote area. That was about an hour drive from their town. People believed that praying and lightening a candle at the sacred place in the church meant the prayers heard and answered. Vivek and Mahima believed what others believed.

It was a cold winter day. The roads were covered with white snow and driving on those slippery roads could be very dangerous. Slipping and sliding on those roads, they arrived at the church premises. All bundled up in winter clothes, coats, hats, gloves and snow boots, they made their entrance into the prayer room. There were countless candles burning in flames and warming up the surroundings. They also placed theirs besides the others. Mahima kept a strong faith in prayers and had a firm belief that if their love was true, the strongest power in this world would not be able to destroy it and by lighting the candles in a holy place was a symbolic way for her to ask God's mercy upon them.

"Mahima, if you also come along with me, they will have to accept."

"Why don't you ask me to stay and not go?"

"No, Vivek. You should go, meet everyone in your family, tell you father everything clearly, get his permission and blessings and come back. He will understand."

Vivek hesitated to face his father. Mahima believed that it was impossible to unite in a sacred relationship against the will of the elders. Mahima saw only blackness before her eyes. She saw an uncertain future. How would they ever be able to live a happy life--a life with opposition, a life with the highlighted religious differences?

The day of his departure arrived. Vivek packed his suitcase. He and Mahima sat in his room. Perhaps—this was the most difficult test for them. *"Vivek should be bold enough to pick the phone and tell his father."* That was her unspoken desire, which she was not able to express to him. Nonetheless she left the decision to him. It was time for them to depart for the airport. He was uncertain, got up from the couch and started pacing back and forth in the room, unable to make a firm decision.

"Mahima! Alright! I will go. You keep your trust in me and I will come back to you."

He picked up his suitcase and both walked out the door. He loaded his suitcase in the trunk of the car and they were ready, him on the driver's seat and her as a passenger. He started the car. The car sped up and was on the highway to the airport. Neither of them had any words to exchange. She was sobbing. Her hand was in his hand and both of their fingers were tightly locked. That was the day, she saw tears in his eyes, heard him sobbing.

"Vivek! Please stay strong. Go and beg your father. He will respect it. I will be very proud of you. Spend some time with your father and come back soon. I will count each and every moment as I await your return."

She kept holding his hand tight—very tightly. She did not want to let go even for a second. They arrived at the check-in counter and found that the plane had already left the gate. Vivek missed his flight by just a few minutes. The next flight to Chicago International airport was scheduled to depart an hour later. They had another hour to spend with each other. They sat in front of the gate holding each other, so no one could dare to separate them. That hour of their lives flew away in a blink of an eye. The announcement for the flight departure was made and the boarding began. One by one all the passengers boarded the plane. Vivek separated her from him, gently, very gently. He took her face in his hand, kissed her goodbye and gave her some words of hope and assurance;

"Mahima, promise me… you will not be afraid… I will return back soon. I will write to you. Please pray and wait for me."

Those words had confidence, power, hope, and a promise. They were filled with profoundness and an absolute loyalty. She giggled with joy in the midst of sobbing, wiped her tears, hid in his arms for the last time and then did let him go. He stepped towards the gate, turned around, looked at her, waved and disappeared. She felt like her soul left her body. She sat on the chair placed nearby. She was helpless. The rivers of tears flooded from her eyes.

After a few minutes, she stood up and walked to the viewing window and kept gazing at his plane without even blinking her eyes. The attachment connecting to the door of the plane detached. She hoped that he was watching her through his window, if he got the window seat. Her eyes moved with the movement of the plane. It backed up away from the gate. In just a few moments it was on the runway and sped off fast. She was able to view every movement of the plane clearly. The wheels left the ground and rolled back in the big body of the plane and finally it vanished in its own clouds of smoke.

Vivek was flying up in the air and she was sitting by the viewing window at the airport. The feeling of emptiness within her was unbearable. She felt like a dead person, an object with no life. She stayed on that chair to try to get some strength back and get herself together. Her life took another turn once again. She got up and walked to the parking lot, unlocked the car and sat on the driver's seat. She had to drive alone. Both of her hands were on the steering wheel, holding it tight. She never drove the car alone without him. How would she do it—she did not know? How would she take the car on the highway—she did not know? She was not quite ready to start the car. She closed her eyes and was lost in the past time spent with Vivek.

"Vivek, please Vivek, I want to learn to drive, please!" She begged him and begged him the day they were returning from their routine shopping.

"Certainly, let us find a big vacant parking lot."

"Good idea. Let us go to the Forest Park and find an open lot."

She was jumping up and down as Vivek agreed upon teaching her driving. In no time they were inside a big parking lot.

"Remember, today on you are my student and you have to obey me. Understand!"

"Yes, Sir. I respect your command!" She raised her arm and saluted her temporary instructor.

"First lesson; you come and sit on my seat and I will sit on yours."

"Oh, really! I thought I could drive sitting on the passenger seat."

She jumped out of the car, ran around it, came to the other side and sat in front of the steering wheel on the driver's seat. She held the steering wheel in both her hands and held it real tight, dreaming that soon she will be on the road.

"The first lesson for today is that you have to locate the brakes and the accelerator, the rear view mirror and the side mirrors, and then start the engine." Vivek indicated.

"But Vivek, I already know all of it. I know where they are. Now tell me, how am I going to move the car forward?"

"Now, listen to your teacher. On Monday, we will go to take the written test for driving, get the learning permit and then the training to move the car will start. Now, come back to your seat."

"Yes, Sir!"

Very reluctantly, she got off the driver's seat and sat back on the passenger seat. In next two days she had to prepare for a written driving test. He drove her to his apartment and found his old driving guide to prepare her for the upcoming test. He guided her through all the driving rules and regulations and then she was ready to take the test. Monday afternoon was the time for her big test and they were there.

"Ready for it Yaddee?" Vivek called her 'Yaddee' means 'buddy'.

"Yeah, Guru ji!" She proceeded to the room to take her test.

He waited outside the testing room. She passed the test and came out in ten minutes.

"Yup Yup Yup." She was happy.

"Now on the guru will sit on the passenger's side and you will drive." Vivek announced looking at her permit.

Mahima practiced driving with Vivek to get ready for the road test to obtain a real drivers' license. Her driving training was in full swing. She drove enough in the parking lot and then gradually moved onto the road.

"Yaddee! Are you ready for the driving test?"

"Very much." She was confident.

"So, let us go and practice parallel parking."

Which meant fitting the car in between two parked cars by moving the car back and forth only in three trials. That was the hardest task for Mahima. She practiced and practiced several times parking in between the two coke cans and knocked them off repeatedly.

She was on the driver's seat and the officer on the passenger's carrying a pen and a score sheet in his hands. She looked in the front, in the back using the rear-view mirror, fixed her side mirror and fastened the seat belt as she was required to do. The officer observed each and every one of her actions. After the officer's 'go' signal, she drove the car on the road and followed his commands. No mistake was made. It was a perfect going. The last hurdle of the test was the parallel parking in between two poles which were not more than three feet in height.

"Oh, my heavens! How will I be able to see these short poles from my mirrors? Lord! Please help me!"

And those were the exact thoughts in her head. She was nervous. The front pole was visible, but the pole behind the car was no where to be seen.

"Why didn't they put the pole on one side, so at least I could see it from the rear view mirror?" She murmured in her head. She tried. She guessed.

"How in the world I could park the car in three strikes...no way!" She talked to herself.

She switched the gear into reverse and reversed the car. In a fraction of a second, the car hit the pole and the pole flew and it dropped a few yards away from the car.

"Miss! You must practice parallel parking more and come back again after you feel that you are ready."

There was a funny smile on the officer's face. He meant, and meant very clearly that she failed the driving test. Vivek was waiting impatiently to hear the word. She returned with the officer. Vivek looked at her and her disappointed face looked hideous which spoke louder than the words. He could not control himself, started laughing and giggling loud.

"How funny!" She was upset.

"Come on Mahima. Don't be upset. We will practice more and come back." They walked to their car parked by the road side.

She was totally lost in her past spent with Vivek. She was still at the airport parking lot, locked inside Vivek's car. The noisy environment, the loudness of planes landing and taking off did not bother her.

After practicing more and more, finally she got her driver's license—a real license, so she could drive independently. She loved driving. She drove and Vivek enjoyed the rides. He never did get upset at Mahima even if she made mistakes and that showed his confidence in her. He was her strength and her motivation.

All those old memories were roaming through her mind. One day, both were coming back from their routine shopping trip and she was driving. She had to take a right turn on a busy intersection. Her right blinker was on and she being a careful new driver waited a little longer to make that turn. Some impatient driver honked from behind, made her nervous and instead of the brakes, she pushed the accelerator on the turn. She could not control the car. The car hit the curb and climbed up on the side walk and in no time hit a big tree on the other side. The front of the car got totally damaged. That accident traumatized them both, but neither was physically hurt. In a few moments after catching his breath Vivek got out of the car and walked towards Mahima who sat stunned on the driver's seat.

"Are you Okay?"

"Yes." She shook her head.

"Come on…"

She opened the door and came out. She was trembling in fear. He took her into his arms.

"Don't be afraid, go on the other side; I will pull the car back."

"Don't be afraid."

Vivek had told her several times not to be afraid.

"Perhaps, Vivek will not be afraid of his father and will talk to him boldly, convince him and come back."

She got herself together and started the engine and drove home. The whole world looked like a big wilderness to her. She felt like she was lost in a maze—alone--so very lonely. Her own room did not look like her own. She threw her purse on the chair, splashed some cold water on her face and laid on her bed—totally exhausted.

Chapter 17
Vivek's Promise

*T*he promising words spoken by Vivek at the airport were her strength, her hope, her future in that time of loneliness. She missed him. Every day in the morning she crossed out the date in the calendar hanging by her bedside; it meant one less day before his return to be with her. Each passing moment became a blessing and shortened the time of her long wait for him. Every evening after coming back from her department, the very first thing after opening the main door was to check her mail box. Seven days after his departure she received a blue inland letter from him. She picked it up and looked all the sides of that envelope and smelled it. The landlady and her son sitting on the couch at the entrance observed her crazy actions.

"Look, I got a letter from him."

She jumped on the stair case, hopping and running on those steps, entered into her room and locked it from inside. She threw her books on the bed, sat on the floor, kissed the letter several times and opened it. He wrote about his journey and also that he told his father about him and her. Also that he would be returning soon.

"I told you Vivek, if you tell your father about us, he would do any thing to keep you happy." She kept talking to herself.

Vivek's letter gave her high hopes. She could hardly wait to see him and be with him. Without any delay she picked up the letter pad and a pen and wrote a reply to him. That was the day she was flying like a bird, chirping like a bird and was the happiest girl in the world. She had to mail the letter right away before the last pick up. The landlady observed her intently.

"Mahima! Be careful honey. It is darn cold outside."

"I will be just fine, don't you worry. This letter has to be mailed today." And she flew outside.

How happy was she that day! Her prayers were answered. She was excited to be with him soon. In her room, she stood in front of a long mirror hanging on the wall, posed and looked at her image. She found herself to be the most beautiful woman on the face of the earth. She tried several outfits and modeled in front of the mirror.

"The day Vivek arrives, I will dress up in his favorite blue sari, role my hair up and pick him up from the airport."

His letters kept flowing every single day. She kept replying immediately and mailing them before the last pick up. Only one week was left in his return. She could hardly wait. Just like every day in the evening, she came back from her department, but on that day there was no letter in the mail box. A thousand weird thoughts invaded her mind. *'Perhaps, the postman placed her letter into some other mail box or perhaps Vivek could not post it before the mail pick up in India.'* She had no alternative but to wait for the next day, which was not easy for her to do. After a long day of classes and her research work, she rushed back to her apartment and to the mail box. Nothing was there, not even a piece of junk mail. Three days have passed by, and there was no message from Vivek.

"*Perchance, he is busy in the preparations to come back.*"

"*He will never break his promise.*"

"*What if his father changed his mind?*"

Her trust in him was absolutely grounded. Contemplating both sides of her wandering imagination, she refused to believe any negative part of her thoughts. They were there in her mind to puzzle her, to confuse her, and to torture her. She had an absolute trust in him.

"*He will come back—no matter what.*"

Four days later a blue envelope arrived in the mail. She saw it in the midst of the other junk mail in her mail box. She picked the whole stack and proceeded towards the stair case. Her hands trembled, her legs had no strength, and she felt feeble climbing up the steps. She was not sure, if she really wanted to open that letter or not, but she did.

"This marriage was arranged by my father a long time ago."

The message was clear and transparent. Vivek was being forced to marry a girl of his father's choice because his father gave a word to the girl's parents a long time ago. For his father, the words given a decade or more ago weighed way more than his son's true love and his future happiness. Why not? According to the traditions and human rules, his father's only concern was his own dignity, his own self respect in the society and to top it all, to honor the firm business deal made between him and the girl's parents a long time ago. That deal had to be honored by his son. The simple order dictated by his father had to be obeyed. A father refused to foresee the future and ignored the fragility of the situation before announcing the ignoble decision, which was made by him and him only. An honorable father did not even think that his son traveled from so far away to get his blessings and to beg for his mercy. In return, the reward given to a son was to make him a prisoner in his own father's house.

Mahima was well aware of those traditions and customs and the values given to them. Many children offered a sacrifice of their love for the sake of their parents' demands and to maintain their somewhat artificial image in society. She still had a hope and she desired Vivek to win that battle with his father and come back to her as he promised. She continued reading the letter.

"My best friend is helping me out. If my father doesn't listen to me, he will help me to escape out and bring me to the airport."

How all of it would happen? It did not sound that easy. Why did he have to have a plan to escape out of his own house? She failed to find the answers to all those 'whys'. All she could do was wait for the next letter. She was extremely confused and puzzled; nonetheless, her hope was still alive.

"*Perhaps—Vivek is with his friends or may be on the way to the airport.*"

"*How could he marry any other girl? This is not a game of dolls being played by little children.*"

"*This marriage cannot be forced upon him.*"

"*I hope he is not miserable. That his father is not emotionally black mailing him.*"

She felt like her whole body was trapped and tightened into thick chains and she was unable to move a single limb of her body or breathe. She was totally paralyzed and there was no way for her to talk to Vivek.

Vivek's expected arrival date passed, the last weekend in January. She was lonely, she was depressed. Nothing in the world could enliven her. The whole universe seemed to be like a big dense and dark jungle filled with all wild animals. The snow covered roads, cars, trees, frozen lakes, all were meaningless to her. She was afraid to stay alone in her tiny room for two long days of the weekend. She phoned her friend, and the friend was kind enough to invite her for the weekend. She took no time to get out of the house, cleaned the snow covered car parked by the street and took off. Skidding and slipping, she arrived at Rajni's house. Rajni and her husband Naveen were her friends from the Bible study group. They knew Mahima and Vivek well and also their relationship.

"Why did you let Vivek go to India?" Naveen posed that question to her without even thinking the sentiments behind it, without any hesitation.

"No, Naveen, it does not matter. He will come back. He is just facing some difficulties at the moment."

She was confident and she convinced Naveen. Naveen kept gazing at her face. Perhaps, he wanted to tell her not to fool herself as she had made the biggest mistake by letting him to go.

"Yes, Mahima, I don't think he should have gone. You know, how forceful the parents are in India and their controlling and dictating power for their children."

Rajni agreed with what her husband had just said. Nothing could ease

Mahima's restlessness. All she knew was that Vivek would not break his promise.

"No, nothing happened to him. He vowed. He promised that he will come back to me. Yes, it is true and would be the best if he hadn't gone, but he has been writing to me constantly." And she broke into tears. Rajni walked her in her room and put her arms around her.

"Rajni, why can't you believe me? I am telling you, he will come back to me and no one can deny this fact."

Rajni and Naveen invited her to stay at their place until Vivek returned from India. She drove back and forth to her university from their house. Every evening on her way back from the university, she stopped by at her apartment to check the mail before continuing to Rajni's house. She was never a quitter and she never wanted to be one. Her hopes were alive and she did not accept not even for a fraction of a moment that Vivek had been taken away from her.

The month of February began. There was no news from Vivek. Mahima suffered through a crucial period of pain and agony during that phase of her life. Naveen and Rajni maintained a silence. They were convinced that Vivek's marriage took place in those past days. They tried several different ways to prepare Mahima to accept the reality.

The first week of February was brutally cold. It snowed and the whole city was covered with white snow and frozen sheets of ice. It was late at night. Mahima was studying in her bedroom at Rajni's house. Naveen and Rajni were in their room--asleep. All of a sudden their house phone rang.

"It must be Vivek. Who else would call that late?" Mahima became alert.

Naveen answered the phone. She heard him talking and a few minutes later she also heard him hanging up the phone. The short conversation was over and after that established an absolute silence. She sensed that something was not right. Just a few minutes later she heard a knock at her door. Rajni stepped into her room and sat on her bed by her side. Mahima's heart was out of her chest. *'So late, in the middle of the night, what could be that urgent?'*

"What is wrong Rajni?" She asked.

Rajni was absolutely quiet. She just kept gazing at Mahima's face.

"Rajni... please say something. Is every thing alright?"

Rajni's face was expressionless, white as snow, speechless and totally blank.

"Why are you staring at me? What happened? For God sake, please say something." She almost screamed. Naveen also entered into her room.

"What is happening? Why aren't you guys talking to me? Please! Naveen."

"Vivek got married."

Naveen announced bluntly and instantly. She heard the news. No word or sound of words came out of her mouth. She remained sitting on her bed like a lifeless statue. She kept gazing at Naveen's face as if he was the biggest liar she had ever met in her life. Then she turned towards Rajni in a hope to hear that whatever Naveen had just said was not true.

"Why are you playing games with me? Why are you lying to me?"

She could hardly speak those words. They were feeble; they had no power in them.

"Naveen. Please don't joke with me."

She looked at Naveen's face. His face appeared like a devil's face to her. He came close to her, held her from her shoulders and shook her as if she was having a nightmare.

"Mahima! Listen to me. Vivek is married, he got married two days ago."

Naveen was determined to make her believe in the real news.

"The phone call, just a few minutes ago was from his father from India, who gave us the news. He also asked us to convey it to you."

Once again, Mahima was shattered. The whole world of hers burned in front of her own eyes. Her dreams were cruelly crushed under foot by the unconscionable societal traditions. The meaning of the word 'promise' vanished from her vocabulary. Naveen and Rajni helped Mahima during her critical time and kept her as a guest for several days in their house. Finally, she accepted the bitter truth once more and went to her apartment, ripped the calendar and threw it away, and started collecting the scattered pieces of her life.

After a few days, Vivek phoned her.

"I am coming in the evening to pick up my car."

He came to her room. She handed him his car keys and without saying a word, he left. She stood stunned watching him. *How could he act like a total stranger? Why didn't he say any thing to console me? Perhaps, he will call and talk.*

Mahima was told by some common friends that Vivek was sick and hospitalized. She could not even go to see him as he was a married man, married to someone else. Soon after that Vivek and his wife were called back to India by his father. Mahima accepted the reality. She had no way to know if Vivek kept in a good health, if he was a happy married man or not. All those negative thoughts created a big cavity inside her and weakened her physically. The future journey without him seemed impossible. All of that was beyond her imagination. Also beyond her imagination was how parents could force their children into such a sacred institution of marriage against their desires, against their wishes. All Mahima could think was that the meaning of 'love' was perhaps non-existent or no one cared about finding the true meaning of it.

"Does Vivek hold his wife's hand as he used to hold Mahima's?"

"Does he love her?"

"Does she love him?"

"Does she go with him everywhere?"

All those thoughts ripped her into pieces. She felt helpless. *Why did Vivek break his promise?*

Chapter 18
A MATCH FOR MAHIMA

*M*onths passed by. The pressure of finding a suitable match for Mahima became her Mamma's first priority. In the middle of her education, there was no way for her to go back and settle in India. She was determined to finish her degree, find a suitable job after finishing it and settle in the US.

The elders of the household were worried about her, mainly worried about her being alone and obviously lonely. Traditionally it was time for her to get married and settle in her life and that was the heart felt desire of her parents. When Mahima was in India before coming to the States, Ateet's parents had approached her parents just like other Indian parents typically do. Ateet's parents' house being not too far from her parents, constant trips were made by them to her house. Mahima met Ateet on different occasions when she was in India not knowing that the match making meetings were taking place without her consent. She was told about the secret a little before she left India. She had no interest in Ateet. So very straightforwardly but respectfully she gave her nonacceptance to Mamma. The day Mahima was about to leave for the U.S. Ateet handed his resume to her to pass it on and also to help him be admitted to an American University. Mahima did so to help him and he was fortunate to be admitted to a university one hundred miles away from hers.

Letters after letters kept flooding her mail box. All were written by her Mamma. All had just one headline, "Ateet."

Her mother bombarded her with questions after questions with one common theme, 'if she would be interested in getting married with Ateet.' Getting married to a person, who she hardly knew, met only a couple of times was totally against her desire. How could he be her future husband? Being in a country so far away from her family was not easy for her especially in that crucial time of her life. She was not ready for any relation or commitment after losing Vivek. She had to finish her dissertation within a year, which seemed to be impossible under the circumstances she was going through. She was traumatized and felt feeble both physically and emotionally. She was in a constant battle with herself and God.

Ateet was a Christian man. His parents were very much interested in arranging their son's marriage to Mahima. She was beautiful and educated and a good arranged match for their son. The two main requirements of having the same religious background and good education of both matched perfectly, which made Mahima's Mamma very happy. Mamma's two matched identities and Pappa's words of wisdom, 'A Hindu family will never accept a Christian girl.' kept echoing in her mind all the time. Ateet kept phoning her and reminding her of what their parents and family members were planning in India for both of them.

The undeniable truth was that Mahima was away from her home, alone, deeply hurt, and lost all her senses to think about herself. Perhaps, that was her fate to marry the one recommended by her Mamma. Her Pappa was absolutely against that arrangement with Ateet for some unknown reason or maybe he had no intentions to pressure her. The same Mahima who convincingly told her Mamma that she will find her own Raja and will never marry some unknown person arranged by someone else, lost the battle, surrendered, and gave up at that phase of her journey. She reluctantly accepted the offer and handed over the string of her life to her Mamma. She obeyed her Mamma. Her engagement to Ateet took place that summer. The wedding date was set for three months after the engagement. Ateet's university was a two hour driving distance from hers and he was very particular in visiting her, his future wife over the weekend. Usually his visits were motivated by his desire to find out and investigate Mahima's past with no concern for her at all.

"Mahima, when I was in India, I had a girl as one of my best friends."

"That's good." She replied.

"I know Mahima! But Julie wanted to marry me." He continued telling Mahima about his past love affair.

"Really! How about you?"

"I never thought about it that way during my friendship with her."

"Did you love her?" Mahima asked with no reservations.

"The night of my flight, she was with me and before leaving for the airport, I took her back to her house." He gave her a convoluted answer.

"I hope, you did not make any promises to her." Mahima joked and laughed.

"Oh, no. Not at all, but she still writes letters to me."

"Really! Do you reply?" She became curious.

"Yes, I did and slowing down little by little."

Mahima could sense that Ateet was not completely honest with her.

"Ateet! Nothing has finalized as of yet for me and for you. We are not married yet, and frankly, our relationship has been arranged by our parents."

Before Mahima could finish what she wanted to convey, he pulled a letter written by Julie out of his pocket and made her read it. The whole letter was filled with complaints of Ateet's parents that she went to see them and they insulted her and were not nice to her. Mahima finished reading the long letter.

"It looks like the two of you were in a serious relationship and your parents were also involved."

"Yes, we were, but my mummy and papa never liked her." Ateet was still trying his best to convince her of something.

"Did you like her?"

He kept a silence.

"Look Ateet! You and I hardly know each other. Her letter is very clear and it looks like she will be waiting for you. I would like you not to rush into any commitment with me and think about it."

Mahima could empathize with Julie. She herself faced a big and cruel injustice. She hoped that the same was not happening with Julie.

"Ateet! Please! Don't take this step of marrying me just to please your mummy and papa. You have to spend your married life with your wife, not with them."

"No, Mahima, I knew—they were talking about you and me for a long time. I met Julie a few months ago and the friendship just grew. I will not keep any contact with her any more."

"What if you receive another letter from her?"

"I will not reply. I am telling you."

That communication with Ateet left her conflicted. Not a fragment in her body wanted someone else to go through the same trauma as she did after her relationship with Vivek ended so cruelly. Oh! What an unbearable painful experience for her that was.

The fact of the matter was that Mahima and Ateet were arranged to be married with a very weak bonding. Mahima could sense Julie's pain and she had no strength to take the blame of that injustice which was about to happen. She decided to tell everything about her past to Ateet the very next time he came. She hoped, perhaps, after learning about her past he will refuse to marry her and will go back to Julie somehow or the other.

Ateet started being very open to Mahima about his relationship with Julie. He also told her that he went through a lot of uncertainty up until the last moment before he left India to come to U.S. He was not sure, if he wanted to stay there and marry Julie or go abroad. Also, he told her that Julie was with him the night he was about to leave.

A couple of weeks later he came again to talk to Mahima and she went to pick him up from the bus stop in the used car she purchased.

"Not many days left for the wedding."

"Just a bit over one month." Mahima responded.

"We will go and pick some invitation cards and give them for printing. What do you think?" He was in a shopping mood.

"It seems like a good idea."

"Did you get any letter from Julie?" She started the topic again.

"No, Mahima!" He replied in two words and tried to stop any conversation about Julie.

"You know my friend Vivek, right Ateet?" She was fully prepared to tell Ateet every thing about her past and her relationship with Vivek.

"Yes, the guy with whom you came to the airport to pick me up?"

"Oh, yes. He was Vivek."

"It came to me through some friends that he was more than a friend to you?" Ateet asked in a very sarcastic tone. She was shocked to hear him.

"Yes, I myself wanted to tell you all about my relation with him."

She told everything to Ateet about her and Vivek. How they met and from the beginning to the end and how Vivek's father forced him into a marriage against Vivek's will. She kept telling and he kept listening.

"Ateet, please don't take any pressure from anyone to marry me. This has to be your decision and not your parents'. From my side, you are free."

"No, Mahima that was our past. Both of us will have to forget it and start a new beginning."

And those words spoken by Ateet gave her a new hope and a new promise for a new future. The cards were picked up and sent to the printing press.

A week later the invitation cards were to be picked up from the printing press. Ateet came back for the weekend to continue on the next project to mail them to all the guests in time and the project was successfully done. He constantly kept asking every tiny detail about Vivek and her relation with him and she kept answering all his questions with no hesitation. She had no intentions to keep any secrets from her prospective husband, but the feelings of jealousy incubating inside him were transparent.

"Look Ateet, it is not too late as of yet. If you are not happy, I will understand, but I really don't like you asking repeatedly about Vivek as I have already told you everything very explicitly."

"And you were the one who assured me that we have to put our past behind and move on to a new beginning."

She was done with her response. She was totally against revisiting their past. She did not want to know more about Julie and also she did not want to talk about Vivek any more in the future. She conveyed to Ateet very clearly that for a happy married life they should not be bringing their past at all.

The wedding date was coming closer and closer; just two more weeks were left. The invited guests started making arrangements to be the part of the wedding. The Bible study group gave them a wedding shower on the weekend before the wedding date. After the wedding shower on Friday night, he stayed at his friend's house and came to her apartment on Saturday afternoon to visit her.

"Would you like me to cook something for you?" She asked.

"Sure." He sounded like he was hungry.

She started cooking, but felt really weird observing his behavior, and a harsh body language.

"Mahima!" His tone was loud and filled with anger.

"Yes." She responded.

Her heart was in her throat and hands started trembling. His blood red eyes reflected anger and jealousy. He got up from his chair and came close to her.

"Mahima!" He almost shouted.

"I was thinking about your relation with Vivek."

The same topic was started again. The agreement took place a while ago, a promise not to dig into the past, start a new future--were all forgotten. He could not control himself. His possessiveness and jealousy took a toll. She stood shocked in front of him and tried to avoid his question, but he waited for her response standing close to her and gazing at her without blinking his eyes.

"I have told you... many-many times... very explicitly. Please don't keep asking same thing over and over again." She had no option but to respond.

"What are all places did you go with him?" He totally ignored what she had just said and continued.

"To the movies... parks... in the town... outside the town... tell me." He was shouting.

"Ateet! Please! If you are so suspicious, you can still cancel this marriage or postpone it, but please don't repeat the same thing over and over."

She continued her cooking. She was trembling and her hands were shaking. Again, Ateet did not pay any attention to her and screamed on the top of his lungs.

"Did you sleep with him?"

She covered her ears. She could not believe what she had just heard. He was in an explosive rage of jealousy, an uncontrollable anger. She did not say a word. She took a deep breath and kept rinsing the dishes in the sink. He was not in a mood to quit, desperate for her response.

"I did not cross that boundary." She spoke in a firm voice.

He moved very close to her. His body was brushing against her back. She felt like she was trapped; sink in the front and him behind her. She kept washing the dishes and the dishes kept slipping out of her soapy trembling hands.

"You... bitch... lying to me." He grabbed her braid in his hand, pulled her by it, turned her face towards him and screamed again.

"You! The biggest liar." And he slapped her on her left cheek with a full force.

"Ahhhh!" She could not even scream.

Holding her braid, he tried to pull her and hit more.

"Stop it."

And he pushed her towards the sink.

Almost impossible to be believed! A barbarous act took place. The act which should and could never be tolerated occurred. Instantly, she felt low, worthless, a lifeless object. She was burning in anger. She had a glass in her hand. She threw it in the sink filled with glasses and plates. The dishes shattered into pieces. Holding her face with both of her hands, she slid against the wall and sat by the sink. She was terrified. After a few moments, she got up, washed her hands, wiped them in a towel, and picked her car keys and the purse.

"I will not marry you. I am going out. And before I return, I want you out of my apartment and please never ever dare to come back."

She slammed the door behind her, ran down the steps and to her car parked by the road. Her whole body was shaking, shivering and the rivers of tears were flowing from her eyes. She felt weak and her whole body felt drained out. She stayed in her car for a few minutes and got herself together. Her hands trembled holding the starting wheel. *Ah! How would she be able to drive the car? Where will she go?*

She wanted to run away, far away from him, far away from this world. With an unknown destination in her mind, she pulled the car on the street and soon she was on the highway. The car was running on the highway at seventy miles an hour. She took the exit to the park, the same park she used to go with Vivek, parked it at the corner of the same lake where Vivek and her used to go for boating. She looked her reflection in the mirror hanging in front of her. Her swollen face, left bruised cheek, swollen big eyes, messy uncombed long hair were telling the true story of her shattered achy heart. She stayed inside the car. She felt like she was her own enemy. That was the time in her life she felt that her life was meaningless, she was a useless creature living in this world. That slap did not only hurt her cheek, but that was a slap on her self respect and self confidence and her inner-self. First time in her life, she doubted her ability, her beauty, and the reason of her existence in this world. She kept on looking at her face in the mirror, sobbing, rolling her fingers on it in an effort to recognize herself and her reflection.

"Ateet hit me. He slapped me. He slapped my past love. He made fun of my

true love." She had no control on her tears. She was out of breath. That day was also the day when she was really angry at Vivek.

"*Why didn't Vivek leave this world for me?*"

"*Why?*"

"*Never ever did Vivek touch me in anger. He never even looked at me in anger.*"

"*Who is this Ateet?*"

"*Why did he hit me?*"

Sitting inside the car for a long time, hiding from this world as if the whole world was gazing upon her and laughing at her, making fun of her, she felt broken into pieces. The moments spent with Vivek were vivid just like she was with him yesterday. If Mahima had a tiny head ache, Vivek gave her the pain pill and a glass of water and made her swallow the pill. He sat by her with her head resting on his lap and gently ran his fingers through her hair until she fell asleep. When she woke up from her little nap, he made chai and served her.

She was in a grocery store with Vivek and they saw a stack of fresh coconuts, a tropical fruit in an American store. They were thrilled and picked one. They came home and could hardly wait to crack open it. Vivek found a hammer from somewhere in his apartment. He hammered the hard shell of the coconut and broke it into two several little pieces. She tried to get the meat out from the hard shelled piece holding it in her left hand and scraping with a sharp knife in her right hand. The knife slipped and poked into her left palm under the thumb. Instantly, a stream of bright red blood covered her whole palm. She was agonized, panicked, and clueless about what should have been done to stop the blood gushing out of her hand. Her vision started getting blurry and she started feeling lightheaded seeing her own blood dripping from the cut. Vivek saw the whole episode. He threw away the piece of coconut and his knife, held her hand and placed his thumb on the cut to put a tight pressure, and did not let go until the bleeding stopped. Then he ran into his room, brought some cotton and a piece of cloth, and wrapped her whole hand tightly.

She spent several hours in the park by the lake. The wound given by Ateet a few hours ago crushed her spirits, her soul. She knew that the scar of that wound would leave a permanent mark and never fade away. After spending a long time in her car she drove to her apartment hoping that by that time Ateet may have left. She hoped wrong. Soon after opening the door of her room she saw him sitting inside waiting for her. He jumped from his chair immediately, pulled her inside the room by her hand and wrapped his arms around her. He was a figure of remorse. A drastic change in his personality had taken place.

"Mahima! Please forgive me." He begged.

She did not say a word. She had nothing to say.

"Mahima! My dear Mahima! Please forgive me." He begged again.

"I will never lay my hands upon you… never… ever. If it happened again, I would rather cut them off." He begged, rolled his fingers on Mahima's cheek, which still was red, gazed at his right hand as if the hand was to be blamed.

Mahima was sobbing like an innocent baby, surrendered herself, believed in each and every word he just said, and believed that he meant it. It was convincing from his side that what happened that morning will never happen again in the future. She kept that episode within her and tried to forget all about it. Once again he made a promise not to dig into the past and she trusted him and the journey continued.

That was a defining moment of her journey. All her friends from her Bible study, students from her department, family friends were excited and were looking forward to be a part of their big day. The Bible study group being very helpful divided the responsibilities amongst themselves. Mahima's hair dresser, her friend, visited her several times at her apartment to try different hair styles on her. Bridesmaids and flower girls got busy shopping. The women were assigned to decorate the chapel and the men from the group got busy in helping the women. Not a single person had any idea of the battle raging within Mahima. There was no one in this world to talk to, to open her heart and show the pain she was going through. No one knew that Ateet had hit her, no one but her. Though she tried to put it behind her, the episode kept frightening her. It crushed the desires any young bride would have. It took away the sparkle of the future hope a young bride possesses in her eyes. She was helpless, she was paralyzed. How would she be able to spend her whole life with a man who hit her two weeks before the wedding date? How? A major conflict was going on inside her. In the midst of all those struggles, a voice of hope would tell her, "Everything will be fine and he will never do that again."

Chapter 19
Her Wedding Day

*S*aturday, the day of the wedding arrived. Friends decorated the chapel. Rajni picked Mahima up from her room to take her to the chapel a few hours before the wedding—to dress her up as a bride. Her hair was rolled up in a French style by Rajni-- her favorite hairdo, with light curls hanging on both sides. Her friend Rajni was not only a friend but she played her beautician too. Rajni also made her up in a very light make-up, a light lipstick and some blush on her cheeks. Her dark big brown eyes looked beautiful without mascara or shadow or any eye make up. She put on her white wedding gown, the veil and the wreath and sat on the chair looking at the clock ticking. If her Mamma or her Pappa or her Bhaiya had any hint of the episode that took place two weeks ago, they would have opposed the wedding. Nothing and nothing could have been done at that point. It was too late. She was trapped in the chains of obligations, culture and traditions.

It was her wedding day. Her Mamma and Pappa and all must be celebrating in India, must be thinking that their youngest child was no longer a child. She is a young woman and getting married. She wished Mamma and Pappa were with her, by her side, touching her, hugging her, admiring her beauty and how beautiful she looked in that white wedding gown. The clock kept ticking rapidly, it seemed, and it was four in the afternoon. She got-up. Rajni gave a final touch to her gown, hair and handed the bouquet of pink roses to her. The journey into a new life began.

The bridesmaid took her position behind her and the two flower girls in front. Rajni escorted all the participants to the main gate of the chapel, where an elderly university professor in her father's role waited for her. He gave his arm to Mahima. She held it with her right hand, holding the bouquet in her left. As soon as she took her first step into the chapel, the organist hit the first key on the organ, the guests stood up as is the custom and the slow procession down the aisle began. The organ started playing to its fullest and her heart pounding to the loudest. She carried that beautiful smile on her face. She kept taking one step at a time, each step over the petals of pink roses spread by the little flower girls on her path. The bridesmaid carrying her long veil behind her also looked elegant in her pink long dress. Each step she took brought her closer and closer to Ateet who was standing in front with the pastor and his best-man on one side. All eyes in the chapel were glued upon Mahima. From the entrance of the chapel to the pulpit seemed to be the longest and the toughest journey of her life and was completed only in minutes. The marriage ceremony was performed. The marriage certificates were signed and now Mahima was declared a married woman.

Down the steps in the same chapel, the wedding reception was set to be held. Her friends had set up the hall with tables, chairs and flower arrangements with candles. A special table was decorated with the wedding cake and roses especially for Mahima and Ateet. Her Mamma had sent her a beautiful silk sari to be worn at the reception. Rajni helped her with getting dressed in the authentic Indian costume with authentic Indian gold jewelery.

A brand new Indian beautiful bride walked in the reception hall with her husband. The guests welcomed the new couple with clapping and laughter. No one had any idea about the weeping heart of the beautiful bride who was carrying a beautiful smile on her face.

"After marriage the love between the two grows by itself."

Those were Mamma's words of wisdom, but Mamma never told her 'how?' How could something grow when there was nothing to start with? The wound of the slap just a few days ago was still very fresh and making her heart bleed day and night. Oh! What an excruciating, unbearable pain it caused deep within her!

The guests were enjoying the light music playing in the background along with the food served. Some were dancing and some were eating. Mahima and Ateet holding each others' hands were meeting with the guests and thanking them for being a part of their celebration. The guests were congratulating them and wishing them a happy married life. She felt like she was a con artist performing amongst so many in the audience. No one could even guess what she was going through on the big day of her life. The harder she tried to put that slap behind her, the tougher it became. After meeting with everybody, both climbed up on the stage and sat on those big chairs especially decorated for them in front of a tall decorated wedding cake.

She sat on her chair with her eyes down, just like a shy Indian bride. She was in her own dreams. Once upon a time, a long time ago, she was one of the flower girls in her oldest sister, Jaya didi's wedding. It was didi's *mehndi* (henna) ceremony, a day before her marriage. Jaya didi and all the other sisters sat on a rug around their Mamma. Mamma acted like a chief commander, placing the orders and giving her motherly instructions to everybody in the family. Mahima was only nine years old at that time.

"Mamma, please, please tell us, how did you meet Pappa?" Jaya didi was in a mood to tease Mamma.

"Oh! No beta, not now." Twenty four years of living together with Pappa,

Mamma blushed. Her face glistened with a glorious shy smile. All six daughters giggled and giggled and did not want to leave Mamma alone.

"Okay! Girls, if you insist." Mamma started her story. All six sisters stopped giggling. They sat around her gazing curiously at her in a complete silence that one could hear a pin drop in the room.

"After my teachers' training, I got a teaching job in a Christian school. The principal of that school was friends with your pappa and family. The very first time your pappa came to see me with his father; we saw each other in the principal's office."

"And love at first sight." Jaya didi interrupted.

"Why not? Why not? So handsome and tall is our Pappa. How could she have refused?" Another sister added her own opinion and again the whole room filled with their laughter.

"Okay… Okay… everybody. Be quiet. So, what happened after that Mamma?" Jaya didi was anxious.

"Then we got engaged." Mamma replied without wasting a second.

"Did you see him after the engagement?" Jaya didi wanted to hear all in detail.

"Oh, yes. Oh yes. Every Sunday, when we teachers used to take the girls living in the hostel to the church services, he was there, always sat in the back row."

"How romantic!" One of the sisters threw in her comment and there was a big laughter again.

Mahima's house was filled with laughter and giggles. Her Pappa and Mamma were always together in good and in bad times. It was just an amazing bond of love in between them. Would Ateet be able to give her that much love and make her forget the pain of that slap which he gave her two weeks ago?

The wedding celebrations were over. All the guests left. The first night together of a newly wedded couple is called 'Suhaag Raat'. That night is defined as the most memorable night for the bride and groom; the night of promises given and taken, the night to assure each other that they are one and will be one for the rest of their lives. Ateet and Mahima planned to spend that night in a hotel. In a hotel, alone at night with Ateet, she was afraid. She had no excitement or feelings a new bride should have. She was terrified. 'What if he hits her again?' Hiding that fear inside her she stepped into the room. Ateet locked the door from inside and both met. That was the night Ateet believed in her virginity, which he had doubted before.

After their marriage, for a couple of months, they lived separately in their own towns. Then Ateet was transferred to the same town with Mahima but at a different university. They started their lives together in a one bed room apartment which was on the fifth floor of the university housing and very close to her department. Both stayed busy. She wrote her Master's thesis and he took classes towards his doctorate. Two months of living together passed in a normal way.

Her university organized an annual international function with dinner and dancing. All the students dressed up in their native clothes. Mahima wore her plain pink chiffon sari, and a matching embroidered blouse. She rolled her long dark hair in her favorite French style with the curls hanging behind her ears. Delicate white pearls dangling earrings with a matching necklace added to the glistening of her face. Both her wrists were full with her favorite glass bangles and she was all ready to go to the function with her husband. The first part of the function was dinner. The variety of international potluck dishes were arranged at a big table. Mahima made baskets full of Indian *jalebis* as a sweet dish. The hall was full of international students and some professors with their families. Mahima sat with Ateet and some other friends. Everyone was in a festive mood, enjoying and having a good time, eating and dancing.

"May I take your wife for a dance?" One graduate student from her department came to Ateet and requested.

Ateet gave his permission. Mahima had never danced before particularly with a guy. She was hesitant and reluctant. The gentleman held her by her hand and she had no choice but to go with him. She took a few dance steps for just a couple of minutes, came back and sat with Ateet. After the party was over, both walked back to their apartment. She stepped into the bedroom to change her clothes and started unwrapping her sari. All of a sudden Ateet came in the room and stood right in front of her.

"What do you think about yourself? A great dancer?" He was full of sarcasm.

"Tell me." He screamed to the loudest and slapped her again.

"Ahhh!"

Her sari slipped out of her hands and she fell right there on the carpet covering her face with both of her hands.

"Get up… you bitch." He pulled her half wrapped sari, threw it in the corner of the room, grabbed her shoulders tight, pulled her and made her stand up. Still the rage of anger was at its peak and he pushed her on the bed.

"Why couldn't you say no to him? You bitch, you dancer! Is he also your old lover?" Screaming and yelling, he got out of the room.

Next day, very early in the morning, she got up, brushed her teeth, splashed some water on her face and changed. He was still deep asleep on the couch. She got out of the apartment quietly. The only place she could go was her department. That early hour of morning, there was not even a single soul in or outside her department building. She was totally drained after another sleepless night, totally exhausted. That was the period when she was busy doing her dissertation work. How could she have focused on her research? She opened the journals to read and write, but was unable to do so, unable to concentrate, unable to take her mind off the night's episode. After consuming a few cups of coffee she picked up her papers and books and headed towards the main library in a hope that a change of setting might help her focus.

She spent the whole day in the university library. She did not want to go back to her apartment. But if not there, where had she gone? She was furious of her own husband. She was puzzled and failed to find any solution. She dropped her head on the papers and books spread at the desk in front of her in the library and closed her eyes. When she woke up, it was already eight o'clock at night and dark outside. She picked up her books and walked towards her apartment. There was a deep uncertainty within her. There was no other easy road for her. Very reluctantly she entered into the elevator and pushed '4'. She was not sure if she wanted to go to her apartment or somewhere else, and find some help, perhaps from her friends. A dense shadow of uncertainty cast upon her. She debated; whether to tell others about that low level act by Ateet. She was afraid that telling someone else would bring nothing but an embarrassment and insult upon her. So, she proceeded forward, unlocked her apartment and entered inside.

"How come you are so late? I have been waiting for you for a long time." He came at the door and spoke very gently.

"Come here Mahima!"

"I am very sorry."

"I don't know why did I do that last night? Why did I lose control? I am very sorry. I love you very much Mahima!"

He begged and begged for forgiveness once more and she trusted him once more. Mahima was never in favor of sharing that ugly experience of her life with other people even for the sake of finding some help. It was again a very shameful and ruthless event. She had to suffer alone. Her self confidence was shattered and her trust was demolished. How could she have told that to her Mamma, who was so far away from her, and her Pappa, who would not be able to endure the news of the suffering of his daughter, his soul and his love.

Ateet's abusive behavior did not stop. Indian traditions took a toll; once you are married, you are married. Only death could separate you—nothing else, so the culture and traditions dictate. She lived under the same roof with her husband in constant fear, as a prisoner, as a moving body with a dead soul. After the long day of classes and research, her routine became to go to the library to sit in a quiet environment and write her thesis. Then, she went back to her department to type the hand written pages into the computer. She had no desire to go home. She was deeply hurt and was afraid to face her husband, and tried her best to spend the minimum time at her apartment. She worked on her thesis till late at night and collapsed on the couch placed in the ladies room of the department to get her sleep. In those months, she lost weight and all that was left of her was skin and bones. A beautiful girl turned into a skeleton.

That phase of her journey was difficult and the road was rocky and treacherous. She could see nothing but darkness around her and everywhere. She had no one in this country with who she could share, talk and get some advice. Also she feared that if Ateet had found out that she was seeking outside help, he would have made her life even more miserable.

The department secretary Mona was Mahima's good friend. One early in the morning Mahima was working at her desk, reading her research papers. Mona walked in the research room.

"Do you have a lot of work to be done today?" Mona placed her hands on Mahima's shoulders.

"Not really Mona. I am trying my best to finish my dissertation as soon as I can."

"Would you like to go to lunch with me, if you have some time?" Mona's apartment was just across the campus.

"Certainly. Is there any occasion?" Mahima was thrilled receiving an unexpected invitation.

"No occasion. You have been working day and night. Just to give you a little break." Mona clarified with a smile at her face.

As promised Mona came to her carrel at lunch time and they walked to her apartment. She made some sandwiches for Mahima and herself. They set across the coffee table placed by the window in front of the kitchen. Mona started the conversation right away. She was concerned. She came straight to the point with no hesitations whatsoever.

"Mahima! The department fellows and I have been concerned about you and want to make sure that you are keeping well."

Mahima's department fellows; all the graduate students, secretaries, technicians, professors were like a big family. They had known Mahima as a happy, contented girl. Most of them attended her wedding with much excitement. A genuine concern in those few spoken words by Mona was enough for Mahima to explode. Her burning heart exploded like a hot volcano, uncontrollable tears started flooding from her eyes and she shared with Mona.

"You have to take care of yourself. Just think, if you won't, who will?" Mona got up and gave her a hug.

"You are right Mona but I have no family in this country to help me." Mahima kept sobbing.

"Look Mahima! You and Ateet need some counseling."

"But Ateet will not agree to it. I am very afraid that he will make a big fuss about it."

Mahima was afraid, afraid that Ateet may rebel against the idea of counseling.

"Now listen to me. You have to stop being afraid of him. He knows your weakness. He will frighten you more and more if you don't become strong. You should talk to Mark. He may be a good person to counsel with and let him contact Ateet."

Mahima was persuaded by Mona's suggestion. Yes, Mona was right. She had to take some step; otherwise, she may get depressed or may die. She gathered all the courage and called Mark for help with no further delay and the counseling sessions started for both of them.

Chapter 20
THE PAIN OF HOME COMING

"Ateet, it has been a long time for both of us away from our families. Why don't we plan a trip to India?"

She was keen to see her Pappa and Mamma and all her siblings and their families. She had been away from them for the last three years.

"Sounds like a good idea. How about during the winter break? After giving a moment's thought he replied.

"Excellent! But we will have to work on our travel expenses." She suggested.

It was the month of May. There were plenty of summer jobs on campus. They had to find one suitable for both.

"Let us try to find some extra on campus summer job for our travel costs."

"What kind of job are you thinking about?" Ateet asked.

"You know that dormitory manager, sits at the front desk, let us talk to him. He must know about on campus jobs." She had high hopes.

"Good idea! I will talk to him tomorrow first thing in the morning."

Early next morning, Ateet went downstairs at the front desk to talk to the manager and came back just in five minutes. He looked happy.

"We got the job." He broke the news.

"What kind? Yeah! Both of us... right?"

"Yes. And the job is to paint the dorm rooms."

"All the undergraduate students are gone for summer. The rooms need to be cleaned and painted before the beginning of the fall semester. And you know the wages, five dollars an hour." He explained.

"But Ateet, how are we going to paint so many rooms just ourselves?"

"Oh no, there are many other students working on this project."

Mahima's dreams were coming true. She was excited to go to India with her husband, the very first time as a married woman. She was excited that she would meet everyone, would stay with her in-laws for the first time in their house. And also how happy all the family members would be to see her and Ateet together for the very first time. After visiting with the families she planned to travel and do some site-seeing trips with her husband. In her mind and in her thoughts, she imagined that their India trip would give both of them a perfect opportunity to come close to each other as a husband and a wife. It is commonly held that every marriage takes some time for adjustments, and she had absolute belief in that and she was hopeful.

The summer break began and so did their painting job. Both got up early in the morning. Ateet carried a ladder and couple of paint boxes in his hands and Mahima carried some paint brushes and rags. Both walked to the undergraduate dormitory building early every morning. They took a little radio along with them for some entertainment while painting. The rooms were filthy. Some rooms were painted black, some dark red and all other different colors. Several of them had weird art work done on the walls by the young undergraduate students. Their project was to convert all the walls into white color. That was not an easy task and it required several coats of the primer and the paint. They painted the rooms for three hours from five until eight o'clock every morning. After painting, they rushed to their own apartment to clean up and take a quick shower before heading towards their universities for their daytime research job. Then again in the evening, after a quick cup of tea with some snacks, they painted for another three hours and continued until nine o'clock at night. Working day and night for all three months of summer break was a record breaker for both of them. They saved plenty of money to buy their tickets and some gifts to be taken for the family members in India.

During that summer her oldest sister, Jaya didi died. Mahima received the sad news through a letter written by her Pappa. The news was unexpected and mournful. How could that happen? It was just a few days ago, Mahima received a letter written by her Jaya didi. There were no indications of her being sick or anything else. The letter described the whole episode. Jaya didi fainted while working in the house. She was rushed to the hospital and was diagnosed with a brain tumor. Immediate surgery was necessary and she could not make it through and died during the operation. Mahima was saddened not being able to give a send off to her Jaya didi. Her last meeting with her didi was at the airport when she came to say good bye to her little sister, and Mahima had the last glimpse upon her when she was tip towing to wave her good-buy.

Summer break was gone in a twinkling of an eye, between painting and doing the research work. The Fall Semester started. Only three months were left before their planned trip to India. They started buying gifts, a little some thing for each of the family members.

In those three months she finished the project of writing her thesis. It was edited on time, printed and all bound. She submitted the copies of her thesis before leaving for India. Her graduation commencement date was in mid January and there was no way that she could make her first trip short and come back for her commencement ceremonies. Her plans were to obtain the certificate after returning from her India trip and then plan the future.

The newly wedded couple landed at the Delhi airport. A multitude of relatives from both families were at the gate to welcome them. Some of them held the marigold garlands in their hands to offer to the couple, a distinct but a traditional welcoming. Poor Pappa always volunteered to stay back and take care of the house and the dogs. Mahima met with all her relatives, Mamma, sisters, brother and their families at the airport. According to the traditions, she had to go with her in-laws. So she said good-bye to her family members and went to her in-laws who were waiting for her in their car.

Ateet and her families lived in the same city, a short walking distance from each other. Three years ago, she traveled to the airport with her family and relatives and that day she was on the same road with an unknown family—her in-laws, and she was going to their house. Her hopes were high and her heart was full of desires. She wished a happy married life. She hoped for a transformation in her life with Ateet. Everyone in the car was catching up on lost sleep from the night before other than the driver. Mahima was also wide awake. She was enjoying the aroma of the morning fresh breeze and her Pappa was in her thoughts. She was anxious to see him, to be with him and talk to him.

The five hours journey was over. It was early in the morning, when they reached home. It was still dawning and the neighborhood was still asleep. They unloaded the car and straight to their beds. Mahima laid on the bed with the rest of the family with her eyes wide open. She waited for the first ray of light to enter into the room.

"I want to go see Pappa. He must be waiting." She whispered in Ateet's ears.

"Go, but come back soon."

Without any delay, she got up quietly, went to the bathroom, splashed some water on her face, hid behind the curtain and changed her clothes. Very slowly, without interrupting the sleeping people, she got out of the house, shut the main gate quietly, and then started her brisk walk towards her own house. She almost started running towards the place where twenty four years of her life were spent. She suspected to observe some changes occurred in the past three years. Her anxiety kept building up at each step she took. She could not stop thinking about her past spent in that house. A long time ago when she sewed the curtains and decorated the windows and doors. Her Pappa joked,

"Mahima beta, you could have used this fabric to sew your petticoats."

Her house was surrounded by the high boundary walls on the three sides. The main entrance gate was all the way to the other side of the boundary walls.

One boundary wall was along the street and the branches of the guava tree hung against it. She leaned on that wall.

"Pappa!"

Pappa was sitting in the veranda on his favorite wicker rocking chair and reading his newspaper. As soon as he heard her, he threw down the newspaper and ran towards the main gate. She also ran along the other two boundary walls to reach to the gate to meet him.

"Come beta come!" He filled her up in his arms just like a little baby and held her face in both of his hands and asked,

"Beta, are you alright?"

And the tears of joy welled up in his eyes.

"Yes, yes Paa, I am quite alright."

He gently took his eye glasses off and wiped his streaming tears. He looked weak and old. He was alone at home. Mamma and the rest of the family were traveling back from the airport.

"Beta, would you like a cup of chai?" Pappa was an expert in making tea for everyone in the morning and enjoyed serving it.

"Yeah, let us make some chai"

It was a day of celebration for Mahima and her Pappa. They were the happiest two people in the world. She forgot all about Ateet's words, 'come back soon.' Both had their morning cup of tea together and after that her Pappa was in a mood to eat a big breakfast with his baby daughter.

"Let us make some special breakfast."

"What would you like to eat?"

"No one can make as good bread *pakodas* (potatoes stuffed deep fried bread rolls) as you used to." He was referring to her Bhaabi and Mamma.

"Tell me Paa, would you like me to make bread *pakodas*?"

"Yes, beta, you got it."

"I will boil the potatoes and rest of the job is yours." He got up and put the potatoes on the stove to boil.

The potatoes were boiling, Pappa was sipping his second cup of tea, and Mahima' eyes were focused at his grieved face. He began the conversation about Jaya didi--his first born child. His heart was bleeding tears. Mahima could feel his pain. How could a father endure the pain of losing his own child?

"Yes, Paa, three years ago, she came to the airport to see me off and she was waving good bye to me. I remember it all."

"Yes, she loved you very much."

"Do you know that she brought an embroidered piece of art for me, which she made herself. She gifted me that at the airport? I framed it and it is hanging as a wall decoration in my apartment."

Mahima kept gazing at her father's face; a smile, which was trying to hide the sorrow within, a fulfillment covering the emptiness of losing his eldest child. The same Pappa, who taught his children to stay strong in all circumstances, appeared like a feeble soldier.

"When you were little, she used to sew the frocks for you."

"Yes, yes. That picture of mine in the frilled frock was sewn by her. I think, I was ten years old that time."

"I was her flower girl in her wedding and that pink satin frock I wore was also sewn by her."

Pappa was lost in those old times.

"And one funny episode I can never forget." Mahima continued.

"What is that? Mahima!"

"Remember, how much she wept during her *bidaai* (going to the in-laws after the marriage ceremonies) and you packed me with her as her dowry and to give her company."

They laughed.

How could Mahima forget? She traveled overnight by train with her didi, didi's in-laws, friends and relatives and stayed with didi at her in-laws house for a few days.

"I received a letter from her just two weeks before she left us."

Mahima told her Pappa about her didi's last letter written to her. Both father and daughter had a good time of sharing.

"Okay, Pappa! Now, time to get up and make your favorite bread *pakodas*."

She changed the subject and walked into the kitchen, prepared the potatoes filling, rolled into the bread and deep fried in hot oil. Both enjoyed the special breakfast with some more hot tea and Pappa ate the *pakodas* with much appreciation and as if there was no tomorrow. Her heart rejoiced to see that contentment in her Pappa's face.

"I should go back now. Mamma will be back by tomorrow."

She was running late and totally forgot about her husband's orders to return soon.

"Go, beta. When will you come back?"

"Tomorrow."

Once again he took her face into both of his hands, lifted it up, and looked into her eyes as if he was searching the depth of her heart, and kissed her on her forehead. She felt like the happiest daughter on this earth and walked back happily towards her in-laws' house. She entered through the main gate and all the way inside the house. Her smile disappeared instantly when she observed that none of the family members even looked at her. They acted as if they did not even know her. She received a total cold distancing from them. No one asked about her Pappa or about her visit with Pappa. They made it so obvious that they did not appreciate Mahima visiting her father. It did not take her long to sense the feeling of jealousy in each and every member of the family. Ateet was still resting under the blankets on the big bed. He sat up resting his back against the pillows. His expressions reflected anger.

"Why did you take that long?" He spoke in a nasty tone.

"I was chatting with Pappa, and we made his favorite bread *pakodas* for breakfast. He was alone in the house as Mamma will come back tomorrow. So, I decided to spend some time with him." She explained the whole story in a few words.

"Alright, be careful next time."

He ordered again in a demanding manner in front of his family members. She did not like that tone of her husband, and felt insulted.

"Yes, Mahima! Ateet is right and this is your house now." The mother-in-law added to Ateet's order.

She heard both very clearly, mother and son. She stood stunned as if she was standing in front of the head mistress of her primary school. A welcome to a new family member, a new daughter-in-law was nothing but implausible.

"What do they mean? Do they want me to ignore my own Pappa and Mamma? How absurd? It is not going to happen." A spark of defiance ran through her.

Ateet's parents and family lived in a small house like that of Mahima's parents. They had one big room. One side of the room was used as a bedroom with one big bed laid dressed with the sheets and four pillows. A sofa with table and other furniture was nicely adjusted to fill the other parts of the room. There was a little veranda. On one side of the veranda they had a tiny room with a TV and sofa-bed in it and the kitchen was on the other side. The courtyard was surrounded by the boundary walls, and the backyard with several beds of vegetables.

The first day passed in cooking and eating and entertaining the visitors, who were keen to see the new bride of the house. The night came—Mahima's first night at her in-laws. All the family members, one by one slipped in the backyard and she was left alone in the TV room, sitting on the sofa-cum-bed and watching TV. The private meeting without her began and continued for thirty minutes. The very first day at her in-laws and she was declared as an outsider in that family. The meeting was adjourned and all came back inside the house. The sleeping arrangements were announced by the mother-in-law. On that big bed, the extreme right side was allotted to Mahima with Ateet on her left side. Next to Ateet was his mother's space and sister in the end. His father and the brother were assigned the folding beds on the other side of the room. Four adults including a newly married couple were on one bed and six people in one room. The tiny room with sofa-bed was empty and locked. Poor

Mahima—never knew that her in-laws are so much in love with each other including her that they shared their bed with a new daughter-in-law and her husband! The little privacy at night, the dream of lying by her husband and talking in private was over for her the very first night. The doors were shut and the lights were turned off. In the silence of the night, all one could hear was the echoing of the breathing sounds. She pulled her blanket, tucked herself and hid her face under the blanket. Partially the jet-leg and partially the sleeping arrangements—she could not fall asleep. She retreated to her past.

Four years ago, before going to U.S., her brother got married. She lived with her Mamma, Pappa and brother and sisters in a house with three small rooms. Before Bhaabi, her brother's wife came as a new bride in the house; Mamma told Mahima and one other sister to clean the corner room for Bhaabi and Bhaiya. Both the sisters started their assigned job. They did not only clean, they hung new fresh curtains, bought new bed sheets and decorated the little room to welcome their new Bhaabi. The very first day, after getting married to Mahima's brother, Bhaabi in a beautiful red silk sari stepped into the house. The whole household was running all over and was welcoming. Bhaabi was the focus of attention and all the activities in the house revolved around her. Mahima and her sister took Bhaabi to her room. How happy and important Bhaabi felt that day as if she was the queen of the house.

As the time went on, Bhaabi being the same age as Mahima became best friends. She was just like another sister for all the other sisters and an important member of the family. Nothing took place in the house without her involvement. Mahima brought a sari from America for her Bhaabi and hoped she would like it. Thinking all this, she fell asleep.

Early next morning, the morning chai was prepared by Ateet's mother. Holding their tea cups in their hands, each of the family members, one by one, slipped to the back of the house again for some kind of secret meeting. The only member not invited again to the meeting was Mahima. This was the second day in her in-laws house. Their attitude was very transparent; she was not accepted as a family member. Ateet's attitude changed instantly. He seemed to be brain washed. He did not favor Mahima in any thing. He tried to prove his dominance by putting her down and insulting her in front of his family. He made it very clear that he did not and does not care for his wife. So much in just one day, she experienced. 'How would she be able to stay in such a stressful environment for the whole month?' Her thoughts created turbulence in her mind. That was their first trip home after their marriage and so many struggles she had to go through, she never imagined, all within twenty four hours.

The old friends invited the newly wedded couple for lunches and dinners. Mahima loved to go out here and there, anywhere away from home. After their return, the family members refused to talk to her or him, conveying the message that they did not appreciate Ateet taking care of or going out with his wife. Her former research supervisor and his wife also invited both of them for dinner. All of them talked about their old memories, food, movies and a lot of other events. They had a great time of fun and laughter. It was late at night when they returned home. Ateet's sister was mad at them and could not control herself. She screamed and yelled at the top of her lungs.

"You are taking your wife everywhere as if you are her servant. Are we dead for you? This woman has made us orphans." And she kept mumbling.

What wrong has Mahima done? What was her fault? Why were these people in fits of anger? Why did they arrange this marriage? Perhaps, they felt insecure or maybe they were too possessive of him. Perhaps, his sister was jealous of Mahima's beauty and/or could not tolerate 'the other woman' by her brother's side. The sister always stayed ready with her sleeves rolled up to find some excuse and create a big scene at home. She cried, screamed aloud just like a crazy woman several times during the day. Mahima had to see and cope with her drama all day and night. Ateet was afraid of his family. He had to obey them to avoid the arguments. At times, they fought with each other. None of them had a soft voice. They were always in a mood to attack each other. What a peculiar environment in that house, certainly strange for Mahima. Each day she thanked God that one more day less of her stay in that house and kept counting the days to returning to the U.S.

A husband should be like a protective umbrella. But Ateet's attitude was entirely the opposite. He could not and did not dare to tell his folks once and just once that he was married to Mahima, that she was his wife and no one had any right to treat her cruelly. How could he say? He himself had abused her in the past even before he was married to her. All the attempts made by Mahima to forget the past cruelty given to her by Ateet failed. She could easily see that Ateet belonged to an abusive dysfunctional family. She started getting suffocated living in his house. At the same time, she firmly believed that getting raised in an abusive family cannot be an excuse to become abusive. Her Mamma and Pappa's house was so close, but she was not allowed to make frequent visits to them.

Two weeks prior to flying back to the United States both of them had to go back to New Delhi to re-confirm their return air tickets. That was a good chance to spend some time alone with her husband or that's what she thought. She was happy that she would get a day or two traveling with him, some time to chat with him on the bus, do some shopping with him, and also some sight seeing with him. All those dreams of a young married girl, she fantasized. She also had some doubts deep down in her heart that there would be any opportunity for them to spend any time alone with each other or travel together. They did not even get a room to sleep together, how they could be allowed to travel together. In the midst of that chaos, after several attempts, Mahima was successful in finding a moment to talk to her husband in private.

"We have to go to Delhi for our tickets and stuff. I would love if just the two of us could go."

"That's fine." He replied.

"I would like to go for some sight seeing with you also." She got excited after hearing a 'yes' to her first request.

"Okay, let me ask my father."

The request was moved to his father for an approval and the response was,

"Yes, Ateet, you haven't taken your sister and brother anywhere. Take them also along with you." His father gave a pronouncement in no time.

Not letting them sleep together, not letting them visit their friends together, and not even leaving them alone for a second together. What kind of people were they? Why was Ateet allowing them to control his and his wife's life? Why didn't he tell his father that the trip was only for him and his wife?

Question after question spun in her head. She was left speechless, unable to seek the answers to all those whys. She covered her face under the blanket and fell asleep. Early in the morning in order to catch the early bus to go to Delhi, all rose early. His brother could not go, but the sister tagged along with them like a spy. Mahima endured and struggled within her not to reflect any disagreements or emotions.

All three with just one carry on bag left the house in one rickshaw to go to the bus stop. At the bus stop, getting off from the rickshaw, his sister picked up the carrying bag and immediately as always, Ateet declared,

"Oh! No! You don't have to carry it." He grabbed the bag from her hands.

"Give it to Mahima. She will hold it."

And even before the trip started, it was ruined.

That contemptuous rude action by Ateet pierced her heart. That was another attack on her self esteem. He always found some way or other to insult her and put her down. He treated her like a servant. He always tried to prove something by hurting her emotionally. Perhaps, that was his way of showing to his folks that as if Mahima was like the dirt of his shoes and perhaps his people got contentment and pleasure to see all that nonsense. Treating her like rubbish maybe made them proud that their son and brother had control over his wife and made them happy that he treated her like a slave-maid.

She reluctantly took the bag from his hands, but her reactions and feelings became obvious. She did not even want to talk to her own husband. She regretted and felt as if she had committed a crime by making the plans of that trip. Everything went on in entirely opposite directions than what she had thought and desired. That was not a demand for gold and silver, but an urge to spend some time with her husband.

Mahima was not allowed to visit her parents frequently during her stay in India with her in-laws. She had no intentions of reflecting the grief of her unhappy marriage during the little time spent with her parents. How could she? The final decision to be married with Ateet was hers. She could have refused the marriage proposal. Though in reality, that was not an easy task either, perhaps this was all in retrospect. She never told her family members about the physical abuse she coped with and was coping with at the peak time of her youth as a married young woman. The extreme brutality she received from her husband as a marriage gift was kept a secret, hidden inside of her. The news of the youngest child being beaten up cruelly—would be way beyond the limit of tolerance and endurance of any parent.

The vacation came to an end and the day of their departure arrived. Mahima's heart was bleeding tears. She was not able to spend much time with her Mamma and Pappa. She could not make the bread-*pakodas* for her Pappa for more than once. She was not able to sleep with her Mamma with her arms around her neck and her right leg on her tummy. Her hope that Ateet might change his brutal behavior after meeting other family members from her and his side of the family, shattered. Her trust that Ateet's elders may be helpful in re-building their marriage, crushed. The trip became a trip of distress and nightmares.

She walked to her parent's home to say goodbye. The house where she spent her childhood, enjoyed guavas, mangoes, pears, grapes, grew up with a tender loving care for the twenty four years of her life was not hers any more according to her in-laws. On the day of the departure she was allowed to touch her house for a few moments and then go back to her in-laws, who were to go to the airport with her and Ateet.

Pappa could sense that his Mahima, who was nothing but a source of joy, who diffused her fragrance into the whole household; the house that echoed with her laughter and giggles, was changed. She was not the same Mahima any more. She lost that bright shimmer in her eyes. She lost the glorious smile of her face. Pappa stood in front of her with tears in his eyes and tried to hide those behind his glasses. He kept looking into her eyes, but was unable to express his heartfelt feelings. His little daughter was not his any more. She belonged to Ateet and his family like an owned piece of property. He could not control himself. He filled Mahima into his arms.

"Mahima! My beta, I want to see you happy." Pappa's deep voice came from his heart.

"Yes, Pappa, trust me, I am very happy. Why do you worry so much?" And she lied.

How could she hurt him more by telling the truth and the whole truth? She could not say more. She held her Pappa tight. She did not want to separate herself from him, started sobbing in his arms.

"Please, Pappa! Please! Somehow or the other... pull me out of this hell."

And those were her unspoken words to her Pappa. Her eyes flooded and her heart bled, but she was totally helpless. In the last few years, in her blossoming days, her petals were pulled with brutal cruelty. The same Mahima, who was untouched and raised like a delicate flower was beaten up with brutality, and constantly ridiculed. Pappa had no knowledge of her suffering and not a fragment of Mahima's body or soul wanted to distress her Pappa, to crush his soul. It was that time of separation, a separation for an indefinite period, where no one knew when would be the next time she would return and spend some time with her family.

"Beta, stay happy, and that is my prayer to our Lord. Make sure to drop a letter soon after you reach there."

Pappa said a prayer, told her to stay happy, but he did not tell her how?

That was her second time; Mahima was going away from her home. All of her sisters and their families arrived at the airport from their cities to see her off. Bhaiya-Bhaabi and Mamma also arrived. She went with her in-laws, in their car. It was different than the last time. She was not alone, she was with Ateet—her husband. Her relatives were not worried about her traveling alone. They knew that she was with her husband, who was there to protect her. No one and none was able to hear the screams of her storming heart. How anxious was she? How hard she tried to establish a normal relation with her husband? How many hopes, she brought with her. But after the treatment she received by Ateet and his family in one month, she lost it. She lost that hope and could not see any light at the end of the tunnel. What a maze—a confusing maze, she was in at that juncture of the journey of her life.

Chapter 21
FIRSTBORN SON

*U*pon their return to United States, Mahima was officially awarded the diploma for her Masters degree and she had to plan her future. She had only two alternatives in her mind; to take some more classes and continue on her doctorate or apply for a job in her field. The companies came to the University for the Job Interviews. She did not have her permanent residency status, neither did Ateet. Both of them possessed students' visa. Ateet had another two years before he would get his doctorate. She had some job opportunities outside and away from the city they lived in, but it was not practical for her as a married woman to move out of the city away from her husband. She needed some professional career counseling. She set up an appointment to see her counselor at the university.

The counselor was aware that in addition to the master's degree from Saint Louis University, she had another masters in Physics from India. Also, having three majors in Physics, Chemistry, and Math, in her college, she was well qualified to teach high school. He was very impressed by her educational background. After evaluating her situation, the counselor advised her to find a job in the city with some company who could also sponsor her to obtain the permanent residency.

"So, you would like to stay in this town." The counselor asked.

"Yes Sir."

"Would you consider a High School teaching job?"

"Yes, by all means." She shook her head.

Wow! She was thrilled by the option and perhaps opportunity suggested by her counselor. Her mother was also a school teacher, a head mistress of a Primary School back home. Physics and Math were her favorite subjects. Chemistry was not one of her favorites, but she was totally capable of teaching it.

"I would be interested. My mother was also a school teacher." She accepted his advice.

"Good! We are facing a nationwide shortage of teachers, especially Math and Science teachers and based upon your educational background you should not have any problems finding a teaching job in this town."

The counselor sounded convincing and Mahima sensed a hope in his promising words. The meeting with the counselor showed her a light into a new direction. Her hopes were getting higher and higher minute by minute. After flipping through the pages of some documents he asked.

"Would you like to teach in a Catholic school?."

"Yes Sir."

"Good."

He found the phone number from the local phone directory and phoned the school system right at that moment.

"Go to the head office and fill out their application forms as soon as possible. They have an opening for a Math teacher."

The shortage of Math and Science teachers during that time was certainly in her favor. She did not delay at all, went to the office of the Catholic School System, and completed the application form. That was in done in the month of April. Meanwhile she continued her research towards her doctorate. She never let her faith go, she had a hope, a hope for a better tomorrow and whatever tomorrow brings, will be good for her.

After a short while, she was contacted by the principal of that school and the date for an interview was scheduled. Mahima did not possess a teaching certificate and had no teaching experience. She had some tutoring experience as she tutored high school students during her college years in India. Also she had some public speaking experience as she presented some research papers in the conferences and meetings. She spoke fluent English and possessed good communication skills. A teaching job, at least for three years made perfect sense to her and Ateet. By the end of three years, they expected that Ateet would also finish his degree and then both could move elsewhere, where she could also find a job in her field of seismology; so were their dreams.

The day of her interview, the Principal, Vice Principal, the board members of the Catholic School Systems, a Math teacher and a Science teacher were on the panel showering question after question on Mahima. In her graduate schools, those kinds of discussions with other students and professors took place once a week. She faced the panel boldly. The panel members appreciated the level of her confidence. Perhaps she inherited her teaching skills from her Mamma, who started her career as a teacher and retired as a teacher.

The first part of the interview went well and was successful. The second part was practical, which meant, teaching two or three classes in the presence of the Principal and Vice Principal. They needed an assurance that an Indian girl would be capable of teaching and controlling the group of young high school girls. She passed her teaching test with no problems at all. The authorities were very impressed by her way of teaching, and she was offered the position the very same day. Her goal was to work hard and be a successful teacher.

For the first year of teaching, she was assigned to teach senior level Math and Physics, her two favorite subjects. She got up early in the morning and dressed in her professional clothes with her long black hair rolled up in her favorite French style or at times she wore it down. The high heel shoes were needed to add some inches to her petite body. Instead of the paint brush and rags, she carried a nice pocket book along with the books and notebooks. Her life style changed. She was a teacher, just like her Mamma. Her class size was about twenty girls in each section. There were some challenging students as well. Mahima got a deep contentment sharing a fraction of her life with those beautiful young girls. She herself was twenty eight years of age at that time. She preferred to sit with her students in the lunch room during the lunch time just to mingle with them and get a chance to know them. Those young innocent girls were keen to learn about Mahima, her family, how she ended up in the U.S.A. Their enthusiasm was amazing, their willingness to learn about the Indian culture, clothes, jewelry, movies, and marriages was incredible. The year of teaching the girls flew by quick.

The second year, she was transferred to the all boys high school, which belonged to the same Catholic School System. The school was a College Preparatory. Again, she was assigned to teach the college level Math, Physics and Chemistry. Most of the boys were much interested in the Math and Science subjects, and that was rewarding for Mahima as she always loved those subjects in her high school and college, and also she was passionate to teach them. She enjoyed teaching the boys and the boys loved her as one of their favorite teachers. She roll played in her classrooms. She sat at one of the student's desks in the midst of them and made the boys go in the front at the chalk board. They enjoyed being a teacher and Mahima helped them by having them explain the homework problems to the rest of the class.

The indelible memories of her teaching years still abide in her. The students waited for Ms. Mahima in the parking lot of the school in the mornings. As soon as she parked her car, they came running to her to open the door for her. They carried her books and notebooks and escorted her all the way to the staff room. She accepted the royal treatment she received from her students gladly.

The Principal, Father Joseph was a man of integrity, morality, spirituality and an absolute example of humility. He was aware of Mahima's residency status and had no hesitation in sponsoring her to receive the permanent resident status. The papers were filed with Father's help and submitted to the immigration service department. As the saying goes 'when it rains, it pours' came to be true in her life. She became pregnant right after starting her new job. *'What now?'* Just as she began a new job, how would she manage? How would she apply for the maternity leave at the end of the school year? She was fearful. A deep cloud of uncertainty entered her.

She was three months pregnant and started showing a little. It was impossible for her to hide her pregnancy. Not having any other options, she decided to announce the news to Father Joseph. Indeed, it was not an easy moment. With all the courage, she walked to his office and after a knock or two, she entered inside. Father Joseph immediately stood up, invited her inside and pulled a chair for her to sit. They talked about her classes, students, and their progress. He was pleased with Mahima's performance and interaction with the boys.

Somehow or the other, she had to tell Father that she was pregnant. She looked at him. He was waiting for her to tell him the real reason of that office visit all of a sudden.

"Father, I am pregnant."

"Wow! This is a good news. When is the baby arriving?"

"In the beginning of May."

Father had no questionable expressions on his face, but just an expression of happiness and all the support she could have hoped for. She thanked God for sending so many angels on this earth to help her and support her. She got up, thanked Father and left his office. The fear of losing her job demolished. She could not be happier by the response. Father called an urgent teachers' meeting. He made an announcement of her pregnancy. Not only Father and other staff members, but the students gave extra attention and care to Mahima. How special she felt during that time—she could not describe in words.

Some events of one's life become life long memories, some good and perhaps some not too good. To this day, she could not forget the wonderful experiences she had during her teaching years. At lunch time in the cafeteria, while sitting around the table with other teachers, one teacher brought an extra box of milk every day and placed in her tray.

"Mahima, remember, milk is good for bones, you should drink a lot of it for you and the junior in you."

Unimaginable, unbelievable care she got in that school. Students were like her shadow, protecting her, carrying her heavy books, helping her climbing the steps, holding her hand walking from the parking lot to the building on the snowy-slippery walk-way. She looked forward to going to her school and be around those loving and caring people.

Her delivery due date was in the beginning of May. She and Ateet got busy shopping for the new arrival. The crib, mattress, sheets, milk bottles, diapers and all the immediate supplies for the new baby were supposed to be ready before the due date. There were just two months left before she became a Maa and Ateet a Paa. The last period of her pregnancy was tough for her just like any other pregnant women. She came home after a long day of teaching and made sure that she got enough rest. She stretched on the couch to relax and felt the movements of the baby inside her, and also saw the waves of those movements outside her tummy. Her life was filled with hope and joy and excitement during that phase of her journey, and she was absolutely convinced that the baby within her was a baby boy.

Ateet went with Mahima for all the routine examinations and also to the child birth classes. Once again, she began seeing rays of hope. The first three years of her married life were not pleasant. She had not felt a true love of a husband and was often mistreated. Her husband did not consider her a part of him and did not love her. She hoped that perhaps she would be loved by her husband as a mother, a mother of his very own child—and a new reason for a hope awakened into her heart.

She desired to work all the way until her due delivery date, which was almost to the end of the school year. The three months of summer break right after the baby's birth was just perfect to take care of her baby without worrying about going to work.

One month before her due date in April, she was sitting and grading the students' test papers in the faculty lounge. All of a sudden, she felt distressed and discomfort. She could not sit or stand still and started pacing in and out of the staff room. She had just one class left to be taught that day. She could not wait and walked to Father Joseph's office, knocked at the door and without him inviting her inside, sat on the chair placed across his desk.

"Are you alright Mahima?" Father was surprised to see her at that hour of the day in his office.

"No, Father, I am feeling very restless, exhausted."

"Would you like me to phone Ateet?" Father got a bit worried.

"I don't think so. I have only one class left to teach. May I please go home a bit early today?"

"Yes, Yes Mahima. You go home and rest. I will ask Jim to take care of your class."

"Thanks a lot Father. I will leave all the class assignments with Jim on my way out."

And she proceeded towards the staff room. Jim was sitting in the staff room and getting ready for his class. Jim was the one who showed his care to a pregnant co-teacher, always brought an extra container of milk for her during the lunch time. He was a kind and happy person. He saw Mahima coming to him.

"How is the junior doing today?"

"I don't know Jim. I am not feeling well. Please Jim, would you watch my class? I already have spoken with Father."

"Sure! Sure! It looks like the junior is coming." He joked again.

"No Jim, please don't say that. There is one month more to go."

She gave all her class assignments to Jim and left for the day to go home and rest.

"I felt weird at school, came home early and still not feeling good." She passed the news to Ateet.

"I hope you did not eat any thing strange."

"I don't think so. All I had was a glass of milk."

"Why don't you go to the bedroom and rest? I will bring something for dinner."

He stepped out to get dinner. Resting was out of the question for her. She could not even remain in one place for more than a few seconds. She kept pacing in and out of her apartment all evening followed by a rough night, a night of turning and tossing. Somehow or the other, she managed until six in the morning, early Friday morning. She went to the bathroom and discharged what seemed like buckets of water, involuntarily. She had absolutely no idea what was going on with her. She got out of the bathroom, totally panicked and nervous.

"Ateet, I don't know what is happening with me? A lot of water gushed out and I could not even control it."

"Don't worry! Let me call the doctor."

Ateet ran to the phone and called the doctor.

"Is Mahima's suitcase ready?" That was the only question asked by the doctor.

"Pick up the suitcase and bring her to the hospital immediately. Go to the emergency room and I will meet you there."

The instructions by their doctor were to be followed. Upon their arrival in the emergency room a nurse walked to them with a wheel chair.

"Sir, you may take care of the registration and paper work and I will take Mahima inside."

"Thanks, but I don't need the wheel chair. I will walk with you."

The nurse gazed at her.

"Ms. Mahima! Please sit in the wheel chair."

She did as she was told. She looked into the nurse's eyes and saw no room to negotiate. Like an obedient child, the very first time in her life, she sat in the wheel chair, thinking that the nurse was crazy. A baby in the tummy, by no means made her handicapped that she could not walk. She was embarrassed to be pushed by someone else. It did not make any sense to her. She was wheeled into the elevator and was taken somewhere on one of the top floors of the hospital, and then to the patient's room. She was given a bed to rest. Lying on the bed, again, an uncontrollable, unlimited amount of water began to gush from her, and that's when she realized the necessity of the wheel chair. Immediately, with no delays whatsoever, the nurse started the intravenous access into her wrist, which was connected to a bag full of saline running into it. The idea was to prevent dehydration and also to make it accessible if she needed any more medicines to be injected in her. Also within a few minutes her tummy and chest areas were patched up and leads connected to the monitor to monitor her and her baby's heart rate. The doctor entered into her room.

"Hello Mahima?"

After greeting her, he did not take any time to begin explaining the whole process to her.

"The water you discharged in the past hour or so was filled in a big sack with the baby in it and that sack of water acts like a shock absorber for the baby to keep him safe. So, the sack popped somehow or the other and the water gushed out."

She kept looking at his smiling face and expressions. He looked calm and assuring.

"But we still have one month before the due date."

"Yes, Mahima—you are right, but we will have to have the baby today."

"How could that be?"

She questioned her doctor. She was shocked to hear the doctor's response. She had known that it could be dangerous for the mother as well as for the baby, if the baby came before the due time. She started weeping.

"Mahima, do you know, how many new born babies there are in our nursery?"

"No."

"So, listen to me. From a pound and a half to twelve pounds and that's why this hospital is called a baby factory."

She kept listening to her doctor, who did not lose his smile for a second.

"You must be worried that you baby may face some dangers as he is coming early."

"Yes." She responded immediately.

"The baby, who weighs a pound and a half is quite safe and is in the incubator, well attended and gaining weight day and night. Very soon, he too will go home with his family." Thus, her doctor reassured her.

"Wow!"

"Yes my dear. And the one jumping in you is more than five pounds. You wait and see, he will be a football player." The doctor rubbed her big tummy with his hands and they laughed.

She felt relieved after talking with her doctor. Ateet walked in the room after taking care of all the paper work.

"Now, both of you listen to me." The doctor looked at Ateet and then at her.

"All the water from the baby's sack is gone, which means that the baby has no protection any more. So, we will have to give you a medicine through your intravenous line to induce the contractions to ease up the delivery process and get your baby out."

The nurse walked into the room and started infusing the medicine. Both Mahima and her baby's heart rates were being monitored constantly. The increasing heart rate of the baby with the induced contractions was not good for the baby as was told by her nurse. It could have been risky. After a few minutes of observing the monitoring, the doctor stepped into her room again.

"Mahima and Ateet, the baby is in stress." He announced.

They were unable to grasp the meaning of what doctor just did say.

"What does it mean doctor?" She asked anxiously.

"We will have to take the baby out immediately by c-section."

In a fraction of a second the nurse and a few more hospital employees came into the room. She was transferred onto the other stretcher and the stretcher was wheeled by several people towards the operating room. Ateet was being very attentive to her and was by her side constantly. He was puzzled. He tried to console her as she was absolutely frightened by the thought of the surgery. Her tummy had to be cut open. She had to receive anesthesia and on and on. During the journey from her preparation room to the surgical unit, the doctor kept on explaining the whole procedure though she did not want to hear it.

The lower part of her body had to be numbed by giving an epidural injection in between the space of the two lower vertebrae of her back bone. The doctor showed her a big, long needle, which was to be poked into her back by the anesthesiologist. It seemed very scary. Mahima stayed strong. She was transferred on the operating table. Ateet sat behind her holding her shoulders. The numbing medicine was infused and she had no sensation below her chest. She was surrounded by the nurses and a surgeon. One of the nurses pulled a curtain in the middle of her body to hide the lower part where the incision was about to take place. The doctor and the nurses began operating on her. Ateet was curious and tried to peek at what was taking place behind the curtain. As soon as he saw Mahima's tummy wide open, his eyes began to close and his face turned pale. Immediately, one of the nurses walked him out of the room. He almost fainted after having a glimpse of the bloody site of that fresh incision. Mahima did not feel any pain at all. She had no idea, when they cut her tummy open. She kept a constant conversation with the people around her during the procedure.

"So, what is your baby's name?"

"Aaron." She replied immediately.

"What if the baby is a little girl?"

"Oh no, it is a boy."

And she felt some pressure on her tummy. She could feel the doctor's hands trying to pull the baby out of her tummy.

"Come on dear baby." The doctor kept talking from behind his mask. She could only see his eyes through the protective goggles he had on.

"One…two…and three."

"It is a boy!"

A spark of joy ran into the room. Aaron cried hanging upside down in doctor's hands. The news was given to Ateet, and he rushed into the room. A new father was congratulated by the crew and was the happiest father in the world.

The neonatal nurse wrapped Aaron into a little blue blanket and placed him over Mahima's neck, and that was the most joyful and fulfilling moment in their life; simply unbelievable and miraculous. A cute little boy came into the world and was already trying to open and close his eyes in the search of food. Aaron was a blessing and the most precious gift for both of them. Mahima held little Aaron with both her hands and the nurse rolled the stretcher to the recovery room. The nurse picked Aaron up from her neck and Ateet was happy to hold his son in his lap. He kissed him and hugged him and wrapped him in his arms.

"It is time for baby's bath and food. You may rest meanwhile."

Aaron was taken to his nursery and Mahima to her private room. She still was not quite awake. She was under the influence of strong pain killers and anesthesia. After a while Aaron returned to her with his nurse. He was wrapped in a blue blanket, wore a little blue hat, and tiny blue booties on his tiny feet. He was curled up on the padded mat on the top of a small cart. He appeared like a tiny angel, a heavenly gift Mahima and Ateet ever got in their married life.

Ateet became a father and perhaps a responsible father. Mahima hoped that his responsibilities as a father may change him and bring him close to her. She also wished to see completeness in her life as a loved and cared for wife and a mother. She always thrived for a better tomorrow and perhaps raising a new baby will bring a better future for both of them, and that's what she hoped for. She picked up Aaron in her arms with the nurse's help. The nurse sat by her side and gave her lesson to nursing her baby, the technique to hold a new born, and several other fundamentals. After Aaron was fed, she took him back to his baby nursery.

It was not even one day after her major surgery and she was instructed by her doctor to get up and take a walk with the help of her nurse. She had no energy in her legs, could not even turn over on her side or sit up without help. How would she be able to walk? It was a major surgery and she lost a good amount of blood from her body, she was helpless, and had to depend upon someone else—unlike her.

"I will try my best."

Her doctor stood in front of her and continued talking.

"Aaron is one month premature, so for a few days, we will have to transfer him to the intensive care unit and monitor him constantly."

"In the intensive care unit?"

"There is nothing to worry about. As you know that I would like Aaron to be a strong boy before he goes home with you."

He left and in a few minutes the nurse walked into her room. With her help Mahima sat up by her bed side. That was a tedious process for her and it left her breathless. She felt like she would never be able to walk again.

"I have no energy in me. How am I going to walk?"

"You have to go for a little walk. It is essential. Come on dear and hold my hand." The nurse made it very clear.

"Now, take some deep breaths and stand up."

"Ah! Maa."

Mahima was hurting. She stood up holding the nurse's hand, took one step and then two and in no time she was out of her room. She made one round of the unit and came back huffing and puffing to her room.

Aaron stayed in the intensive care unit for seven days in a tiny incubator, intravenous line poked in his little foot and small patches all over his tiny body to monitor his little heart. He faced the tough challenges of life very bravely. Mahima was taken to him in a wheel chair every three hours for feedings.

"Good news for you guys." The doctor entered her room with a big smile on his face.

Aaron was announced to be a perfectly healthy baby. All the tests done on him came out to be with good results. The doctor wrote the discharge orders with some instructions, and the family of three began a new phase of their journey.

Ateet brought the car to the main entrance of the hospital. The nurse rolled Mahima in a wheel chair with Aaron in her arms. Aaron was buckled up in his car-seat and in no time the family of three was on the road. Ateet drove and she sat next to Aaron on the back seat. It was a miraculous experience for both of them. One week ago, two came to the hospital and that day three were heading home. Aaron slept through the ride. He had no idea that how much joy he brought into his parents' lives.

They arrived home and parked at the main entrance of the apartment complex. That was the happiest day for her and a very fulfilling one too as a new mother. Ateet unbuckled Aaron from his car-seat, picked him up very gently, took him inside the apartment and laid him in his new crib, which was all ready, dressed and decorated. Then he came back to give a hand to her and to walk her inside.

Chapter 22
SHATTERING OF HOPES...AGAIN

$\mathcal{A}$ family of three people thus began living in a small one bedroom apartment. Mahima had three months of summer break. She spent those months taking care of her new born, giving him all the attention, bathing him, playing with him, and also taking care of the house work. The whole agenda of the household revolved around Aaron and his activities. When Aaron was asleep, Mahima did her cooking and cleaning. When he was awake, she fed him, cleaned him and played with him. Ateet started going back to his department early in the morning and return in the evening. He had a great deal of pressure to catch up on his pending research work. His university being close to the apartment, there were days that he came home for lunch and also helped her as much as he could. She started recovering slowly but surely, and she was able to take care of all the chores. She also started going for a drive with Aaron fastened up in his car-seat.

Aaron was about three months old when her next school session started. She had a short meeting with Father Joseph at the school. Father was concerned about Mahima's day care situation for Aaron.

"I have found a real nice lady in our neighborhood. She takes care of two other little ones."

"Great!" He responded.

"Your last class will end at 1:30."

Blessing after blessing showered upon her. She felt overwhelmed by Father's generosity and thoughtfulness. Two hours early dismissal every day; she was pleased. How miraculously God was at work in her life. She could spend more time with Aaron. Father, staff members, young students, everyone, cared deeply for a new young mother. All that affection and care further convinced her of the existence of a little heaven on this earth and served also to recall the unforgettable biblical words reinforced by her Pappa. *"God will always protect you and will never leave your hand; you just have to trust in Him."*

The school year started. Mahima's day started with getting Aaron's diaper bag ready for the baby sitter. Ateet dropped him at the sitter every morning on the way to his university and she picked him up every afternoon, fed him and rested with him. After a little afternoon nap, she checked some school work before cooking dinner. Their routine was to go for a short walk after dinner with Aaron in his stroller. The last duty for her was to bathe him, feed him his bed time milk and he slept through the night. The days kept fleeting away. Along with the other things in her life, she also began working hard towards the process of getting permanent residency in the country, so she could continue to work. The process was supposed to take a whole year and was already started with great help and support from Father Joseph.

The winter season was upon them before long and also the snow—a lot of fluffy white snow. Eight month old Aaron was thrilled to see the white snow on the ground and always keen to go and play in it. He also started connecting words to make short sentences. In his vocabulary, he conveyed to his mother that he wanted to go and play in the snow one afternoon. Both mother and son played in the snow for a long time behind their apartment complex. Mahima was unable to cook dinner that night. She was changing her and Aaron's wet snowy clothes when Ateet walked into the apartment.

"What did you cook today?" This was the very first question he asked after seeing her and Aaron.

"Oh, Ateet, Aaron and I played out in the snow. I am very tired today. Why don't we order pizza for dinner tonight?"

"What do you mean you did not cook? So, it means that there will be no cooking in this house any more." He was out of control.

She looked at him. Again, once again, seeing his bloody eyes filled with anger, she started trembling in fear. He came close to her, picked up Aaron, took him into the bedroom, put him in his crib, shut the bedroom door and came back to her. He grabbed her tight by her arm and pulled her into the kitchen.

"Dammit, open your ears and listen carefully. I will not order any food from anywhere. Cook at home."

She stayed in the kitchen and cooked. Abruptly and dramatically her hopes were shattered again.

"Why does Ateet treat her like a slave? He never cares for her. He never shows any concerns like a husband would show to his wife. He never tells her that if she is tired, he will cook or order food from outside. Why?"

Mahima worked outside the house, in the house, took care of an infant—an infant who required absolute attention, never complained about anything. She deserved the best, but the truth was not what she deserved. She was abused; physically, verbally and emotionally. Her efforts, to love him, serve him and to keep the family together failed, not one time or two times, but several times. His cruel behavior kept pushing her away from him. He repeated the same nefarious act again, did not change over the years, even after he became a father. At that point of her journey a hatred for Ateet began to incubate in her heart involuntarily. She was helpless. A beautiful working woman, a young mother of a beautiful child was being treated like rubbish. She felt humiliated, insulted, a creature of low self esteem and hollowness inside of her. She was frightened of her own husband and his unpredictable threats and attacks on her. A woman should be treated like a blossoming flower—if one petal of the flower is plucked, the flower dies slowly and that was exactly how she felt, dying slowly. The dinner was cooked and both ate. Aaron was bathed and already asleep in his crib. Mahima, laid in her bed on her side, motionless, with him on the other side of the bed. Her big brown eyes were wide open and kept trying to search some ray of the light somewhere in that dark room. Her Mamma's spoken words echoed her mind. *"After the baby comes in this world, every thing comes out to be just fine."*

The hope in Mamma's words of wisdom was fading away. She felt like she was being punished for some crime she has not even committed. Ateet was a father of a beautiful baby son, who was just a few months old. What would happen in future, when Aaron grows up? Mahima refused to marry him after his first slap on her cheek before the marriage. Why did he come back to her? Why did he ask for forgiveness? Why did he give her a fake promise that he will never lay his hands upon her? Why? Why did she believe him? All those thoughts kept brain storming her.

He was sound asleep, lying on the other side of the same bed, and she felt like a dying flower, which did not even blossom to its fullness. The night's episode left her shocked and bewildered. Should she share his behavior with her family friends? The answer to that question was 'no', as it would be nothing but a great embarrassment. After each abusive episode, some way or the other, she convinced herself to believe that that was the last one and he would never do that again. Again and again she was proven wrong.

That happened sometime at the beginning of December; when she was planning to get a Christmas tree, decorate it with Ateet and Aaron. She was more excited because it was Aaron's first Christmas. She planned on wrapping several gifts for Aaron and putting them under the decorated tree. She was so happy to celebrate Christmas with her little one, but Ateet's uncontrollable behavior took away all the thrill of the season. It crossed the boundaries of her endurance. Once again, she called Mark the leader of her Bible study group for his help in her marriage. The counseling sessions started for both of them. She felt like her marriage was nothing more than a sham and she was hanging on to the marriage for no real reason. She was helpless. She had no elders or relatives of her own living in the country to help her and give some guidance.

They all went to the Christmas Eve services. Aaron sat in their laps and enjoyed the colors and the singing. On Christmas morning, Aaron opened his little gifts placed under the decorated Christmas tree, wrapped in colorful wrapping papers. Little stuffed animals, baby books, and small toys made little Aaron jump up and down with joy. His favorite gift turned out to be a four wheel toy car. He pulled it out from under the tree and sat on the seat holding the steering wheel and kept pushing it back and forth on the kitchen floor and everywhere in the apartment. The crawling little eight month old considered himself to be the best driver in the world. That little car made him the happiest little boy in the whole world. Aaron had fun all day with his new toys and Mahima and Ateet had fun watching him playing with them. She prepared the meal with authentic Indian dishes and they enjoyed a special Christmas dinner. After some time of relaxation, Aaron was ready to go to his bed. Both husband and wife sat on the couch and turned the TV on. The joy of Christmas did not take long to turn into a nightmare. She could easily sense and see that transformation in her husband's attitude. His facial expressions had a reflection of anger and grudges. His blood red eyes looked ready to explode. She sensed it and her heart began fluttering with fear. She knew that whatever it was that created that mood, he would find some excuse starting a fight. The television was on but neither of them was really watching it. He could not control himself anymore and broke the silence.

"What was the point of buying so many toys?" There was anger and a threat in his tone.

She tried her best to suppress his anger.

"How happy Aaron was? Did you see how much he was giggling while opening them, jumping up and down? Well, those toys were not expensive at all. I found some good sales before I purchased them." She gave the best explanation as good as she could.

"You watch, in two-three days he will break and dump them."

"That is very true. The little car with four wheels; he was really enjoying pushing it back and fourth with his feet. Did you see how he was trying to stand up holding the steering in his hands?"

Ateet kept quiet. He did not even respond. They sat there in complete silence watching the TV. She tried to put all her efforts in hiding her emotions in her heart. She was frightened, afraid, and hoping that that was not the silence before a big storm. It was a very cold night. She got up and stepped into the kitchen.

"I am making a cup of tea for myself. Would you like to have some?" She made two cups of tea and brought the cups in the living room. They started sipping.

"Mahima! Tell me the truth about the relationship between you and Vivek."

Out of nowhere, he again raised the forgotten subject, the repetition of the same question asked several times before. She kept quiet in an effort to ignore and not to continue the discussion about the same old past. She did not like his attitude, which was nothing but an intentional attempt to emotionally blackmail her, exploit her, dominate her, or seeing the relationship with Vivek as her vulnerable point to torture her periodically. She kept sipping her tea. She knew that Ateet was waiting for her response and any second he will provoke her.

"I am asking you something. Don't you have ears to hear?" He screamed.

She tried to get up from the couch with the cup of tea in her hand. He grabbed her by her arm and pulled her back. The hot tea spilled on her.

"Leave me… you are hurting me."

"I am asking you, what was in between you and Vivek? Answer me, you dumb bitch." He screamed louder.

"Why do you keep digging up the past over and over again? It has been four years into our marriage and didn't I already tell you everything several times ?"

That firm response by Mahima did not satisfy him. He got totally out of control. He pushed her harshly on the couch and lifted his right hand to hit her.

"Stop it. If you lay your hand upon me, I will not tolerate it."

And she grabbed his strong arm with both of her hands. A miracle happened and she felt an amazing strength in her body. She was not afraid of him any more.

"What will you do?" He pulled his arm out of her hands.

"I will call the police." And she continued.

"And now, listen to me very carefully, and I mean it. This was the last time you pushed me and tried to hit me, but don't you dare to do it again."

The burning volcano inside of her exploded. She warned him. Perhaps, that was the day, he learned about Mahima's strength. He stepped out of the room and went to the bed room. The same nasty episode which shouldn't have happened repeated itself again and the same drama of forgiveness was played again the very next morning.

Though she became emotionally feeble, the innocent person within convinced her again that the previous night's episode was the last episode and it will not repeat again. She became the source of her own comfort and kept continuing her journey with Ateet. Aaron was her hope and goal for a happy future. She would raise her son in the best way, she would give him the best of the world, and that was the promise she made to herself. Aaron was her whole world. She crawled with him, walked with him, talked to him in his baby language, took him to the park and spent all the time with him. Aaron took his first step when he was ten months old.

Chapter 23
TRIP TO INDIA

$\mathcal{A}$teet completed his doctorate and was offered a post doctoral fellowship in another city, which meant that, that would be the last year of teaching for Mahima. They got the permanent residency on time and moved to the other city. The past three years she worked as a teacher and he worked on his doctorate. In those years the teaching assistant-ship he received was used to pay his tuition and the other expenses related to his graduate studies. They kept a joint bank account. Moving to a new city meant that she had no job that year. That was the year of a big transition for both of them. In a new city, they moved in a new apartment and they needed a new bank too. Ateet went to the new bank and opened a new account with the little savings they had. The account had only his name, his name only. Her name was nowhere, which simply meant that she had no right to any money. She sat on the chair with Aaron in her arms, rocking him, thinking about her past and trying to find the answers to the unanswered 'whys'.

Ateet received all his mail at his department address including the letters from India written by his family members. He never shared any of those letters with her. She accidentally found a letter in his jeans pocket while doing the laundry. That one was written by his mother after their recent trip to India. She read the whole letter. His mother gave her son very clear instructions,

"Never let Mahima have any control on any money. Keep all the money in your control. If she gets any letter from her family, make sure you read it. When you send any dollars to us, wrap them in a carbon paper before putting in the mail."

How could a mother poison her son against his own wife? How could a mother be that manipulative? The letter crossed the limits of her tolerance. She made up her mind not to take any more abuse from him or his family.

"This is your mother's letter. I found it in your pants pockets." She tried hard to control herself though she was boiling inside. He snatched that letter from her hands without any delay thinking that she had not read the letter.

"I already read the letter." She declared boldly. A big bubble of anger built inside her exploded.

"Did you write a reply to this letter?" She asked.

"No, what reply? There is nothing to reply to." He answered ignorantly.

"Yes, there is. You should remind your mother that now you are a married man and very capable of taking care of yourself and your finances. She has no right to control our lives." Mahima was still boiling with anger.

"Well, listening to the suggestions and following them are two different things." He again tried to be defensive and justify himself.

"Have you ever thought that she should not interfere in our lives? Who is she to tell you, how to manage our money and life? My Mamma never does those things. Doesn't she know that we are working hard to make our living, barely surviving and she continues with her demands?"

At the time of that episode, both were students and Aaron was not even born. Ateet was totally in his mother's control. He could never dare to disobey her under any circumstances. The letter made it very obvious and transparent that he and his entire family pursued wealth at all cost.

Those old episodes came back vividly in her memory. In so many years of their marriage, he never cared for his wife or her very basic needs. They always had a joint bank account. For three years, Mahima worked as a teacher and he was a student, she earned more than him and they had a joint account. The living expenses, electricity, water, rent, all were paid from that account. The first year and the first time of her life she had no job because she had to move with him to another city and he excluded her from the bank account, though most of the transferred money in a little savings account was from her past earnings. It was like a funeral of her rights as a wife and a mother. She swallowed that bitter poison and did not say a word. She devoted herself to little Aaron's care. The only money which was her own was the wage earned by baby sitting a little girl for just a few hours every day. The new town was a small university town. The only outlet for her was to walk to the mall across her apartment complex after lunch with Aaron in his stroller and the little four year old girl, who she baby sat. Walking to the mall and inside of it along with playing with the kids in the playground were the two workout activities for her.

Three months later in the new town, she found that she was pregnant and again her due date was in the beginning of May. She was a housewife that year. She thought about going to India for a few months so she would be well taken care off by her family during her pregnancy. Also she would not have to worry about running after Aaron, who was just eighteen months old and a very active little boy. Ateet willingly agreed on the plan; Aaron with Mahima leaving in the month of October, him joining them in December and all three would travel back home together. It had been a period of four long years since she had seen her Pappa and Mamma and all. She was anxious to go and meet with all her sisters, brother and their families. Her Pappa had been asking about Aaron in his letters all the time and he would be the happiest grandpa to see his grandson. The preparations began. Aaron's diapers, his baby food, clothes, toys, vitamins, juice, milk cans, all of his supply for three months was to be packed and all the suitcases were totally packed with his stuff. The day of their departure arrived. Aaron's was excited to be on the plane. He was thrilled to see the planes at the airport. She was excited as she had three months to spend in India with her and his families.

The plane landed at the airport. After immigration and the baggage check out areas they wended towards the exit. Just like the last time, the whole household was eagerly waiting to see Aaron and of course Mahima as a mother. His aunts, uncles, cousins, all were keen to pick him and hold him and Aaron enjoyed the special attention he received. Another five hour journey they had ahead on the road to reach her parent's house. Aaron called them Nana and Nani. He was jet lagged. For many days in the beginning, he slept during the day and was wide awake all night. Not only that, he kept everyone awake. He wanted to run around and play in the middle of the night. Poor Nana, not caring about his night time rest enjoyed playing with him, while the rest could sleep.

Nana and Nani had a little poultry farm with some hens and roosters, just enough to fulfill the supply of eggs for the household consumption. Early every morning, the chickens were allowed to roam in the courtyard of the house and that was a big entertainment for Aaron. Chasing those chickens with a stick in his hands was the morning entertainment and a good workout for him. All the toys packed in the suitcases brought all the way from United States were not worth a penny. They stayed unpacked in the suitcases. His duty was to feed the chickens with Nani and help her fill up their water containers for the day. The rewarding part of his duties was to pick up the eggs and arrange them in a basket to bring them in the kitchen. Omelets for the daily breakfast were made from the home produced eggs.

Late every morning a big herd of cows crossed the mud road in front of his Nana and Nani's house. Aaron waited each morning to meet the cows. He jumped into Nana's lap and Nana lifted him up, sat him on his shoulders and both stayed by the road side to welcome the herd. Aaron had never seen a cow before. His jumping and clapping with joy on his Nana's shoulders, seeing so many cows walking on the street was a joy for Mahima also. Perhaps, his little brain imagined an open zoo in India. After an escorted trip to the 'zoo on the street', every single day, the mobile toy-wallah, with balloons, plastic toys, whistles and many other toys hanging on a long stick showed up in the courtyard of the house. The toy-wallah became Aaron's best friend in a short time. Aaron placed his hands on the toys and his Nana bought them for him. As a result, Aaron turned out to be the best toy-wallah customer. He fell in love with Indian toys. He played with them, broke them in no time and was ready to buy another the very next day.

"*Alu… Gobhi… Palak… Moolee… Chane ka saag.*" The sale calls by the vegetable and the fruit sales man fascinated Aaron the most. The vegetable man came every day before lunch time rolling his cart and calling the names of the fresh produce he had on his cart, so the whole neighborhood could hear him. As soon as Aaron heard his loud melodious voice, he ran after him and imitated him in his baby vocabulary,

"*Alu… Dobhee… Moolee… Palak… Chhane ta chhaag.*"

The vegetable man pushed his cart. Aaron chased him everywhere in the inner streets and it became a free entertainment show for the whole neighborhood. As a result, Aaron became the marketing person for the vegetable man and the vegetable man's business picked up in no time. Aaron was rewarded with a handful of his favorite grapes. The vegetable man had no other option, but to make sure that he brought grapes for little Aaron every single day.

Nana and Aaron became the best buddies. Both played football in the fields in front of the house. Aaron woke him up in the middle of the night and both talked whispering in each other's ears lying side by side in Nana's bed inside the mosquito net.

The month of October was still summer like weather in India, warm but comfortable after the monsoon rains. Mahima gave Aaron a bath every morning after breakfast and left him in his diapers and a light under shirt. His favorite sport was to run up and down on the stone stair case in front of the house. One morning as he was playing he hit his left leg against the hard concrete of those steps. He started crying. Apparently, he hurt himself badly.

"Pappa, go get a rickshaw please." Mamma screamed loudly.

Pappa not knowing the reason of that urgent call, ran to the street and found a rickshaw wallah. Mahima jumped and climbed up on the rickshaw. Mamma put Aaron in her lap and then sat with them.

"Beta, make sure, his leg doesn't move." Her mother straightened Aaron's leg in her lap.

Rickshaw wallah rode his rickshaw gently avoiding the pot-holes on the street, and they headed towards the local clinic.

"*Mem-sahib!* Did *Gudda* (the little boy) get hurt badly?" And they made it to the clinic.

"*Mem-sahi*b, you get *Gudda* checked. I will sit and wait in my rickshaw and take you back too."

All three got off the rickshaw and entered into the clinic; the same clinic with the same doctor Mahima used to visit in her childhood. The doctor being a family friend was amused to seeing all of them in front of his clinic.

"Beta! Mahima! Is that you! Is everything all right with you?" For some reason, the doctor speculated that some thing happened to Mahima.

"Yes, Doctor, I am all right, but Aaron was jumping up and down on the stairs and he hit his leg."

"Come on inside." He took all three inside his examining room.

"Let us check our little Aaron." Doctor consoled Aaron.

"Aaron, honey, tell me where is it hurting?"

Aaron kept sobbing and gazing at the doctor constantly, grabbed his mom. He placed his little hand on the lower leg, where the pain was.

The doctor suspected that he may have fractured his leg.

"Alright, Mahima, I think we will have to get an X ray of his leg."

An X-ray was done and as suspected they found a hairline fracture in Aaron's leg bone. "*What now?*" Mahima was away from her home. Ateet was not there. She was pregnant. Would she be able to take care of Aaron? The doctor assured them as it was a hair line fracture, would not take long to heal. Before long Aaron was in a full hard cast from his toe all the way up. Ateet's family was informed. She informed Ateet through a letter about Aaron's accident. Ateet's father, Aaron's grandpa loved Aaron very much as he was his first grandson, came to Mahima's house almost every day to visit Aaron. He was also aware of Aaron's love for grapes and brought grapes for him every single day. Aaron enjoyed stuffing his mouth with grapes before chewing them.

The original plans to visit the sisters and their families were canceled. Instead, the sisters took turns to visit Mahima and help her with Aaron. Aaron was not able to walk at all. The little active boy became inactive and disabled to play and run around as he was accustomed to doing. Mahima could not even lift her son up with that heavy cast on his leg as she had to be careful during the second trimester of her pregnancy.

Aaron's best friend, his Nana spent hours and hours with his injured grandson. Mahima enjoyed their baby talk.

"Aaron beta, how are you doing?" Nana asked in Hindi.

Aaron, in his sweet broken Hindi replied,

"Aaron *bikkool theek hae Nana.* (Aaron is perfectly alright Nana...)"

"Nana, when will my pants come off?"

Aaron thought of that hard cast as his pants.

"Soon."

"Okay, Nana."

In the beginning of December, Aaron's cast was removed. He recovered rapidly, forgot all about his injury and started running around again like nothing had happened. The days drifted by and it was almost time for Ateet's arrival to join Aaron and Mahima in India. A few days before Ateet's arrival, both mother and son moved to his parents, her in-laws house. Ateet's flight landed late at night. Mahima, Aaron and Ateet's family were at the airport to pick him up. Aaron was asleep in Mahima's laps throughout the ride and at the airport. Ateet came out at the receiving end of the international arrivals at Delhi airport. His desperation to see his son after a separation of over two months was very reflective on his face. He came straight to Mahima and cuddled Aaron in his arms. Aaron was still asleep. In the transition of switching laps, he woke up and opened his eyes, looked at his dad for a moment to make sure that he was in his dad's laps, half awake-half asleep, and whispered joyfully,

"Dadda!"

Aaron enjoyed to be in his dad's laps and she pushed the cart with his luggage in it. All came out of the airport and got situated in the car. Everyone was tired. Ateet was exhausted after a long journey. Aaron slept again in his lap and Mahima told him the whole story about his accident word by word. The five hour journey got over quickly by talking, sipping the tea and cruising through the dense smog and fog. The last month out of three was planned to be spent at Ateet's house with his family. His house being so close to her parent's, she kept making frequent short trips to them also. Aaron kept her busy. She hand washed his clothes and diapers as there were no laundry machines. She cooked special food for Aaron as the supply of his baby food was finished in the first two months of their stay in India. She stayed occupied all of her day. She also had to take some breaks to catch her breath as the baby inside her was also growing day and night.

One month with his family passed by with a normal life. They were unable to get the same return flight because of a peak traveling season. Ateet took his flight two days prior to Aaron and Mahima. She was happy that all three had a good time with their families and Aaron was fully recovered from his injury. Perhaps, her in-laws accepted her because she was the mother of their first grandchild—a grandson, and was also the other one on the way. Perhaps—they had realized that their son was not only a husband but also a father.

Chapter 24
Birth of Sarah

$\mathcal{A}$ teet drove two hours to pick Aaron and Mahima up from the airport. They were on the highway going back home. Aaron was buckled up in his car seat in the back and sleeping after a long weary journey. Mahima was also trying to get some rest sitting on the passenger seat with her eyes closed. All of a sudden he started the conversation.

"Where were you when Aaron got hurt climbing those steps?"

"Mamma and I were sitting there on the cot and watching him." She replied in her weary voice and continued explaining.

"Those steps were fun for him. He loved jumping up and down. It was a nice and sunny spot for him to play every morning. Mamma and I sat there in the sun and watched him playing."

She kept talking as she understood his concern, a father's concern for his son.

"Anyhow, it is very fortunate for us that it was only a hair line fracture. Aaron is just perfect, back to his running and jumping. So nothing to worry about, accidents do happen."

"But, my sister told me that it happened because of your carelessness."

That statement of accusation by Ateet pierced her heart, hit her like a lightning, and burnt her inside and out. Her tiredness turned into a bitter anger.

"*How?*"

"*How could Ateet make such an accusation? I am a mother. He again believed his ruthless, trouble creating sister and her complaint, a complaint against his own wife. How dare she poisons him? This is his entire fault that he believes in all the nonsense told to him and that's why his folks keep poisoning my own husband against me.*" All those thoughts slipped into her mind. She could not stay quiet, tried to control on her emotions and an anger building inside of her.

"What else did your dear sister tell you against me?"

"She told me that whenever she passed through your parent's house, she saw Aaron running around in his diapers and you were never around him…"

Again, his jealous sister did not fail to find a cheap complaint to poison her brother against his wife. Why did he believe her? This was an immoral attack on Mahima's motherhood.

"Ateet! I am not hurt or worried thinking why your sister made this story. I am hurt that you believed her. You believed her knowing that she does not only cause problems in between you and me, she causes fights in between your own parents and other people too. You believed her, knowing how much this little Aaron means to me, knowing that he is my life and my soul."

That day was another sad day for Mahima. Those two hours from the airport to their home after a long flight became a nightmare for her. How hard had she tried to strengthen the weak bond between her and her husband, and her in-laws tried harder to break it. All the plots made by his family against her kept echoing in her mind all through the two hours of that road journey.

"We all are dead for you. You made us orphans. All the time, you roam around your wife like a servant." His sister yelled out of jealousy in front of Mahima after the couple came back from the dinner at a friend's house.

"Do not listen to her. Do what ever you think. If you listen to her once, you will be like her servant all through your life." These were his mother's words against Mahima written to him in a letter.

"My brother is not happy with you at all. He will divorce you and marry an American girl." That's what Mahima was told by his sister, the very first time she was at her in-laws house after her marriage and those words were spoken in front of Ateet and Ateet played dumb and ignorant.

Her rights were being snatched away from her and she could not do anything. She realized that Ateet would never care for her or listen to her. He was totally controlled by his family. Those cheap allegations against her by them were adding up to create a big wall between them. How in the world could she ignore and neglect her own child? Has Ateet ever thought about that?

How could she? Why were those words spoken? Why did Ateet believe in such a reckless allegation?

Both of them took Aaron to the pediatrician for his first check up after his birth. Aaron got a routine vaccination. At the sight of the injection there was a tiny droplet of blood and as soon as she saw that droplet of his blood, she became light headed. Ateet was with her all the time. He was the one who ran outside the examining room and got a glass of water for her. He was not with her when Aaron fractured his leg in India. He did not even try to think, how much agony and pain his pregnant wife went through. All she wished was that he would have trusted her and could feel a fraction of that pain that she felt. He did not even think about her fragility during her pregnancy, and without a second thought, he believed his sister who very cleverly turned an accident into an allegation of carelessness on Mahima. Mahima was at a stage where she wanted to say something but remained speechless. Again, it was a reminder to her that her husband had no maturity and he was absolutely influenced by his controlling family back home.

The car was speeding away on the highway and her mind was wandering into her past. During her last trip, a few years ago, when both of them went to visit their families for the first time after their marriage, Ateet declared very adamantly and devastatingly to his parents.

"Who cares about her (Mahima)."

Oh, what unbearable pain that declaration caused in Mahima's heart! How openly her husband declared her an outsider in his parent's house.

After a long plane journey of several hours with two little ones, one inside her and the other one sleeping in his car seat, she was dead tired and exhausted, but her husband showed no concern for her or for her well being. Ateet not only attacked her as a person, but her motherhood, the depth of her feelings, the emotions of a young mother.

"We should never forget that we are giving our daughter to the family, not only to Ateet."

Her Pappa could foresee her future and was not in favor of giving his daughter into that family.

"But Ateet is in America and his family is here in India. You know that Ateet is a well educated boy. He would keep Mahima happy and I am sure he will not tolerate any interference by his family." Mamma's reply was confident as well.

How confidently her Mamma convinced Pappa!

"I wish Ateet had taken this marriage seriously. Up until now, he hasn't. He has neither afforded me my rights nor has he taken care of me. He keeps inflicting pain on me intentionally. I am married to him and according to Indian traditions; I have to live with him always, for the rest of my life, happy or unhappy. I have to forget all the mistreatment given by him in the past and erase them completely out of my memory."

And they arrived at their destination.

Aaron turned two and only one month was left for the new baby's arrival. Aaron knew that the new baby in his Mom's tummy was about to come out any time. He was involved with his mother in the preparations to welcome the new baby. A new little bed was bought for him and she dressed it with the comforters, sheets, pillows and stuffed animals. Mickey Mouse, his favorite cartoon character was the theme of his bed. Aaron loved his new bed and he helped his Mom to decorate the crib for the new baby.

The anticipation to receive a new baby for all three of them kept building up. She was well prepared. She had no fear of delivery at all. Her doctor had already told her that because of the transverse position of the new baby, she will have to go through other c-section. The delivery day arrived and she started having contraction pains; it was time for them to check in the hospital. She coped with those pains bravely as an experienced mother. Ateet dropped Aaron at their friend's house and took Mahima to the hospital just like he did two years before. After all the surgical preparations, she was in her doctor's hands and the same story repeated itself.

"So, Mahima! What is your baby's name?" Just like before, the doctor asked.

"Sarah."

"What if it is baby boy?" The question was repeated again.

"No, it is a girl."

Lo and behold, she was right. Soon after coming into this world, Sarah started crying with her full energy and strength and filled up the operating room with the echo of her beautiful cry.

Nurses, doctor, Ateet and Mahima—all were joyful. The nurse wrapped Sarah in a little blanket and laid her at Mahima's neck. It was again an amazing sight. Sarah was wide awake. She looked around, had an eye contact with everyone in the room, and gave her own introduction. She was an alert and a happy baby. She was also the biggest Mother's Day gift Mahima had ever received. Her big brother came to see her in the hospital several times and asked in his innocent voice,

"Mom, when are we taking Sarah home with us?"

The doctor's orders were to keep Sarah and Mahima in the hospital for two more days for their full recovery. She was a blessed mother of two little ones, who were nothing but God's greatest gifts in her life. Ateet was not only the father of a little boy but also a father of a little girl.

It was a stormy day when all four drove home from the hospital. Instead of one, there were two car seats in the back; Sarah in one and Aaron in the other. Ateet had two tiny lives and a new mother with him in the car to take home safely. He drove slowly and carefully. The apartment was on the second floor. To connect the two apartment buildings, there was a bridge and the staircase to go up on the bridge. It rained cats and dogs that day. He brought the car all the way under the bridge and parked it on the grass. He made three trips up and down the steps to take Sarah, Aaron and Mahima into the apartment. All three being dependent upon him, he was the only support for them. Mahima never let her hopes be dead, rather she stayed strong and hopeful taking care of her duties as a wife and a mother of two. She dreamt a bright and glorious future for her little ones. She found her joy and happiness in them. She was married for six years, but she was still hungry for her husband's true love. She still had some hope, a lingering hope for years and years to be loved by her husband, to be embraced by him in appreciation, to be cared as a mother of their two beautiful children, who she loved abundantly.

Chapter 25
TRAINING

*O*ne year passed with Ateet doing his fellowship and Mahima taking care of the two little ones. He was offered another year of fellowship in the northeast part of U.S.A. She had to give up her planned career. She remained as a housewife along with taking care of Sarah and Aaron. She followed her husband to the places where he got a job or a fellowship. Sarah was just a new born baby in the middle of that summer, when they packed and moved to the northeast part of the country. Once again to another new town, new people, new every thing and they had to adjust to a brand new life style again. Her desire was either to find a teaching job again or to go for some short term training. In that part of the country there were no jobs for her in the field of her interest in which she had a Masters degree. Also it was not possible for her to move elsewhere given the family's responsibilities with her two little children. She decided to discuss and express her interests to Ateet.

"I would also like to find a job or at least do some kind of training."

She was not acquainted with the city or the surroundings. She needed his opinion and help.

"Sounds like a good idea. Would you like to teach?"

"That would be great, if I can find a teaching job."

"I will bring the local directory. Find out if there are some schools in the area."

The very next day, she noted some phone numbers of the area schools from the local directory and made several phone calls. All she got was total disappointment. The area schools had already started or about to start their sessions, and all the vacancies were filled as the hiring was done before the beginning of summer.

"Why don't you think about doing some kind of short training in health care?" He suggested to her as his research was also hospital based.

"I like this idea of exploring some possibilities in the hospital."

"But, Ateet, I am not sure what kind of job I will be able to get in the hospital, and even if I am offered a job, will I be able to do it? I have no experience in that area at all."

Obviously, at that point Mahima had no idea about the nature of the jobs suitable for her in the hospitals.

She thought it would not hurt if she at least went and visit the hospital he was working in. She did not hesitate to call them and scheduled a meeting with the hospital authority. The head of the department showed her around and gave her an orientation tour to familiarize her with the work done in that area. He also introduced her to some of his employees working in the department. She found that based upon her past education, she needed only a year training. After the completion of the training, the requirement was to pass the board exam to be certified and be able to work in any hospital with that department with a handsome salary. The deal was fabulous but the path did not seem to be that easy taking the children into consideration.

"So, you visited the hospital. How did you like it?" Ateet asked her.

"I liked the hospital. I think I will enjoy working with the patients."

"When will the training start?"

"Next week and I have to register very soon."

"Wow! That is quick."

"Now we will have to find a baby sitter for Aaron and Sarah."

"The lady downstairs baby sits a child. Let us go and talk to her." She suggested.

Mahima registered for her classes and the clinical training. She was a bit nervous and uncertain realizing that that was an entirely new and very different approach for her. The big question lingering in her mind was, "*Would she be able to do it?*"

The very first day of her training, along with the other uncertainties, she was worried about Aaron and Sarah. She hoped that they were well taken care and happy with their baby sitter. '*Did they eat? Did they play with her? Did they take a nap?*' With all those questions, she was unable to focus on her classes.

After a long first day of the classes, she took the public transport back to her apartment and went straight to the sitter. The situation was entirely opposite than what she expected. Sarah was sobbing. Her eyes were swollen and her nose was stuffed up and runny. Mahima picked her up in her arms and instantly Sarah grabbed her tight around her neck and rested that little face on her shoulder. The message by little Sarah could not be more clear and transparent; she did not have a good day. She was only three months old, but amazingly very wise to recognize the people around her. Aaron was fine as he was used to staying at the sitters in the past but he also showed his unhappiness when he saw his baby sister in tears. That evening both the kids went to bed early and fell asleep.

"Sarah and Aaron don't seem to be happy at the sitter. What should we do now?"

"In a day or too, they will be just fine. Obviously they are new to the sitter. Let us give them some time, perhaps a week to get adjusted."

That was a sensible suggestion by Ateet. She requested the sitter to put both of them in their stroller and take them out to the park which was in the apartment complex. One week passed. There were no improvements. Sarah was not happy with the sitter. She did not look forward to going to the sitter. She conveyed her unwillingness by crying even before going down stairs.

"Why don't we leave Aaron at the sitter and take Sarah to Mummy. I hope, my Mom will be happy to take care of her, and hopefully Sarah will also be fine with her." Ateet suggested.

Ateet's mother was visiting his younger brother and his wife, and she was helping them to take care of their baby son. They lived about two hours of driving distance. That seemed like a good solution and in their favor. Who could take better care of the children other than their own grandmother? Under those circumstances and the complexity, Ateet's mother was the best choice.

The plans were finalized and the weekend was set to take Sarah to her grandmother. Her suitcase was all packed along with her baby food and toys and what not. The anxiety of separation from her little baby daughter was intense. The choice was not easy, but was the only alternative. Mahima, Ateet and Aaron had to stay apart from Sarah for the time being and they hoped that that time would pass quickly and everything after that would be normal.

Early Saturday morning, all four packed into their car and took off. Little Sarah had no clue, where was she going or what was going to happen next. Perhaps she thought that she was going for a car ride somewhere. The whole family spent the weekend together until Sunday evening. That evening was the evening to leave Sarah with her grandmother. It was not easy for anyone, Ateet, Mahima or Aaron. The plans were to visit Sarah every weekend from Friday evening to Sunday evening. The five days of the week without Sarah seemed impossible. Positivity in the midst of uncertainty was that Sarah had a cousin of her age to look at or perhaps to play with.

Sunday evening came and that was the evening to apart from Sarah. The goodbye hugs and kisses were given to Sarah and the return journey for the rest began. The three came downstairs, sat in their car with heavy heart and headed back to their town.

"Why is Sarah not with us? Why did we leave her at Uncle's house?" Aaron questioned frequently over the journey.

The distance between them and Sarah kept increasing and so did Mahima's restlessness. She felt like a piece of her body was taken away from her. Each fraction of each moment was filled with thoughts of Sarah. *What if Sarah hasn't slept? What if she was crying? Was that a big mistake on her part to go for that training? Wouldn't it be just fine for her to forget about the training, stay home and take care of her children?'* She was unable to focus on anything but Sarah, her baby, who could not speak up for self and unable to say a word in her defense; *'why should she be punished so harshly? Was her little brain thinking that her mother abandoned her?'* How wise that little soul was? She knew who her father and mother were and also her older brother. She recognized the three important people in her life very well. Immediately after arriving back to their place, Mahima phoned her mother-in-law.

"Sarah has been crying non-stop and all of us are trying our best to calm her down." Sarah's grandmother conveyed the message with no hesitation at all and she sounded helpless.

"Oh! Lord! Please have mercy upon us."

That was the very first night. What was next? There were five more days to the next weekend. Her restlessness became unbearable.

"Ateet, we need help." She felt totally incapacitated.

"Why don't I ask my mother? We can write her a letter explaining our situation. If she is able to come stay with us and help us with our children, all the problems will be resolved." Her mother lived in India.

That was the last alternative left and if that failed for some reason, any reason, she would have to forget about her training. Both agreed upon the idea to request her Mamma to come, stay with them and help them with the children during Mahima's training. They contacted and made the request to her Mamma through a letter. Mamma already had a passport. All she had to do was to go to New Delhi to the embassy to get the visa stamped on her passport. They were sure that her Pappa would be supportive to send her willingly. If she was granted a visa, all she needed then was ticket. According to their calculations, if every thing went well as planned, it would take at least two weeks before Mamma would be able to travel.

Out of five days, two were crossed off. Sarah was not willing to compromise with the arrangement, which meant that she did not show any signs or symptoms to surrender and accept living at her Uncle's with grandma taking care of her. Early Wednesday morning, Mahima dropped Aaron at the sitter and drove to the hospital. That unforgettable Wednesday was the third day of her training program. She was anxious, extremely worried and restless. She was firm and her mind was made up. She was determined to place everything in this world in second place, and pick Sarah up in the evening of that day and bring her home. She had no patience left in her. Her motherly instinct kept intensifying moment after moment. She was in her morning session of training at the hospital, but was consumed with finalizing the plans to bring her daughter back home, and consult with her husband. On her ten minute morning break she phoned Ateet.

"If my mother is willing to come to help us, it will take at least two weeks or more."

"Yes, that is very obvious." He replied.

"I have been thinking about it and I am going to talk to my supervisor about our situation. I have decided, no matter what he says, we will drive to your brother's house and bring Sarah back home tonight." Mahima's plans were firm and nonnegotiable.

"And then what?" Ateet asked with curiosity.

"For tomorrow and day after, I will request for some time off and also for the next week. After the next week, you take a week or so off before Mamma comes, if she can."

"What if your boss refuses to give you time off?" That was a legitimate concern. She was new in that program and chances of her boss refusing the leave were pretty high, but she was willing to take the risk.

"Then to hell with my training. I will have to think about some thing else, but I will not leave Sarah so far away from us with your mother."

Ateet could easily sense her determination. He had nothing much to say or suggest. She could hardly wait until her lunch break to talk to her supervisor. She knocked at his office door with no hesitation whatsoever, explained him the whole situation and she was very fortunate that her request was honored with the commitment to make up for that lost time by putting extra hours during her training period. She immediately relayed the good news to Ateet.

Both of them reached home a little early. She ran to the baby sitter to pick Aaron as quickly as she could and packed in no time. Wasting no time they were on the road racing with other cars on the highway to reach his brother's place. Mahima could never forget those moments when she entered Ateet's brother's apartment. Sarah was lying on her tummy on the couch, just a sweet three months old little Sarah. Mahima came close to her, called her name.

"Sarah!"

And Sarah gently lifted her head, gazed at her mother Mahima for a moment. Her lips quivered as she wanted to verbalize something. Unhappiness was the dominant expression on her innocent face. And she cried in a loud deep voice,

"Maa! Why did you do that to me?" How could Mahima not translate that cry?

Mahima was unable to control her emotions, picked up her daughter in her arms. The two hearts talked and the tears flooded in their eyes. She apologized and promised her tiny three month old baby girl that under no circumstances, she would ever leave her far away from her. Oh! What a moment!

Sarah was back with her family—happy little Sarah.

"What if Mamma could not come to help?"

"What if she does not get her U.S. Visa?"

Mahima had no answer to all those 'what ifs' battling in her mind, but deep down in her heart she felt that her Mamma would be able to come. If she could not, she was determined to quit her training, be with her children and be a house mother. She was willing to offer that sacrifice for her children and forget about her training.

Chapter 26
PAPPA'S MEMORIES

*M*ahima's mother's U.S. visitor's Visa was granted and one way flight ticket was confirmed. Oh! What a relief for her and Ateet. Mamma came, the blessings came. Mamma took care of Sarah and Aaron and Mahima continued her training with full concentration.

Three months of her training passed. She was very confident in performing her duties independently. Her self confidence was evident and observed by her supervisors. She was fortunate to be selected by one of the hospital doctors to work for his research project. The beauty of the opportunity was that she got paid for two hours every evening. She was happy to stay at the hospital for those hours every evening to make some money, plenty for her own pocket money.

Aaron and Sarah were content with their Nani and so was Nani. Nani cooked dinner and fed both the children. Mahima got more time to study. Mamma missed her husband very much. Mahima's oldest sister was responsible for taking care of her Pappa. Both of them kept communicating with each other via letters. There was an amazing love between her parents even to that time of their lives, nothing faded. It sparkled more and more with their age with an absolute strong unbreakable bond between the two of them. The two of them optimized the saying that some marriages are made in heaven. Theirs was. She remembered how much they were made for each other and how much care they took of each other. In times gone by if her Pappa visited her sisters' families, he always made sure that he returned home to Mamma the same day in the evening before late night. He never ever left Mamma alone, no matter what. That was the biggest sacrifice her Pappa made for Mahima that he sent Mamma so far away from him happily and willingly just to help his youngest daughter. What a gift of love she received from her loving Pappa. Thinking of her Pappa's unconditional love for her, Mahima still gets tears of joy in her eyes.

The year went by productively with her mother's help. She completed her training and Ateet also finished one year of his fellowship. He got a job offer in northeast, so they had to move once again. She was also fortunate to find a job. Mamma helped them to settle down in their new place and then she left to go back home, her home in India. She was grateful to her mother and her abundant help in caring for, and raising her young children. Sarah was one and Aaron was three years old when she started her full time job. Their baby sitter lived in the same neighborhood, a nice Indian lady, who had a three year old daughter. Mahima packed Aaron's and Sarah's diaper bags with some food and clothing before going to her job in the morning and Ateet dropped them at the sitter before leaving for his work. She picked them up from the sitter on her way back from her work every afternoon. Both of them became busy with their jobs and children. During that time, occasionally, Ateet flashed his temper, but had not laid his hands upon her.

Both were professionals and possessed full time jobs making decent salaries. So, instead of wasting a big chunk of their money towards the rent every month, they decided to purchase a house of their own, and started going out with the agent who showed the available houses in the area. It was a major project for both of them and they typically got back home late with both the kids after seeing houses for sale in the area. Mahima's mother's presence was a blessing in her life. Her fear of being physically abused by her husband was fading in her presence. Also, both worked hard all day long, came home tired, took care of their children, cooked and cleaned, so there was not much time left. Yet one event took place when both with the kids returned home late after seeing some houses with the real estate agent. The children were fed, but they were hungry.

"What is there to eat?" Ateet asked.

"A little *daal* and some *sabzee* (curried vegetable), left over from last night is in the fridge. I will quickly cook some rice in the pressure cooker."

"No, make some *rotis*." Ateet demanded forcefully.

She looked at his face to confirm he meant it.

"Ateet, I don't even have dough in the fridge and it is too late to make one now. I am tired. Rice will be ready in a few minutes in the pressure cooker." Mahima pleaded while getting both the kids ready for their baths.

"And while I bathe the kids, dinner will be ready."

Aaron and Sarah already had their dinner from a fast food place.

"No, hurry up, bathe the children, put them in their beds, make the dough and make *rotis*."

He refused to compromise and demanded her to obey him. Those harsh orders neither persuaded nor scared her any more. She was not there to take orders and especially out of selfishness and inconsideration.

"I also have to go to work in the morning and I deserve some rest. I told you that it is already late. Why don't you have any concerns or care for me? If you want *rotis,* make yourself. Why didn't you get some fast food for us too? You always force me to cook and you always think about saving your pennies." She blew up and lost control.

Her absolute determination not make *rotis* provoked him and being temperamental, he lost control of himself and that rage of anger did not take too long to appear into his eyes.

"So, you will not make *rotis* today." He yelled.

"No. Not today." She responded in a firm voice.

He got totally out of control, came closer to her and grabbed her arm to push or pull her.

"Ateet, I am telling you... don't you touch me." She screamed.

He acted like a mad man, totally out of control. He did not pay any attention to what she just said, pulled her from her arm and,

"Slap." He slapped her on her cheek.

She was at the bathroom door at that time and watching both of her kids playing in the bathtub. They saw their mother being slapped by their father. They saw her in pain and started crying in panic, a helpless panic. They were terrified, breathless, in tears, and sobs. She rushed and grabbed two towels, wrapped them up and took them in their room. She put on their pajamas and tucked them into their beds, went to the kitchen and made two bottles of milk, handed them their bottles, kissed them good night and shut the bedroom door.

The boundaries were crossed once again. Her endurance was tested once more. She had no other way, but to take a firm step and defend herself and her two little children. She went to the living room, picked up the phone and called the police. At that point of her life, it was absolutely unjust for her to take any physical abuse from her husband and that also in front of those two innocent lives. In the last seven years of their married life she failed repeatedly to convey him the message that she was his wife, a human being, who has a soul and a body, who deserves love and respect. In those seven years, she remained as a weak vessel and forgot her own identity. In those seven years, she allowed her husband to be dominant over her, she allowed him to take advantage of her, take her for granted, and she kept silent.

In a short while a police officer knocked at the door. She opened it and he stepped into the living room. Sarah and Aaron were almost two and four years of age at that time. They were unable to go to sleep. As soon as they realized the presence of someone else in the house, they got out of their beds and stood by the door. They were curious. All they could understand was that something was not normal. Mahima had no tears in her eyes at that time though her cheek was swollen red and eyes were searching for some help, any help from anywhere. She stood firm in front of the officer and told him the details of the whole episode in front of Ateet. Ateet appeared like the most innocent man on this earth with no words in his mouth. The officer asked her if she would like to press any charges against her husband. She looked at her husband and his terrified face, and declined to press any charges. She was aware of the fact that one 'yes' would take him to the jail and how insulting and demoralizing that would be!

That late hour of the night the officer did not want to take any chances and suggested to Mahima not to stay at home but spend that night in a hotel with the kids. He took all three of them in his police car and dropped them in a nearby hotel. Both the kids were traumatized and so was she. She could not stop thinking about her husband's abusive behavior, how harshly he mistreated her over the years. *'What would happen if he adopts the same behavior in future with Aaron and Sarah?'*

Aaron and Sarah were asleep in the hotel room. She kept turning and tossing all night long. Again, a battle kept raging within her with question after question and not a single answer. She could not rest for a moment all night long. She got up early in the morning, looked at her reflection in the mirror hanging in the bathroom. Her very own image did not appear to be hers; it seemed like some stranger standing before her. The swollen eyes and red swollen face with the blue imprints of fingers on the left cheek looked terrifying. How could she have gone to work in that condition? It was already ten o'clock in the morning and the kids were still asleep. She took a long shower in the hotel room, got dressed, woke the kids up and checked out from the hotel. She requested the front desk to call a taxi cab to take them home.

It was already late in the morning and Ateet may have left to go to his work or that's what she hoped for. She unlocked the door of the apartment and saw him sitting on the couch in the living room. He immediately got up, took both the kids in his arms and hugged them. The same old drama of regretting and begging was replayed once more.

If she had left him, where would she go with her two little children? She had no where to go. How would she be able to survive with two youngsters and raise them on her own? Those questions lingered in her head all the time. She felt defeated and again she surrendered herself into the arms of injustice and decided to live her life for the sake of her children's welfare. Their future and the nurturing of their future were in her hands. Not a single fragment of her body and soul wanted her children to be raised in a broken family by a single mother. The woman within her died and she had no other choice but to live her life without that woman; a loveless life with no expectations. On the other hand, she had no intentions for her motherly desires to be dead too. She had to live her life for her children and not for herself. The woman who in last seven years of her married life, in the peak seven years of her youth, got nothing but rejection, humiliation, abuse, how could she have hoped for any betterment in her future? Her hopes were shattered again and again. She even considered leaving Ateet and perhaps leaving the children with him but that thought gave her nothing but chills. The kids needed their mother, and the genuine concern she had was *what if Ateet follows the same pattern of abuse with them.*

The sharpness and the heat of the burning rocky road she was traveling on failed to burn or bruise her feet. She was bold; she kept walking courageously holding the hands of her two little ones. On the other side of the world, her father was seriously sick and there was no way for her to visit him. She was financially constrained, unable to afford a round trip air fair to India and also just about a month old on her new job. It was the end of May, when in the middle of the night the house phone rang. Ringing of the phone in the middle of the night meant a call from India. The bad news was delivered that her Pappa had passed away.

Mahima was aware that her Pappa was sick, but she had no idea that the end was that near. The news left her stunned. *'How could that be?'* She hung up the phone and came into her bed. The last time she saw her father was a little over two years ago. At that time he seemed to be doing well, running around and playing football with Aaron. All those old memories kept slipping into her mind. Her biggest concern at the time was her Mamma. Her father, who never left his wife alone for a single night in years and years, was not with her any more. How would she be able to endure such an excruciating pain of separation? Mahima was unable to go back home for the ceremonies. Knowing the burial traditions back home which should be done within twenty four hours of death, she stayed back and joined her family in her thoughts.

Her deep desire was to get her father to United States at least once, just once to show him around, show him her house, her work place, have her children play with their grandfather, and spend some time with him. That dream never turned into reality. It was a quiet night. Ateet and children were asleep. She laid in her bed with her eyes wandering in the darkness of the room. Before long, she got up, had a glass of warm milk and sat on the couch in the living room. She was not ready to accept that her Pappa was no more in this world. All the old time memories and the time spent with her Pappa came so fresh in her mind.

A long time ago, Mahima and her Pappa used to visit the villages in the vicinity of the town they lived in. Every Sunday, at dawn, her Pappa got up, made some morning tea and woke her up. After a light breakfast, he tied his medicine box on the luggage carrier of his bicycle. One of Mahima's responsibilities was to pack some snacks and drinks in a bag and carry them on the luggage carrier of her bicycle. Pappa was passionate about serving the poor villagers and treat their illnesses and Mahima accompanied him as his helper. He made good friends in those villages over the years of his committed services to them. Every Sunday of the year, with no reservations, under all the weather conditions, was set aside for both of them to provide the social services to the needy. Their mobile dispensary consisted of two chairs, a small table for the medicines, a register to keep the records, and a pen. The dispensary stayed open from the early hours of the morning until late into the evening. The villagers looked forward to receiving those services.

The father and daughter team rode their bicycles through the crowded city; the mud covered streets of the villages and reached their appointed destination. The villagers and friends stayed prepared for the arrival of the mobile clinic every Sunday morning. They had a table with two chairs set up in an open area. A long queue of patients, young and old, men and women, waited to be seen by her Pappa. Pappa wrote the prescriptions and Mahima's job was to fill them. She found the prescribed medicine in the box, made small doses, wrapped them up in tiny pieces of paper, and gave them to the patients with all the verbal instructions. She also warned them with authority that they should not eat or drink anything thirty minutes before and after taking the medicine, she advised them to suck the medicine not to chew them, and let the little white pills dissolve in their mouths just like a candy.

The innocence and the illiteracy of the villagers motivated Mahima to serve them. Some of them were underprivileged and by all means could use some help. There were no schools, no dispensaries, and no doctors in the villages Mahima and her father visited. The men labored in the fields, worked hard all day long to grow their own crops. They saved enough for their household supplies and went to the city market to sell the rest to make a living. The women stayed home, took care of the household work, raised their children, cooked, cleaned, walked to the well to get the supply of water, fed the cows and goats, milked them, and make butter for their daily use. Nothing went to waste in those villages. The women also used the cow dunk to make flat cakes, dry them to make fire for their cooking. They helped their husbands in the fields and carried the lunch bags to feed them, to give them a break from the hard laborious outdoor work. Mahima was young, but she observed their innocence, dedication, not even a tiny trace of selfishness they possessed. As a result they looked absolutely content and happy in their own little world.

The mobile dispensary owned by Mahima and her Pappa was totally free of cost for the villagers and was a gesture of love. The care and affection young Mahima got in return from those villagers was remarkably priceless. A very special lunch was always prepared by the women of the village. That delicious lunch consisted of a nice hot heaping plate of steamed rice, topped off with a big load of home made brown sugar, which came from the village-grown sugar canes and also topped with the home made butter. Having a sweet tooth she thoroughly enjoyed eating that sweet lunch in a specially decorated room, just for her. The little dining room was decorated by the host girls in a traditional style. It had a rug to sit on and a flat stool placed in the front to keep the food plate and a brass cup filled with well water. Pappa's friend's daughter always sat by her side and gave her the pleasure of cool breeze by a hand held swinging fan. Conversing with those young girls was another incentive for her being there.

"What is your name?" Mahima started a conversation with the young girl sitting by her.

"Maya." Maya answered in her soft innocent voice. She was shy, covered her mouth with her *dupatta* (scarf) and started giggling.

"And who is the one sitting outside washing the dishes?" Mahima pointed towards the other beautiful girl who was busy at the time scrubbing the dirty dishes.

"Daya. She is my sister."

"Maya and Daya, very beautiful names you have. Let me guess, who is older."

Maya kept giggling louder and louder gazing at Mahima's face with her big brown eyes.

"Maya! Why are you laughing so much? Aren't you older?" She guessed.

"How do you know?" Shy Maya began talking and tried to be friendly with Mahima.

"You know Maya, my older sister does the same thing. She sits and takes the easy job just like you and sends me to the kitchen to clean the dirty dishes."

All three giggled and giggled and instantly they became good friends.

"Alright Maya, now tell me how old are you?" Mahima was curious to learn more about them.

"Seventeen."

"And Daya is fifteen. Isn't that right?" Mahima guessed Daya's age.

"Yes Didi."

'Didi.' Mahima liked it very much. She liked to be called 'Didi' though she was younger than Maya. The tradition was to call the older sister 'Didi' out of respect, not by the name. Being youngest in her family, no one called her 'Didi' before. After that little conversation with Mahima, Maya was no longer shy. She opened up and enjoyed talking and talking like a chatter box.

"Didi, do you go to school?"

"Yes Maya, I do. This year, I have to prepare for a big exam."

"You know didi, there is no school in our village. We cannot even go to school." Maya sounded a bit sad.

"I did not know that Maya! What do you do all day at home?"

"Working at home, helping in the fields, that is all." Maya replied.

"We have only one school in this village and that is for boys only." Maya lamented.

Mahima was very surprised.

"Why Maya? Why is it so?" Mahima wasn't happy to learn that the girls and boys did not have the same rights.

"The boys are taught just to read and write." Maya explained.

Mahima had never known that there was no girls' school in the village. After some moments of silence Maya started smiling, a smile carried its own loveliness and a hidden shyness within. Her beautiful face glistened.

"Maya, please speak up. I know, you are trying to tell me something."

"Didi! You know what?" And she paused, looked around to make sure, no one else could hear her.

"Next month I am going to get married." Maya announced it with some hesitation and some shyness. She kept on chewing the corner of her *dupatta*, which fell off from her head.

"Wow! This is such joyful news!" Mahima was aware of the fact that in the villages, the girls got married very young. Maya was only seventeen.

"Wow! Maya, I am so very happy for you. Now tell me everything, everything and everything. Where does your would be husband live? What does he do and how does he look?" She bombarded Maya with numerous questions.

"I have not seen him as of yet Didi, and never met him. He is the son of the land-owner of the nearby village. Babu ji (father) told me that he is very good and educated boy and that's all I know about him."

"Okay dear Maya, what is his name? Can you tell me?" Mahima played ignorant. She knew that the village girls do not speak up their mate's name and that was the custom in Maya's family also.

After spending all Sunday with the villagers, typically it was late evening when she and her Pappa returned home dead tired. A good wash and a bath was a must for both of them and also a nice meal cooked by Mamma before they retired for the night. The time she spent with her Pappa was priceless and unforgettable. Pappa always encouraged Mahima and said,

"Mahima beta, I am just a small doctor and I want you to become a big doctor in the future."

Pappa was a figure of humbleness, a man of integrity. He underestimated his own values, his passion to serve others, his capacity and strength hidden deep inside him. He was a man like a deep ocean, who was hiding those precious treasures in him. Mahima kept thinking, how could she be a bigger doctor than him? How would she be able to match her father's passion as a doctor? Who in the world could be a bigger doctor than her father? Her father left his own interests behind and on his day off, just one day off did nothing for himself but served the people, the needy people. In that service there was a true devotion, genuine sacrifice, and a compliance. He did not care if it was scorching hot or freezing cold, every Sunday was dedicated to the villagers, who needed him and anxiously waited for his arrival.

She was immersed in her thoughts. It was not easy to believe that her Pappa was no more. He had finished his journey on this earth and he lies motionless surrounded by all, Bhaiya-Bhaabi, all the sisters and Mamma. Mahima was his only child who could not attend the funeral services and grant him the last goodbye. Her priceless time spent with her dear Pappa, him playing football with his grandson Aaron just two years ago, him enjoying the bread *pakodas*, preparing tea for the household early every morning, singing hymns in the mornings and waking up the whole neighborhood, playing his harmonium, his extraordinary personality, all were so fresh in her mind. He was Mahima's mentor and support at every step of her life. His greatness was beyond description.

Chapter 27
ARRIVAL OF MAMMA

*A*teet and Mahima with their two children moved into their new house. The house was roomy with a fenced backyard. The yard was large enough for the children to play and run around. They also installed a swing set for them.

Any transition or change in her life always brought a sense hope, a hope for a better future. Her definition of a better future was to receive love, care and respect from her husband. The past was gone and nothing could have been done, but she was desperate to create a homey environment with family values in her new house.

Their new house was much bigger than all those apartments they lived in thus far. It had four bedrooms, a family room, a good size kitchen, a formal dining and living room, three bathrooms, a full finished basement, a nice big deck and a front porch. Aaron and Sarah were happy to have their own rooms. The furniture and the household belongings they owned thus far were such that they fit in a little space of the house. One of Mahima's commitments was to keep the house tidy and clean and also nicely decorated. She desired to furnish and decorate the rooms little by little. That hobby of hers kept her busy and also gave her satisfaction and contentment as the lady of the house. They did not have much cash to spend at once, so she started looking for the affordable sale items to make her house look like a home. Ateet was not cooperative or appreciative of her interests and efforts. Rather he taunted her and attacked her self confidence with sarcasm.

"What an interior decorator!"

She also loved to cook for him and the children. She enjoyed trying different recipes and cooked special dishes in a hope that her family will enjoy the meals and her husband would be appreciative. Instead of appreciating her efforts, she was constantly criticized by Ateet.

"This woman is spoiling the children."

On numerous occasions she was criticized by her husband in front of friends and family members. He referred to his wife as 'this woman'. He did not give it a sensitive thought that he was married to 'this woman', who happened to be his wife. She felt like she was a hollow vessel eaten up from inside with no gratitude and no self esteem. She was totally crushed. Years passed, but she was being treated like rubbish still, a slave in her own house. Her husband always found some excuse to hit her, to demoralize her and to control her for little or no reason. She was neither appreciated nor encouraged for her hard work in and outside of the house. Her desires and needs were ignored. She could never understand the reason for his lack of love and care. And that fear kept gnawing away at her--both physically and emotionally. In fact, bitterness developed within her, and hatred for him kept incubating in her. As a result she became rebellious and it seemed impossible to her to develop the bond which should be there between any husband and wife. Her feelings were dead and her soul was crushed.

She felt fortunate that she had a full time job in an area hospital. She looked forward to going to her work place and meeting a diverse group of people, her patients. Talking with her fellow employees and patients gave her a sense of contentment. She met patients with various personalities, some were down to earth and some hot tempered. Some were terminally ill, but hopeful at the same time. She was amazed to meet some who traveled a tough journey but preserved the glittering smiles on their faces. Her work environment was absolutely favorable and inspiring. The appreciation of her work ethic and personal admiration by her colleagues and patients were uplifting to her. Her friendly and charismatic character played an important role at her work place. She loved working with elderly patients, especially the elderly couples. They held each others' hands, walked together, and accompanied their ill spouse. Mr. and Mrs. Smith was a couple of love birds. Mahima called Mrs. Smith, who was sitting in the waiting room. Mr. Smith got up quickly, took his wife by her hand and both started walking slowly together. She walked them to her department, and before starting the procedure on Mrs. Smith, she introduced herself.

"My name is Mahima."

"How lovely, a beautiful name." Mrs. Smith smiled broadly and pleasantly.

"Thank you. Please have a seat." She requested both to get comfortable so that she could explain all about the exam that had to be performed.

"What part of the world are you from Mahima?" Mr. Smith showed his interest in Mahima's nationality.

"I am from India Sir and living here in the United States for the last ten years."

Mr. Smith was ninety and Mrs. Smith eighty seven years old. For some reason Mahima was always keen knowing more about her elderly patients, finding out the secret recipe for their lasting love, especially when she observed a strong bond between them.

"So, Mr. and Mrs. Smith, how many years have you two been married?" Mahima asked casually.

"Sixty seven years." Mrs. Smith did not hesitate in her response and she began the story of her youth immediately.

"We met during our college years, dated for a while, got married and have been together ever since."

Mrs. Smith was lost in her past. She went on and on with her love story. Her face reflected a blush of a newly wedded girl. Her eyes sparkled. Her body language spoke a thousand words. Mr. Smith listened to the story as if he had heard it for the first time. His eyes forgot to blink and were glued on his wife's face. Phenomenal reflection of love sparkled on their faces. It was so obvious to sense that the love between the two was still alive and they preserved it all those years of their time together.

The conversation with them during the procedure left Mahima absolutely speechless. She was totally astonished talking to those love birds. Their ripe age, the ups and downs, society and the rules made by the society, rocky roads, worldly storms, nothing, absolutely nothing could shake the strong foundation of their love.

"We have sixteen grand children and eight great grand children." Mr. Smith delightfully talked about his family tree.

"Wow! How lovely. It means, you must keep a long list for your Christmas shopping." Mahima joked and all three laughed.

Their story paralleled the story of her parents, who also had seventeen grand children. They loved each other and an example of oneness. They were always together and nothing could separate them. After her father's death she thought of getting her mother to the States in a hope that a change of place and surroundings would be good for her and also both the children would be happy to spend time with their Nani.

Aaron and Sarah were happy with their baby sitter, but it was a bit inconvenient especially during the hours when Mahima had to take calls at her hospital. There was uncertainty in her working hours and frequently she had to go to work in the middle of the night. Ateet had to travel out of town frequently. Considering the situation she decided to talk to Ateet.

"I have been thinking about getting my mother here once more to help us"

"Are you thinking because of the children?"

"Yes, and hopefully a change would be good for for her too as she is alone now. She will keep herself busy with the children and at the same time it will be a help to us too." She continued her explanation.

"I also know that the children will be happy to stay with their Nani during summer. Aaron will start school in the Fall, and we will need someone to drop him and pick him up from the bus stop."

"Sounds like a great idea. Why don't you write a letter to your mother and ask her. Obviously we will have to come up with some plans." Ateet agreed to the proposal gladly.

A few years ago, when her Mamma came to take care of the children leaving Pappa behind in India, Ateet was on his best behavior and did not lay his hand on Mahima. So she hoped for the same the second time.

All the dreams of having her mother with them came true when she accepted the invitation gladly and willingly. Her mother flew from India to spend a short time with Ateet and family. Aaron and Sarah were also excited to be with their Nani again. Nani and Sarah's duty was to walk Aaron to the bus stop in the morning and pick him up in the afternoon. She served some afternoon snacks to both the kids and helped Aaron with his homework. She also prepared the dinners for the whole family and cooked a wide variety of Indian dishes. All that meant there was less work for Mahima. Mahima worked at her job with no worries about her children and also regularly went to the gym to swim early in the morning before beginning her day at work. The family ate dinners together, and enjoyed the home made fresh food prepared by her Mamma. Life was wonderful with her Mamma's presence at home.

Mahima took her mother and children for a car ride to the mall or to the park after their long days spent inside the house. Mamma loved to go to the malls. The malls fascinated her as they were very different from the Indian bazaars. She was surprised to see the fixed price stickers on the merchandise versus the bargaining trend with the merchants back home.

Mamma was a social bee and good in making connections. She made some friends of her age group in the Indian community of the area. She also discovered that some of her friends were in fact her distant relatives. She socialized with them in her free time and also kept herself busy chatting with them over the phone. Through her efforts Mahima also got connected with several families, who cared for her and treated her like one of their own.

Ateet's job required out of town and overseas travel frequently. Having her Mamma at home was a major blessing for her especially in those times when he was out of town. She did not have to worry about her children if she had to go to the hospital in the off hours and at times in the middle of the night. Before their bedtime every night she made a routine to bathe them, put their pajamas on, tuck them in their beds, read a little bed time story, pray a little prayer in their ears, turn off the lights and go to her Mamma's bed room. Mamma had severe arthritis in her knees. Mahima made sure to rub the ointment on her knees, give her the pain killer with a warm glass of milk and lay with her in her bed to chat.

"Mamma, I thank you for all your support." She never got tired of conveying a heart felt thanks to her mother. Her mother provided unconditional help, support, a lesson to raise the children with patience, love and tender care.

"Oh, beta, I also love to stay close to you." Perhaps—that was a motherly instinct.

Mamma had a framed picture of Pappa placed on the side table by the table lamp. That picture was taken in his youth. He was dressed in a three piece suit, a fancy tie with a pin, a white handkerchief folded in the coat pocket, debonair in his looks. He was one in a million.

"Mamma, when did Pappa take this picture?"

"This one was taken before we got married." Her eyes sparkled.

"What was that year? I forgot."

"June 12, 1938." She replied instantly and Mahima started counting the years on her fingers.

"53yrs ago."

"Wow! A 54 years old picture and how well you have preserved it… my dear Mamma."

"Yes, you are right. I changed the frame several times. Ever since your Pappa gave it to me, I keep it with me, always."

Remarkable! Her eyes filled with tears. Extraordinary! What an example of true love right in front of her eyes. Her curiosity to learn more about her Pappa was sparked. She continued the conversation.

"I can sense that you loved Pappa very much. Did he love you as much as you loved him?" Mahima kept asking all those innocent questions.

"Yes, my dear! He never left me alone even for a day all these years, and I don't know why he left me alone in this world." Her voice was cracking with emotion.

Mahima was well aware of the sorrow sitting deep down in her mother's heart. Mamma was grieved, but there was not a single drop of tear in her eyes.

"He became very stubborn during the last days. He did not even listen to me." She was totally lost in her past and continued talking.

"He was going down hill, became very weak, but refused to see a specialist, we had to force him, he refused to take the medicines though the doctor who specially came home to see him, warned him to be regular with his medicines and wrote him the necessary prescriptions."

Mamma was talking and Mahima was listening. Perhaps, her heart was being comforted by telling all about Pappa.

"During his last months he became very dependent, stayed in his bed all the time, could not even move by himself. Your didi and I helped him walk to the bathroom. We sponge bathed him. All he could eat was a little light lentil soup and drink some juice. How could he get energy from that! The doctor kept him on such a strict diet."

Mamma's voice started getting deeper and deeper and trembling. She was deep into her thoughts. Perhaps she was totally into some other world with Pappa. She kept relating her story to Mahima. Mahima's eyes were glued to her face, a face, which reflected thousands of unspoken words, a glorious face with beautiful deep dark brown eyes, filled with shimmering tears and very transparent. And she continued…

"Last year, on the 30th of May, he woke up in the morning, asked your didi to make some bed time tea. Just like every other morning, he drank the whole cup of tea with gratitude. After that cup of tea, he looked so energetic, so happy as if he was never sick before and all of us were convinced that the medicines were effective and we got some hope."

After a long pause she continued.

"Then your didi made some oat meal and fed him and he ate the whole bowl unlike other mornings. He made us believe that he was getting his appetite back."

Mahima was listening intently to her Mamma.

"You know that he was in a habit of reading the newspaper daily. Your didi helped him sit up, supported his back with some extra pillows and handed him the daily newspaper."

Mamma's voice started trembling and the stream of tears flowed down on her pink cheeks.

"In just a few minutes, I noticed the newspaper was on the floor by his bed side and his eyes were closed."

"I thought that he fell asleep while reading the paper. I went close to him and shook him, but he did not wake up, he never did."

Mahima failed to control her sobbing any more. She got out of the room, went down stairs in the kitchen and warmed up two glasses of milk for her and her Mamma.

"Mamma, may I please sleep with you in your bed tonight?"

She wrapped her right arm around her Mamma's chest and placed her right leg on her tummy, just like she did in her childhood and both mother and daughter fell asleep.

Mamma's help for Ateet, Mahima and their children could not be described in words. She always enjoyed cooking for them, feeding the children, checking their school work and to top it all refining her daughter's cooking expertise. Sarah and Aaron became their nani's best friends. Ateet was generous to give Mamma some allowance as a gesture of thanks for all her help she provided.

Mamma saved each and every penny of her earnings in a small pouch hidden under her pillow in her bedroom. She went to the mall with Mahima and used her saved pocket money to buy a doll for Sarah and toy cars for Aaron. That unconditional love created a strong bond between Mamma and her grandchildren. That love was not only love, it was an absolute definition of a true and genuine love, that brought big sacrifices, which she offered to her youngest daughter Mahima and her family. Ten months flew by in a blink of an eye. Mamma had to return to India. She had to go as her visitor visa was about to expire and also all her other children were back home.

Chapter 28
BRUTALITY STRIKES AGAIN

*T*wo years passed since Mamma returned to India. It was the late winter of 1994, February, on a Saturday morning, Mahima stayed in bed until late morning. That weekend morning was the only morning of the week when she could rest and relax a little more after a long tiring week. She got up late, made breakfast, served to both children and Ateet. As was the Saturday routine, she started on her house cleaning projects. In the middle of it the house phone rang. It was Ateet's mother phoning from India. Mahima overheard the conversation, which made it obvious that there was some serious problem or urgency. Almost always Ateet's family phoned him at his work over the week days but never at home. The conversation was over and he hung up the phone. Out of concern, she asked him.

"Is every thing alright?"

And that was it. Perhaps, that was the wrong time to show any concern. Instantly, his face turned red in a rage. At that time Aaron and Sarah were watching the Saturday morning cartoons.

"Who the hell are you to hear our conversation?"

He screamed on the top of his lungs with his red eyes popping out, filled with anger and glaring at Mahima. What a mistake she made by asking a simple question. Perhaps it was not simple for him. Twelve years of abuse, hitting, pushing, screaming, being treated like a slave made her lose control of herself and the limits of her endurance were tested again. She took an instant decision not to stay quiet. She felt like a wounded lioness.

"I just asked a question out of concern. What is the big deal about it?" She also screamed.

Immediately, he turned into a devil. She was dusting the dining table. He came close to her to attack her. He grabbed her arm tightly and pulled her away from the table.

"Ateet... leave me... leave me alone... You are hurting me."

"You bitch how you dare argue with me." He lifted his hand up to hit her.

"Don't you hit me... leave me... Ateet... I am telling you...if you hit me I will call the police."

He pulled her cruelly towards him and pushed her harshly into the wall.

Her body hit the wall and she fell down on the floor. The picture frame hanging on the wall fell and crushed into several pieces. The children saw the whole drama and started crying in terror.

She had no tears in her eyes. Her heart was bleeding in pain, burning with smoking flames. The limit of her endurance was long gone. She got up, walked to the phone and phoned the police.

She never ever had imagined in her youth, before her marriage that she would get a husband, who will be so cruel, no less than a devil. What in the world he expected from her? Why? Why did he continuously hit her? Did he ever reflect on reality that Mahima was his wife and the mother of his children? All those questions with no answers again and again stormed her mind.

So much she dreamed about her future husband before her marriage. Before her marriage, she dreamed of her husband like a Raja, who would admire her, her beauty, her talents and would in fact be deeply in love with her. Both would dream of a future together, a family of their own. Their life together would be nothing less than a blooming garden of flowers, spreading its fragrance. She would look elegant, would dress up just for him. She would love her Raja and her Raja would love her. What happened to those dreams? They were shattered, crushed, the very first time when Ateet laid his hands upon her.

She never in her worst dreams thought of calling police against her own husband. That day, once again, she was beaten up by her husband in front of her innocent little kids. It was cruel and unjust for her to see her children crying in terror, standing helpless and sobbing in front of her eyes. How on this earth, any mother could stay strong under that kind of brutality? How?

The police officer came. Once more Mahima refused to press any charges against him. After looking at the two prior police records, Ateet got a warning by the officer that if he hits his wife again, no matter whether she presses the charges or not, he will have to go to jail. Once more, that silence after the storm lingered for a long period after that episode. At that stage of her life more than herself, her concern was for her two young kids. What if in the future he makes the children the target instead of her?

She did not stay quiet this time. The person, who did not even make an effort to understand the needs of his wife in years and years, took advantage of her submissive nature and her physical weakness. Knowing that she will not be able to fight back, he used her weakness as a weapon to show his own physical strength. He kept on emotionally black mailing her. He kept on attacking her by using her love affair before the marriage as his weapon, just to satisfy his manhood. How in the world could such an abusive man even give any happiness to his wife in the future? The little hope inside her died.

Mahima was on the verge of failing to cope with that abuse alone by herself. She raised her voice. She went to the pastor of her church to get some counseling hoping as she failed to change her husband's abusive behavior, perhaps, some outside person; in particular the pastor may be able to work with him. He went for counseling just a couple of times and then quit. The reason he treated his wife brutally could be that his father treated his mother exactly the same way. Perhaps for him, the definition of a wife was 'a man's slave', just like his mother was in the eyes of his father, like a piece of furniture in the house, use it and put it aside before the next use.

Ateet knew that Mahima always respected privacy and believed in morality. He made an assumption that she will suffocate herself in the midst of his brutality, but to preserve her morality and self respect, she would not raise her voice outside the house. He bluntly refused to seek any help or counseling from the pastor of their church. Mahima could not keep the acts of his brutality a secret any more. She gave up after years and years of abuse. She needed some help from somewhere, from any where. She wrote a lengthy letter to her brother in India about her husband's behavior. The news spread into the whole household in no time. It was like a wave from a tsunami, which paralyzed her Mamma and the other family members. The word 'divorce' did not exist according to the family traditional values. No matter what, after the marriage, under no circumstances, the girl could return to her parents' home or leave her in-laws home. The only way to leave her husband or in-laws was in the form of her own funeral. Her brother, Mamma and other family members went to Ateet's house to discuss the issue. His father consoled them by saying a few words.

"We will talk to our son and he will not hit her again."

One thing and just one thing Mahima was happy about was that her Pappa was not alive any more to hear or witness her suffering. At the same time, she thought that maybe if he was alive, he would have had found a way to help his daughter and rescued her out of that wilderness somehow or the other. Ateet refused any counseling. Mahima needed help. She made up her mind to get help from her church pastor. She told him all about the past openly and extensively in order to receive proper help. At that point of her life, she was determined that she would not take any more physical abuse from her husband.

Her pastor was helpful. He assured her that he would keep everything private and confidential. There was absolutely no excuse for Ateet to hit her or abuse her in any form. He discussed the whole situation with Mahima, and explained to her that the husbands who beat their wives, abuse them and control them have no self respect or confidence in them. They have jealousy in them, in particular for the wives who are submissive to them. They desire a submissive wife and if she is not submissive, they take it out on her to satisfy the burning ego deep inside them by hitting her, abusing her and demoralizing her.

They only think that whatever is said or done by their wives has some ambiguous motive in it. They do not see any noble qualities in the woman. They do not trust her. The universal rule of a good relationship between a husband and wife is founded upon respecting each other, but there are those husbands who get jealous seeing their wives happy. If the wife is in a good mood, they become restless and try to spoil her mood by ridiculing her.

They always look for moments to prove her inferior and put her down. They are provocative and at times there is a good possibility that a wife may lose her temper beyond the certain limit of her tolerance and these are the moments those abusive husbands seek to attack their spouses physically, verbally, emotionally or sexually. Their aim is to play with her emotions, hurt them and satisfy their burning controlling power. Their treatment of their wives is akin to a two sided sword—impossible for the wives to face it or fight against it. In that situation, the woman wastes years and years just to prove herself right, but in reality all her efforts are nothing but impotent. Their efforts are to train their wives to forget themselves, their needs, their self esteem and respect and bow down to their potentate husbands' feet day and night like slaves. Those husbands desire to be the absolute focus of attention and they use their wives to quench their sexual lust. Their goal is to prove that they are in control and powerful. They have no self respect and they are eons away from the qualities of real manhood.

Those controlling husbands take advantage of the submissive quality of their wives and treat their submissiveness as their weakness as they fail to control other men or dominating women. They become addicted to power and seek to crush the self esteem of the submissive wives, and they feel victorious. These kind of men show their love for their wives only when they think that the circumstances are out of control—a vacuous and superficial expression.

Mahima totally embraced what her pastor had described. She felt all of that was so true in her life. Ateet always looked for the opportunities to put her down. She lived her life in a constant fear. Ateet went out of town frequently for his work meetings. During those times she was petrified staying alone with the kids, but at the same time she felt relieved.

After all the hard work and time she devoted to her graduate school to accomplish and be a career oriented woman, she did not even get a job in her field because she followed her husband to the places he took his job, and kept the family of four together. She got trained to be able to work in the hospital on his advice because she could have found the hospital job anywhere in the country his job took them. She made a handsome salary, but he did not stop hurting her feelings and continued humiliating her by saying that she was no more than a button pusher and he possessed a Ph.D. She worked hard day and night, and was a committed mother. He did not appreciate, but always accused her of spoiling the kids. For twelve years of marriage he did not stop ridiculing and insulting her by bringing the topic of her relationship with Vivek before marriage. He made fun of her and told her that he had several offers from rich peoples' daughters, doctors in India and he was stuck with her.

Ateet forced Mahima to quench his physical thirst. He kept control on all of their earnings, took account of each and every penny she spent in the grocery store. He constantly threatened her by saying that she was not worthy for him, she was the dust of his feet. He abased her family members back home, who he never even met. Mahima was so tired of his cusses against her and her family. His cussing words that he vowed to destroy her family and her life echoed in her head incessantly. After each abuse he bowed to her feet and asked for forgiveness, treated her gently with appreciation as if she was the most beautiful thing for him in the world and there she melted again. She looked at the two beautiful faces of her children, took a step back and gave herself a false hope again. She made sacrifice after sacrifice to keep the family together. At that stage of her life, she felt feeble as if she was being eaten up from inside and losing her soul.

She kept going to the pastor for counseling. That was the only way for her to protect herself from possible stress or other health problems.

Chapter 29
Her heart in Flames

*A*aron turned ten and Sarah eight. Both started their new session at school. Just like before they were enrolled in childcare for before and after school. Mahima dropped them early every morning at seven o'clock on the way to her work and picked them up in the evening around six. Both of them were happy at their childcare center. They enjoyed playing with other children of their age, and loved the afternoon snacks provided by the childcare. They also enjoyed doing their homework with other children.

From early childhood Aaron was a very active and athletic little boy. He was in the fifth grade. It was the first week of February and a winter warning was posted in the area with a severe snow storm on its way. People were advised to minimize their commute because of the dangerous road conditions. Driving to the grocery store to get the basic supplies was treacherous on the slippery roads. That day, Mahima called Ateet and asked him to pick up the kids from the day care so she could go to the grocery store to get some food items to see them through the stormy days. She did so and reached home in the evening. The house was completely dark inside and out.

"The children and Ateet should have been at home by that late hour of the day. They should have been home at least an hour ago."

She checked the messages on the answering machine. There was nothing, no messages from Ateet.

"If Ateet was running late, why didn't he leave a message?"

The negative thoughts overpowered her. She made several attempts to call the childcare, there was no answer. All she got were frustrations. Obviously no one was there at that late hour of the day. She managed to find the house phone number of the manager of the childcare. She dialed the number and fortunately got hold of her husband, who conveyed to Mahima that some kid at the childcare got injured and his wife took him to the hospital.

"Who is the child?" She became more curious.

"I don't know."

"Ah! I hope the child is not Aaron." She felt numb. A million thoughts crossed her mind in a fraction of a second. Her motherly instinct was immediately sharpened.

"The child is Aaron."

Her hope nonetheless was that she was wrong. She was helpless, fearful and confused. The only one to share her restlessness was the house dog, who kept pacing behind her. How could she find out? She kept walking back and forth from the main entrance to the telephone and kept looking at each and every car that passed by on the street. Each car's head light coming into the neighborhood appeared to be Ateet's car with the children in it. She had no choice but to stay in the house and wait for a phone call.

The predicted snow storm was at its peak outside. The road in front of her house looked buried under a fluffy layer of white snow. The little hand on the clock hanging in the kitchen passed the number eight and the phone rang.

"Mom, Aaron broke his leg." Sarah conveyed the news.

"Mom, the doctor is saying that Aaron may have to have a surgery."

Sarah told the whole story in her broken, sobbing voice. Little Sarah did not even know the meaning of surgery. All she knew was that her brother was injured and was in pain.

"Ah! My heavens!" Mahima sighed.

"Sarah, I am on my way, and you take good care of your brother."

She said bye to Sarah, placed the phone on the receiver, picked up her car keys and in no time she was on the road. The weather conditions were treacherous. The roads were slick and slippery. The traffic was unbearable. A distance of ten minutes took thirty minutes. She parked her car at the first available spot and rushed towards the entrance of the emergency room of the hospital. As soon as she entered through the main door, she saw Ateet pacing back and forth with Sarah in his arms. He took Mahima to Aaron's room. Aaron was lying on the stretcher with both of his legs stretched. She saw not a single drop of tear in his eyes or any expression of pain on his face. He was brave in coping with the situation and the painful injury. Mahima kissed him and talked to him, then turned her head towards the view box, where his X-rays were hanging. She took a closer look at those X-rays. That was not a hair line fracture like before. There were two broken, totally dislocated bones in his lower leg. She could not believe it. All of a sudden darkness came in front of her eyes and she turned pale, light headed. Ateet walked her out of Aaron's room, and sat her on a bench placed in the hallway. She drank some water, composed herself and went back to her son who was suffering and trying his best not to express it.

"Aaron, is it hurting?"

"No Mom, Doctor gave me a pain killer medicine." He assured his mother.

"How did it happen? Did any one tell you any thing about it" She asked Ateet.

"Yes, the manager of the childcare center told me the story. Aaron was playing football with the other kids and the counselor. Aaron was running and his childcare counselor was behind him. He tripped over and the counselor fell on top of his leg. When I arrived to pick Sarah and him, the care taker told me about the accident and also that they called the ambulance to take Aaron to the hospital."

Sarah was trembling in fear with her arms wrapped tightly around her mother's neck. Ten year old Aaron also repeated the story in detail. The doctor stepped into the room and explained more about the X-rays. He assured them that in growing children the broken bones knit together very quickly if they are aligned properly. He also assured them that he will do his best to settle the bones into the correct position. That was an encouraging and promising prognosis by the doctor for the whole family.

All but Aaron's nurse were asked to leave the room. Those orders by the physician were honored by all three of them. Aaron was in good hands. They stepped out and sat in the adjacent waiting room which was filled with several people. There was a tense silence in that room. Perhaps those people were other families and friends of the patients being treated in the emergency room just like them.

Mahima sat with Sarah in her lap. Ateet could not sit for a second. He kept pacing in and out of the waiting area. Within a matter of a few moments a loud scream of Aaron echoed through the area, and that was when the doctor settled his bones.

"Aaron is doing well and now we are ordering another X-ray to make sure that the bones have aligned properly. All of you can come in the room now."

The nurse and all three walked into Aaron's room. Aaron and his orthopedic doctor were chatting as if they knew each other for a long time and were life long friends. The rest of the plans totally depended on the X-ray report. The doctor was a famous orthopedic surgeon in the area. His articulate confidence and the confident look on his face comforted the family abundantly. The new X-ray films were delivered in a short while and hung by him side by side with the old ones in the view box.

"Oh, Thanks to God." Those were the exact words that came from Mahima's mouth.

Those broken bones were perfectly connected and aligned. Surgery was not needed. Alas! It was nothing but a miracle. She hugged the doctor and had no words to thank him enough. The tears of joy could not stop flowing down Mahima's cheeks. Sarah's face glistened again, and Ateet tried to hide his emotions. Immediately Aaron was taken to the other room and the whole leg was put in a hard cast for eight weeks.

Mahima took some time off from her work to stay with Aaron at home.

Aaron availed a private tutor through his school to stay up to date with his school work. A wheelchair was delivered for him to take him to his follow up check-ups and to move him around. Ateet's mother also helped. Sarah helped her brother and always remembered to pick up his home work assignments from the teachers at the school.

In three months, Aaron was completely healed and started running around and playing football again. The summer break finished and the same school routine resumed. Aaron started the first year of his middle school. Sarah was in the fourth grade. Just like his mother Aaron was very much interested in sports and his favorite sport was ice hockey. He joined a youth hockey league and enjoyed it thoroughly. It was one of the top priorities for Mahima not to miss any of his games. She drove him to his practices, sometimes very early in the morning before going to her job. She made every effort to be at her son's games and support him. Aaron was a good player on his team. He loved his mother being there for him and to see all his moves and skills on the ice. He was well aware that his mother was a great admirer of him and she kept her eyes focused on him during his time on the ice. He frequently lifted his head up to make sure that his mom was watching him. When he scored a goal, he lifted his hockey stick up in the air and looked at Mahima and she gave him a flying kiss.

Sarah's dance classes were equally valuable. During the classes Mahima waited in her car and read her favorite books as there were only certain days a parent was allowed to go in the classroom and watch their daughter dancing. On the day of the recital, Mahima helped her daughter putting on the dancing costumes and some make up on her face. She made sure that the family arrived at the auditorium on time to get the best seats in the front row. It was a fulfilling experience for Mahima and the other parents to see their little daughters dancing on the stage. Just like any other parent, Mahima was a proud mother of two talented beautiful kids.

Her days were spent at work and the evenings with her children; she had a busy life. Helping her children with their school work, cooking dinner for the family, taking children to the places of their extra curricular activities were her activities, and she enjoyed them. Her job along with the night calls kept her busy too. The time seemed to accelerate like an express train. She got exhausted at times especially when she had to go to her job in the middle of the nights unexpectedly. Her dream and goal was to help her children achieving the best and to be able to give them the best education. Perhaps, that is the dream of every parent in this world. She was not fortunate to hear even a few words of encouragement, support or appreciation from her husband, rather there was criticism and sarcasm constantly. Several times he commented, 'So you are going to make your son a hockey player and your daughter a dancer.'

That kind of sarcasm became a part of Mahima's life. She was aware of the fact that her husband wanted all the good things for his children but he did not want to spend money on their activities and at the same time did not want to take the responsibilities of time commitment with them. Her support was her church counselor. She kept taking advice from him. He admired her and appreciated her devotion and efforts to raise her children. That support from him gave Mahima a boost to start building up her self esteem and respect. She was determined that with or without Ateet's help, she will do her best for her children.

Ateet kept his bank account separate and contributed half of the household and children's expenses. She took care of her own financial needs, her own clothes, necessities and every little or big expense. Ateet refused to spend his money on the tiny affordable desires of the children other than the basic necessities. She bought some toys, books, or some special gifts at times and he accused her of spoiling them. He accused her for every little thing which included buying food for them from a restaurant. The main reason was that he was not willing to spend any money from his own pocket. He took advantage of Mahima's motherhood knowing that she would do anything; especially she would not ignore the children's desire to enjoy some special food from restaurants once in a while.

Ateet's constant accusations, yelling and screaming made Mahima very adamant. He did not care for her being tired, not even for a change he took initiative to order the food or take his family out for dinner. He bluntly refused to pay any money for Aaron's hockey supplies and sports related expenses. Very rarely he went to see Aaron's games or took him for practices. His daily routine after coming home from his job was to make two cups of tea and give one to Mahima, watch TV for a while and go to play tennis for two to three hours.

Mahima felt as he was taking total advantage of her and her sacrifices for the family to enjoy his own life. The other new habit Ateet developed was to gamble in the stock market. He knew some of his friends who made money in the stock market so he thought he would also. He started taking pride in his new hobby and estimated that he will be easily able to double or triple his money in a short period of time. In a very short period of time he became addicted to trading the stocks as a day trader and just like a broker. All his talks and conversations with his friends and neighbors stayed focused on the stock market. He was also aware of the fact that Mahima was not supportive and totally against gambling money in the stock market. Though she knew that he would not listen to her anyway, she dared to discuss the matter with him only out of concern.

"I hope that you are not wasting your money in the stock market."

"No. Do you think I am stupid?" In a fraction of a second he picked up the usual loud tone in his voice.

"No, that's not what I have said. I only hope that you are not losing your hard earned money in the stock market."

"Who are you to care about my money? Is it your money? It is my money and I will do whatever I would like to do with it."

Very tactfully he tried to shut her up by raising his voice and reflecting his authority over her. Mahima could easily guess that he was hiding something and something was not right. She was prepared not to end the conversation without knowing the details.

"My money or your money, it does not matter to me at all. Next year Aaron will be in High School and we should have some savings for his and Sarah's education and that is the major concern I have."

At that time Ateet was heavily involved in the stock market. He was losing money left and right. He kept Mahima in the dark by not discussing or telling her anything about his involvement in the stock market. He fantasized about making up his losses and becoming a millionaire overnight. She reached the conclusion that talking to him regarding his addiction to the stock market would be useless as he refused to take her advice or listen to her. Whenever she tried to talk to him he turned the conversation into a big argument, which in no time turned into a fight. So she decided to stay quiet and started putting some money little by little in the bank as a saving for the children's education.

Then one night he seemed to be in a great mood, a very unusual behavior for him. She was surprised to see a drastic change in his attitude, a big happy smile on his face, like something good hidden within him was about to explode any minute. Mahima was admired by him, as if all of a sudden she became the most beautiful woman on the face of this earth, and she was the best mother, the best cook and what not. All those words of appreciation by him left her totally amused and surprised. That sweetness in him made her question herself, how in the world was he converted into such a decent and loving husband...overnight? The family of four ate dinner together and they talked with each other just like a normal couple. After dinner both the kids ran upstairs. She cleaned the kitchen and they sat together at the couch in the living room.

"Did Sarah and Aaron finish their home work?"

"Yes, they did."

"I can see you are so occupied all day at work and stay busy with the children in the evening."

"*Wow! All these concerns, all this love, I hope everything is alright with him.*" Those questions ran through her mind and he continued,

"I bet you must be exhausted by this time of the day."

"Yeah, I am. At least both the kids are old enough to shower by themselves and change by themselves. So, I don't have to worry about that part."

He could not wait for long to discuss the real issue on his mind for which he had created a beautiful caring environment. There was a silence for a while. He held her hand into his and started talking very tactfully.

"The housing prices are going up day by day. They are way up ever since we bought our house."

Mahima's curiosity began turning into a suspicion. '*Why was he talking about the housing market?*' She had no clue. A thousand questions crossed her mind.

"So, what? We are not selling our house."

"No, oh no, I am not talking about selling our house." He clarified and continued.

"I brought some loan papers today. I thought that we will be able to get some home equity loan for the amount of equity on our house."

"Why Ateet? All the expenses are in control. We don't need to get any loans." She made her point clear, but still was unable to solve the riddle.

"Oh, you do not understand Mahima! Within three months, I will double up the amount of the loan money." He announced with a feeling of an absolute confidence in himself.

"The house is in both of our names, so both of us will have to sign these papers." He clarified his scheme.

She looked at him and could not take her eyes off from his face. She could not believe.

"*Did he really say what he just said?*"

"*Did he really mean it?*"

She was left speechless for a while. Perhaps, she did not hear it right, but the reality was that he meant it, he planned it. He was well prepared to get a loan against the equity of the house. He was well prepared to use that money in the stock market to gamble it. She paused and she had no alternative but face another challenge imposed by him. It did not take her long to explode. '*How dare he could think such a thing?*' She lost self control and blew up.

"What did you just say? Sign these papers? Do you think I am stupid, illiterate, and I don't understand the games you are playing on me? How many times in last five years you have doubled, tripled or quadrupled your money? Tell me, how many times? Do you think I have no knowledge of your gambling addiction?"

She was trembling, crying and her voice began cracking.

"God has given me these two hands and thank God that I can work and earn my living; otherwise you would have sent me to the streets, sold me. I know it all; I know your dirty habits. The only reason, I don't say a word and play ignorant is to stay away from your filthy tongue and your ugly, abusive, controlling treatment which you have given to me as a treasure in the last so many years of our married life."

She had completely lost control of herself. Ateet kept looking at her as if he will eat her alive. He was shocked to see Mahima bursting like a hot volcano.

"All my education... my career... I dreamed of... went down the drain. Why? Have you ever taken a second to think about? Obviously no. So listen! To keep this family together I followed you everywhere like a slave. Wherever your career took you... I followed. I have been working day and night in the hospital to earn a living. If I was selfish like you, I would have moved away and found a job... a job of my interest for which I spent over three hard working years of my life. I dumped my career, my dreams just because you... you and you, and you treat me like dirt."

That burning lava within her kept exploding.

"Money, money, and money all the time, you worship money. Now, what are your intentions? You want me to sign these papers so you get the loan money and burn it all. Have you ever thought that how big a chance you are taking? Have you ever thought that this addiction of yours could put us on the streets one day?"

"I will not sign these papers. I am sure that I am very loud and clear in my decision." She tore the papers in several pieces and threw them at his face.

"I am leaving. Put the children in their beds."

She spat the burning fire of her heart, picked the car keys and her pocket book and got out of the house. It was very late at night. Her hands were trembling on the steering wheels, legs were shaking. Her whole body felt like some one squeezed out all the energy from it. She had no clue where was she going. She drove miles and miles on the highway and finally pulled her car into a small area by the side of a hill. No one was around and there was no trace of any human being around her. The darkness of the night surrounded her. Fierceness overpowered her—perhaps a fear of some wild life in that remote area in the midst of the dense trees over the mountains. She quickly locked all the doors and raised all the windows up and turned the engine off. Her arms were wrapped tightly around her chest to protect herself and her eyes kept searching outside which looked just like a big hollow space. In the midst of the hollow darkness, she saw some shimmering lights coming through the windows of some houses located far away in the valley. It did not take her long to realize that that was a little town where after a long day of work people were asleep. Her eyes were focused on the lights of those houses and also rolled around to make sure that no creature or wild animal was close to her car. She sat in her car in that lonely place for hours and hours. In just a little while those shimmering lights vanished and the houses far away in the little town were engulfed darkness. A weird thought crossed her mind that one day, just like those lights, she will also lose that shimmering and it will extinguish and vanish forever.

Her journey was rough and her hopes for any betterment were dead. Up until that day her husband had attacked her physical body and he had beaten her with brutality. That day the attack was on her soul, on her integrity and morality. Years and years have passed in a hope for a better future. She was shattered by her husband's physical and emotional abuse. The power of her endurance was remarkable and her strong character was admirable. That day she felt as if she was nothing but a failure and broken into thousands of pieces, her body was dead with no soul in it. In that darkness of the wilderness she saw a ray of light, what her father told her a long time ago,

"Never be afraid of the storms in your life. Always have faith in our mighty Lord and remember that He will always lift you up if you have fallen."

She could not sit in a locked car in that wilderness for ever and ever. She had no other option but to return home. Also the very next morning she had to at work at seven. She started the car and drove back. All were asleep. She entered quietly in her house and into her bedroom, washed her tired face, changed and laid quietly on her side of the bed. One more time and once again she woke up with a hope within her. The same hope of a better tomorrow, a hope of some extraordinary miracle. She hoped that perhaps one day her husband would wake up and come into his senses, perhaps he will come to a new realization, perhaps he will learn his lesson by falling on his face.

She always found a streak of light in the total darkness so she could move on and keep her family intact. Yet she felt helpless and hollow. She felt feeble, tired all the time, unable to function normally in her day to day life. She felt as if her own body was not her own. She was not as energetic as before. She faced several sleepless nights gazing at the roof, wandering in the darkness. She was unable to hide her distressful condition from the world. The comments and questions from her friends and coworkers were killing her;

"Mahima, is every thing okay with you? You look tired."

And, she had no answers to those comments. She worried about losing her health. She worried about who would take care of the children if something happened to her. She was under tremendous stress.

After a long tiring day, the toughest moment of the day for her was to go to her bedroom, which she did very reluctantly after tucking the children in their beds. She did it quietly, walked into her room and laid on her side of the bed hoping that Ateet was asleep. Her desires for intimacy were buried a long time ago. Sleeping with her husband felt like a punishment she had to cope with. Ateet tried.

"I am very tired today." She tried her best to make some excuse.

"Can't you stay up for thirty more minutes?" He insisted and pressured her.

"No, I don't feel like."

"You stubborn woman, you never feel like." Just like any other night, he attacked her womanliness.

Mahima became more and more adamant and stubborn over a period of time. The fact of the matter was that she was trying hard to fight the hatred towards her husband which was built within her as a result of mistreatment, abuse, torture by him for a number of years. She was a different woman at that stage of her life. She was not anymore the woman who would surrender herself regardless of the situation, and her submissive nature was long gone.

"Yes, you are right... I have no feelings... and how can I have those feelings? Have you ever thought about your wife's desires, her needs? Have you ever cared for your wife or loved her? Have you ever thought that the woman who you are abusing is your own wife? What gives you the right to come to me in the bed?"

"What are your needs, your desires? Don't you have clothes to wear? Are you wandering naked? Aren't you getting food? Are you starving and dying? All the time, you keep singing about your needs and desires." He kept attacking her soul.

"Married for seventeen years, don't you know your wife's needs?" She yelled.

"Why don't you tell?"

"I am eating food because I am earning, wearing these clothes because I buy my own clothes from my own money, and let me also tell you that I don't have any problem taking care of my own needs. Have you ever thought that all I am asking you is to give me my rights, my rights as a wife and a mother, love and respect? Perhaps—you don't even know the definition and value of these words."

"Oh, so you will tell me the meaning of love and care. What do you have? You have nothing. Go and look at your face in the mirror; you ugly wrinkled woman."

Again, he attacked her self esteem and self respect and he did not stop yet.

"You look like a beggar. If I kick you out of the house today, no one in this world will look at you, you bitch."

Those arguments became a routine and their bed became nothing but a battle ground. She grabbed her pillow, stepped out from her room, walked into the guest room and locked it from inside. She had no intentions to return to her bedroom, never--ever at night. She made up her mind to sleep in the guest room, alone, by herself. Years have passed of her being tortured, cussed at, and abused by her husband, but his addiction to treating his wife like rubbish did not change. Those attacks on her appearance and self esteem by her husband made her feel like she was a dead human being. She started thinking of herself as the ugliest woman in this world. Those brutal words of Ateet haunted her like a shadow and created an echo in her head, tormenting her day and night. Just to convince herself, to get over those negative criticisms, many many times she stood in front of the mirror and talked to herself convincing that Ateet lied just to hurt her feelings, to control her, and to destroy her self image. She was not an ugly, wrinkled woman. She became her own counselor and convinced herself that she was the most beautiful woman on the face of this earth.

Her decision to sleep in the guest room was far away from practical. After a few days and her husband's sweet talks she had to go back to her bedroom. Ateet did not stop spitting those bitter words from his mouth. To avoid hearing those words and to rescue her self image, she surrendered her body to him several times to use it, to satisfy his sexual appetite, to quench his thirst.

Her journey with Ateet was difficult. The roads were narrow and rocky, and there was no way out. All she could see was the darkness in the end. It was not only tough but seemed impossible. On several occasions she thought of leaving him, but she could foresee the future of her two little ones without her or their father. She was afraid; what explanation would she give to her two innocent children if she decided to separate from Ateet? How would she be able to take care of them alone by herself? If she left the house, would she be able to live without her children. The reality was that at that tender age her children needed both a father as well as a mother. In that complexity of life she felt exhausted, but never defeated.

She continued her counseling sessions. She made a point to meet with the counselor at least two to three times a month. She had several lingering questions on her mind. In the last seventeen years, she was abused by her husband in many different ways. He hurt her intentionally. He hit her cruelly. He blamed her for his own wrong doings. He did not even spare her family members. He accused and abused them constantly. He cussed her Pappa who was dead. At each and every turn of her journey all she got was humiliation. Could she have kept any hope for any betterment or a hope that her husband would change and come into his senses? Not only her but the counselor was also unable to answer that question. All those years Ateet kept justifying himself and his vulgar acts by putting all the blames on her and suggesting that she deserved that treatment from him. For such an awful act of abuse if there is anyone who is to be blamed it is the abuser. Either he felt insecure or he had jealousy incubating in him and to overcome his shortcomings he attacked and threatened her physically as she was weaker then him. The counselor suggested her to stay firm in her beliefs and never blame herself for her husband's wrongful acts.

At that stage of their lives, Ateet was well aware of the fact that if he laid his hands upon her, she will not tolerate it, and may very well result in a serious trouble for him. So he started attacking her emotions verbally or acting weird in front of her. That act of his was no less painful than the physical abuse she was the victim of for several years of her life. The scars on the body caused by the physical abuse could fade away in time but the scars caused by the emotional abuse may leave a permanent life long marking on the victim's heart and the soul. They could never be healed. The intentions hidden in the emotional abuse are to frighten the person from negative criticism, insulting, putting the person down all the time, never being appreciative, cussing and cursing and a stream of constant threats. As a result, the victim loses self esteem and feels drained out all the time. The thought of all the negativism eats them up like a hidden cancer within the body of the victim. A human thinks of himself or herself as a lifeless object which has no use, no value, and that was exactly how Mahima felt. She became incredibly frail and unable to get out of the situation because of the fear of loneliness. She felt like no matter how much she would sacrifice and how hard she would try to keep the family together, she would never be able to please her husband. She felt like a total failure. Ateet felt like a winner by abusing her, yelling at her, blaming her, controlling and commanding her and what not to destroy her and her inner self.

Chapter 30
AARON'S EDUCATION

*A*aron was about to start High School. During the summer break Mahima and Ateet visited several schools in the area. It was extremely important for them to find a good school, that would meet their son's needs and also affordable. Mahima had more time than Ateet. She managed to take some time off from work and visited the schools. The four years of High School in anyone's life are critical years, determining the future, and a right school had to be found. After several orientations at different schools, she was successful in finding a much respected Catholic school with a good academic reputation. Also, the school was identical to the one at which she taught years ago when Aaron was born. She was excited the day she visited that school and was anxious to tell Ateet about her discovery. She could hardly wait until he came home in the evening.

"You know Ateet; this school is similar to the one at I taught in Missouri."

"That sounds like a very good one." He replied agreeably.

"I brought the application form and I will also try to find out from some people at work if they know more about their academics and teachers."

"The open house is in two weeks. We will certainly learn more about it. Would you like to go? It is in the evening." She desired to go with Ateet as both had to make a decision together.

"That's fine. What time in the evening?" He showed his willingness and cooperation.

"Seven till nine, just two hours." Immediately she replied.

"Sure, I will drive straight from work and join you there."

The day came and both went to the school's open house. The visit and the tour of the school impressed both of them very much. They were also fortunate to see some other parents who they met before through Sarah and Aaron. Aaron waited for them at home and the word was conveyed to him and also that he needed some preparation to take an entrance exam in order to get admission to that school. Aaron studied and prepared himself for the entrance exam. He passed and gained admission. They all were very happy. The only disadvantage was the distance between their home and the school. Again, if parents would not make sacrifices for their children, who will? Both Mahima and Ateet discussed the matter with each other and the responsibilities were divided equally between them. Ateet agreed to drop Aaron off at his school in the morning and Mahima to pick him up in the afternoon after her work. The plans progressed very well.

Aaron's school uniform and books were all purchased. He was excited and ready to go to his new school. Just a few days before the beginning of the school session his tuition bill from the school office came in the mail. She showed Ateet the bill and wanted to discus it.

"Aaron's yearly tuition fee is divided into ten installments and we have to pay the first one before the school starts."

"I will not pay a dime." He answered immediately in his loud dictating voice as if he was prepared for it.

"What did you say?" His response was nothing but a big shocking surprise to her.

"Why can't he go to a public high school?" He questioned.

All of a sudden a change of mind, what is wrong with him.

Such an important decision for their son's future made by the parents at that stage of a child's life suddenly jeopardized. Ateet was well aware of the fact that the public school in the area where they were residing did not meet Aaron's academic needs. An anger started building in her. *A father would like the best for his child. Why was Ateet so different?* She paused and waited to discuss the issue until the children went to their rooms.

"Ateet, you know that the public school in our neighborhood, where Aaron can go free of cost does not meet ours and his needs."

"Why not, don't other kids go there?"

She immediately sensed that he was in an arguing mood. She tried her best to stay calm simply because it was the matter of Aaron's future. She hoped that she may be successful in convincing her husband in that matter.

"Yes, Ateet, other children go there and I know it. What if he gets into some wrong company in this tender age and you also know that there are all kind of kids in that school and the class size is also large."

She kept trying and trying.

"Also, it is not the case that we cannot afford his tuition. Just like we equally share other expenses, we will also share Aaron's tuition and other school expenses."

"If you want to send him to that Catholic school, fine, go for it, but I will not pay a penny."

He was determined and stubborn not to change his decision. She failed to convince him. She concluded that any further discussion would be of no use and may very well end up in an argument or a fight. She also feared that if he came to his screaming and yelling, that would not be good for Aaron or Sarah.

'After sharing half of the household expenses would she be able to pay Aaron's tuition?' It was a pitiful situation. Both of them together earned a pretty handsome salary and could easily afford their son's school's expenses. She had a desire, a dream to give her children the best education they deserved. She had a desire to help them make a bright and happy future, but she was repeatedly devastated not to get her husband's support in any area of her life, even the life associated with her children. She felt deprived of the main ingredient missing in her life— her husband's support. They used different banks and they had separate bank accounts for the last several years. He kept his earnings separate in some bank hidden from her. Her biggest fear was that he was burning his money in the stock market.

There was not much time left to make the tuition payment. Two to three days later she had no alternative but to talk to him again regarding Aaron's schooling. The matter had to be resolved soon.

"Did you give it a second thought about Aaron's tuition?" She asked very politely.

"Yes, send him to the public school." He played stubborn and she could not move him.

"Why? You earn more than me. Why can't you pay half of his tuition?" She had to find the real reason.

"What is the problem sending him to the public school?" He raised his voice.

"You know Ateet, you know the difference between the two school systems, especially where we live."

"I do not have any money to pay for his tuition." He refused again. Her suspicion was turning into a reality. She needed to know the real reason.

"I hope you are not burning your money in the stock market."

"That is my money and I earned it, and I can do whatever I want to with my money."

"It has always been with you; my money and your money. Why can't you understand that the money earned by both of us is our money—yours, mine, Aaron's and Sarah's. It does not matter at all that you are keeping it in a separate account. If you keep doing mine and yours, one day this family will split. Why aren't you trying to understand?"

Tolerance, patience, endurance, and more and more of it seemed to be ending. Each day of her life brought a new puzzle for her. She was confused and tired of coping with new problems added to her life every single day. She had no idea if ever in her lifetime, she would be able to live with those problems or perhaps may end them somehow or the other. Her husband took advantage of her being an earning woman, and he was aware that she would do anything for the children. In fact that was so very true. For her children, for the betterment of her children, she stayed firm. She made up her mind that with or without her husband's help and support she would send Aaron to that private school and work hard by working overtime to pay his tuition.

"Alright, Ateet! You keep gambling in the stock market as you wish and I will pay Aaron's tuition."

The chasm between her and Ateet grew wider and wider. Every episode was presumably the last episode for her, but the reality was very different than her hypothesis. The cloud of uncertainty kept on getting denser and denser. She kept trying her best not to give up. Perhaps—one day, some day in this life Ateet will straighten his messed up priorities and will realize the meaning and the definition of his own family. A realization of the needs of his wife and children will take place one day. One day he will leave the love of money and his selfishness. She lived each and every moment of her life in the hope of that one day.

In her growing up years Mahima could not recall even a single episode of a disagreement over the money earned by her parents. Her father brought his whole earnings and gave it to her mother, who ran the budget of a huge family of nine. Pappa sat back and relaxed in his weekly pocket money with an absolute trust in Mamma. They had the responsibility of seven children on their shoulders. Not a single time in their relationship, Pappa questioned her Mamma about the spending or running the household budget in their joint income. At times Mamma shopped for the groceries and also in her busy time she handed the shopping list along with the money to Pappa and he felt privileged taking that responsibility. She kept a separate stack of money for all the school expenses of all the children. If there was a bit extra money left, the whole family enjoyed some special sweets from the market and during the shortage a simple low budget meals were being prepared. That unselfish love, sharing and caring for each other in good and bad times kept Mahima's family a close knit secure family, away from the world of selfishness.

Her older sister was an excellent student and her dream was to become an English teacher. Living in a small town was disadvantageous for her sister as there was no school with education major within or close to the town. Mahima was young at that time but she had a good recollection of some of those moments. Her sister had no choice but to study away from home for one year after her college to be a certified teacher. Studying away from home meant more expenses for tuition, books, accommodation in the girls' hostel, traveling, extra clothing, etc. Mamma and Pappa were financially weak, but their strength was in their unity, their togetherness, and their mutual agreements. They tackled the challenges and problems in a compromising and wise way. Both decided that their daughter will go for her training no matter what, for the sake of her better future. The day came and Mahima's didi left the town and went away for her teacher's training. That year was the toughest year for everybody especially for Mamma to run the house on a limited and tight budget. The special sweets from the market place had to be forgotten. At times the whole family had to be fed with the home grown produce making casseroles prepared with unripe papayas and cooked mangoes in place of curries. That was a really tough chapter for the whole family. The beauty of that chapter however was their commitment to passing through that short turbulence holding each others' hands with no complaints whatsoever.

The year passed by very quickly and her didi finished her training successfully. One whole year without seeing didi or without being able to talk to her face to face made everyone desperate. The day of her return was a memorable day for every member of the family including the family dog. Her train arrival was very early in the morning. The station was about two miles from the home. The summer was in its full swing. There was just one winding clock but not an alarm clock in the house. Not a single soul in the family had any sleep that night. They, along with Tiger, the family's Labrador left home in the middle of the night to walk the two miles to the train station. It was dark with no street lights by the road sides. Pappa's torch came in very handy. All reached at the train station long before the arrival time of didi's train, bought platform tickets and entered through the gate to the platform. They spread a big blanket and sat on it, enjoyed the tea and some lemonade while waiting for didi's train arrival. The platform became like a park in the middle of the night. They spent their time watching the goods trains and other passenger trains passing by.

Finally, it was her didi's train, arriving on time. All eyes followed the passing bogies, looking through the windows to find didi's bogie. The train came to a complete stop and in a few minutes didi came out. It was a delightful sight for all the family members to see didi after one whole year. All the eyes were focused upon her. She was tired from her overnight journey. Considering the tight budget only one rickshaw was hired for Mamma, didi and her luggage. The luggage was placed on the wooden board of the rickshaw behind the two seats and Mamma and didi on the seat, while the rest of the crew walked home. That was the day of celebration.

Her didi stayed home with the rest of the family just for the summer and she was a full fledged, certified teacher. She was offered a High School teaching job in a town away from home. Didi was kind enough to take another sister with her who was in eighth grade at that time. She stayed with didi and got admission in the same school where her didi was about to begin her new career. Didi's support for the younger sister turned out to be a blessing for Mamma and Pappa, but then there remained two less people in the house. With the help and support of the family the great didi fulfilled her dreams to be a teacher and after getting the teaching job she also helped the other siblings fulfill their dreams too. To cope with such a difficult period joyfully was not only a family's sacrifice, it was indeed a bond of pure love also, which kept them together and taught them the real definition, and value of family unity. The unity, which has no selfish motive, but rather each member of the family looked at the needs of the other members before her or his own needs. They always encouraged each other; to build and respect self esteem and self respect. Instead of casting faults on each other they uplifted each other and they did not hesitate to express appreciation to each other. Without that bond of love in a family, it would not have been easy to cope with the hardship Mahima's family went through.

Aaron started his new school, his High School. The school excelled in academics and sports. He was thrilled to learn that his High School was known for a good ice hockey team with a good coach, and that was a motivation for him. He was also excited to be selected in the hockey team. He liked his new school and showed great enthusiasm towards the studies and sports.

From the very first day his school curriculum was in force. The hockey practices started very early in the morning at least twice a week and the games after school mostly once a week in the season. The days of his practices Mahima and Aaron set their alarm clocks for five in the morning and quickly got ready to be on the road. She made a quick breakfast of Aaron's favorite cinnamon rolls, poured a glass of milk for him and some hot tea for her. Both enjoyed their breakfast while driving. She dropped him at the rink at six and took the back roads to go to her work. She also made her best efforts to go to his games after school which were played at the various skating rinks in the area.

Aaron loved his mother's presence at his games and she was always there to support him. She did not mind even if she had to drive a long distance. She also helped him in his homework, kept in touch with his teachers at school, and was able to pay his tuition including the sports related expenses. Aaron adapted to the new culture of his new school and performed very well. He made new friends and was very happy.

The school year flew by rapidly and the long three months summer break started for both the children--a perfect time for a family vacation. Mahima had a desire to visit her relatives back home in India with her husband and kids. Their previous visit to India was a long time ago when Aaron and Sarah were very young and they hardly remembered their time in India. They had a vague memory of their cousins, aunts, uncles and other relatives, their culture of origin, and also the places their parents grew up. Ateet had been traveling by himself for the past several years to his parents' house during the Christmas break, but Mahima and the children also had a wish to go.

Chapter 31
VISITING INDIA

$\mathcal{T}$he vacation plans to India were finalized for the entire family for a total of three weeks. Out of those three weeks a three day layover in London was planned and the rest of the time taking the children to the relatives located in different cities, along with some sight seeing tours. All were excited. The day of departure was getting closer and closer and the shopping list of the gifts for family members became longer and longer. An air conditioned van with a driver was reserved for the family to travel in the country and also to the different cities to visit the relatives. Sarah and Aaron packed their suitcases and carry-on bags.

The adventurous journey with the children began. After spending three days of sight seeing in London they landed at the New Delhi airport a little after midnight. They completed all the formalities at the Customs and exited through the green light. The month of May in India was the month of scorching heat and smog, especially in the capital city. A tremendous change of temperature they felt immediately after exiting the airport. The driver and her sister's family who made the van reservation were waiting at the airport. Both Aaron and Sarah were quiet and in a state of culture shock. As soon as the driver pulled the air-conditioned van to the gate, both the kids jumped into it. The van stuffed with two families and eight suitcases in the back took off and started rolling on the highways in New Delhi.

According to their plans they had to spend that night or the early morning hours at Mahima's sister who lived in Delhi. Though tired from a long journey, jet-lagged, neither Aaron nor Sarah had any intention to close their eyes and relax. Obviously they did not want to miss any moment of that adventure. Sarah was too young to remember anything, but Aaron had a vague memory of his last trip several years ago.

The van exited the highway and entered into a ghetto area onto the narrow streets of the city. Parked rickshaws, sales people's carts, bullock carts, scooters, bicycles, some piles of trash and to top it all, sleeping cattle on the both sides made those narrow streets narrower. The big van barely did fit to make its way through. Sarah's big eyes were wide open with no signs of sleepiness in them. Her observant character was expressive, and her facial expressions were filled with surprises.

"Aaron, look outside, so many cows! Wow!" Her eyes were focused on a herd of cows resting by the road side.

"Oh yes, don't you get excited! You will get to see a lot more." Aaron spoke with his skillful past experience.

Mahima's sister's house was in a slum area within the boundaries of New Delhi. The van took a turn onto the other dingy and narrow street with the open sewer water collected on both the sides of the street. A bunch of pigs and piglets were asleep in the coolness of that muddy puddle of water. A mother was nursing her little piglets lying on the bed of piled up neighborhood rubbish on the street side.

"Mom, look at that, how cute! Aaron! Hurry up and hand me my camera." Soon, a beautiful picture of a mother pig nursing her hungry little piglets in the middle of the night was stored in Sarah's camera.

The short journey filled up with so much enthusiasm ended at Mahima's sister's house, who lived with her husband and two daughters on the top floor of a family house. The lower levels were shared by her in-laws and they were sound asleep at that late hour of the night. Ateet and family were dead tired but wide awake and jet lagged. They washed up and got ready for dinner. It was the middle of the night. After a long journey they were hungry, and enjoyed freshly cooked authentic delights of puffed *rotis* with *meat-saag* (spinach) prepared by her sister.

After that delicious meal, Mahima's sister and her family departed to their bedrooms all the way to the topmost floor of their house. The main floor was reserved for Mahima and family. The lights were dimmed and it was time to rest. Sarah showed no interest in going to bed and sleep. She sat on a chair placed in the corner of that big room with both of her feet tucked under her bottom, investigating and inspecting every little corner of the room. Her eyes were still wide open and roaming all around the viewing area. All of a sudden she looked panicked, frightened. She screamed and jumped down from the chair and ran to her Maa, pointing her fingers towards the ceiling and there was a lizard crawling into a crack in between the ceiling and the side wall. Mahima herself was not a great fan of those lizards either, but she tried her best to show her courage and lack of phobia.

Sarah was sitting on Mahima's lap holding her tight and her big eyes were filled with big tears. She could not grasp, what in the world was happening and why in the world she got stuck in a place like that.

"Mom, please take me back home."

"Beta, as soon as we turn off the lights, the lizard will go away."

"What if it falls on my bed Mom?" A very practical question she asked in her sobbing voice.

Mahima had a lizard-phobia also. In winter or in summer, any time of the year, if she slept inside the house, she always used a mosquito net not to protect herself from the mosquitoes, but from the thought of the lizards falling on her.

"Let us ask your aunty to take out the mosquito net and we will sleep comfortably in that."

The mosquito net was tucked tightly in between the bed and the cot. Both mother and daughter tried to get some sleep with no fear of the lizards falling on them, but they failed. All night long they whispered into each others ears and Mahima told Sarah a once upon a time story.

"The scorching heat of summer killed all the mosquitoes, but the poor lizards hiding in their heated houses within those cracked holes in the walls need to come out too, to breathe and to eat. We should not be afraid of them. These little creatures know how to crawl on the ceiling up side down on their bellies. They never fall."

"When you were in your Mommy's tummy and your brother was eighteen months old, we came here in the month of October and stayed at your nani's house." Mahima kept whispering as the rest of the family was already asleep.

"What happened then Mom?" Sarah's bright eyes sparkled in the midst of the dim light of the night lamp and had no sign of any tiredness.

"We slept with the mosquito net tucked in—but somehow or the other, the mosquitoes entered inside, and they bit Aaron so much that we had to take him to the doctor."

After that short story Sarah inquired,

"Mom, when are we going back home?"

"Oh, Sarah, we just landed a few hours ago. We have so many plans. We will travel to different places; go for some sight-seeing, take you to the Taj Mahal, we will have a lot of fun at the hill station where it is cool. As soon as everyone wakes up in the morning, we will have breakfast and leave this place to go to your other aunty's."

Mahima's other sister's house was just about three hours from Delhi. She had a big and open house.

"I am sure that you will like it there. Also your nani must be anxious to see you both. We will also call her early in the morning."

Sarah was restless. That experience of seeing a crawling lizard just a few hours after landing was not a pleasant introduction to her or anybody. The plans to leave early morning were finalized with Ateet. They hoped that they will get some rest for a day or two at Mahima's other sister's house and then they will continue their journey.

Mahima's sister in Delhi had two daughters; twenty one year old Ana, and the other was nineteen years old. Ana was an outgoing girl. Her hobbies were to go to the pubs, drink, dance and flirt with boys. That was the lifestyle she had adopted. Mahima was aware of all that, but she also understood that being young, immature, not being able to understanding the consequences of those acts were part of the growing up process. Ana was young and was going through several transitions, just like other growing girls during that phase of their lives. Though Ana was a total contrast with the other young girls in the family, the family had a hope that one day Ana would settle down. Mahima loved her as her own daughter. During her previous visits to India, she took Ana everywhere with her and Ana was also very much attached to her aunt Mahima. In the last few years Ana changed. She was not an innocent little girl any more; she was a young independent woman.

Early that morning of departure her sister prepared delicious traditional Indian breakfast for everybody and all of them had a good time. Ateet talked and talked like an authoritarian in a proud and boastful manner to impress his Indian relatives. He was proud that he was living in U.S.A. He defined himself as the most educated and wealthiest person in the whole family. He always looked down upon Mahima's family and acted arrogantly in front of them. He talked like he was interviewing the family members. His attention was upon Ana and he started a conversation with her.

"So, Ana what are you doing these days?"

"I am working in a call center, Uncle." She replied respectfully.

"You guys did not find a match for Ana as of yet?" Ateet asked Ana's mother.

"Oh, Yes. We are looking for one and as soon as we find someone suitable, we will marry her." She replied and continued.

"Why don't you find a match for her in U.S.?"

"Sure, sure." Instantly he replied in full confidence as if finding a match was a piece of cake for him.

The driver arrived with the car. Sarah was desperate to get out of that house. Perhaps, she had a nightmare of the lizards crawling everywhere during her short sleep. Ateet was busy giving Ana his attention and she was also following him like a shadow. Why wouldn't she? Ateet gave her pseudo hopes by saying that he will find a match for her in the U.S. Mahima got busy with Sarah and Aaron, packing and sending the suitcases downstairs with the driver. The entire luggage was sent to the car. Aaron and Sarah were with Mahima and anxious to leave, but Ateet was no where to be found.

"Perhaps, he is downstairs and helping the driver loading the van." That is what Mahima thought. She went down stairs to the van with her kids, but Ateet was not there. Aaron and Sarah started showing their impatience. They were tired from traveling, lack of sleep and could barely cope with the cultural shock. They jumped in the van and were more than ready to leave. After some

investigation Mahima found out that Ateet went for a walk with Ana. She could not believe it. The driver started the car and turned the air conditioning on for the children. *'Why would he go for a walk with Ana? Ana was still a callow young girl.'* Mahima hoped that Ateet was not fooling her niece or flirting with her. She hoped Ana not to be tempted by his boastful promises though anyone could at that vulnerable age. Ana was just like his own daughter and his inner soul could not fall to such a low level to make him act in any wrongful way with her. All those weird, negative, puzzling thoughts kept crossing her mind. Yet she convinced herself that those emotional feelings do not linger forever. She tried her best to prove her intuitions wrong, but her womanly intuitions overpowered her. *'That day was the first time he met with Ana—why couldn't he talk with her in front of all the family members?'*

Mahima's motive to have a family vacation was in a hope that staying together and having a good time together as a family may help them rebuild their relationship and might bring Ateet close to her as a husband. Also by connecting with other families and observing their life style could make him realize the meaning of the word "wife". It was disappointing to see that her efforts were going into entirely a reverse direction from the very first day of their trip. Was he trying to show everybody that he did not care for Mahima? What was he trying to prove? At least—he should have told her that he was going for a walk.

The journey to the other sister began. The family enjoyed their ride on the Indian highway in an air conditioned van and arrived at the destination in three hours. Both the children were relieved to see a better and clean place. They took a cold shower to cool down, ate lunch and slept through the day and night. Sarah's swollen eyes got some relief. Her bright face sparkled again. She inspected the ceilings and cracks in all the rooms of the house and felt better not to see the crawling lizards and bugs. After a long rest the children looked happy and they did not take long to interact with their cousins and the little nieces. Though there was a language barrier, they managed to communicate with them in their broken Hindi. Their stay was pleasant and fulfilling at their aunt's house.

The next fragment of their journey was planned at nani's house, Mahima's Mamma and the children's favorite person in the world—their lovely and loving nani. The same nani, who took care of both of them in their childhood, was not only their nani but their best friend too. Sarah was only three months and Aaron was a little over two years of age when they first met their nani and bonded with her. Both were desperate to see her and be with her. Aaron's only motive for that trip to India was his nani.

After arriving at nani's house, both the children forgot all about the scorching heat, crawling lizards, the herd of cows and pigs sitting by the road side. Nani was old. She was not as active as before when the kids saw her last. She used a stick to walk around the house. Mahima knowing that her mother needed some walking support, she brought a nice and colorful folding walking stick as a gift from the U.S. Nani loved it, she adored it. She started dancing with that stick and confessed that she never heard of or saw a folding walking stick before. Aaron and Sarah could not stop giggling seeing their old nani dancing with a stick in her hand. The love between them was so unselfish, so innocent and tender; it could not be described in words. Nani, Aaron and Sarah formed a triangle. Nani was waited on by both her grand children. They enjoyed chatting with her, taking her for short walks, one on each side holding her hands—who cared about a new walking stick!

Chapter 32
BEYOND TOLERANCE

*T*wo weeks in India flew by quickly, touring and sight-seeing and the family returned to their home in the United States. Ateet's comments about her family, in particular about Ana made it very obvious that he was in a continuous communication with her by phone and exchanging emails, he was flirting with her and giving her false hopes to bring her to U.S. Mahima did not express her feelings to Ateet or the kids, but she kept all of it within herself. She knew that on the day of their return from India he exchanged the contacts, email address and phone numbers with Ana. Her inner woman kept on telling her that her husband was getting too involved with Ana, talking with her via phone when Mahima was not around and also writing her email messages. In addition she wondered how a person could act so low. Ana was his daughter's age and also a niece. Almost a month passed and the monthly phone bill came in the mail. She opened it, looked at the statement and was shocked to see a sudden high bill. She flipped through the pages and the pages of overseas calls were filled with incoming and outgoing calls with Ana's number. The times on those calls were the early morning hours after Mahima left home for work. Her suspicion was grounded.

Just like any other day he walked into the house in the evening and went straight to the stove to make tea. Mahima could hardly wait to find out what was going on with him and Ana.

"Did you hear from Ana after we came back from our India trip?" She asked.

"Why are you asking me about Ana? What do I have to do with her?"

He answered her question with a question. Just like the other times, in a very defensive, loud and belligerent voice, with an angered facial expression as if he was caught red handed, as indeed he was. He had no clue that Mahima already saw the telephone bill.

"Did you call her or did you talk to her by emails?" She had every right to confront him.

"No, I called her just once after arriving here to tell her that all of us arrived here safely."

Mahima's intuitions were turning into reality. '*Why does he talk with Ana behind Mahima? If he loves her as a niece and like his daughter, why doesn't he talk to her openly? Also, why does she call him when Mahima is not at home?'* She decided to get to the root of what was happening behind her back.

"So, how come the telephone statement is so long?" She placed the bill in front of him at the table.

He was surprised, nervous, but did not stop defending himself.

"Oh yeah, I made just a couple of phone calls to find out how they were doing."

Mahima hoped that before long her husband will come to his senses. The days passed, but his flirting with Ana did not stop. He continued phoning Ana from home as well as from his work, and also emails were being exchanged frequently. His nefarious behavior further destroyed the core of Mahima, made her feel low, worthless, and created hollowness within her. Was that a cheap trick played by him against her or did he try to create some animosity between her and her sister's family. She could not understand. Nonetheless, that was the time when she realized the low moral values her husband possessed, a new trick to crush her again—intentionally.

A woman, a married woman was trapped in the cultural rules and regulations. She tolerated and endured the abuses, threats, negligence, the persistent vilifying of her character doled out to her by her husband during all the years of their so called married life. She was denigrated and there was no end to it. The relationships with other women--was unbearable, beyond her capacity of endurance, burnt her up from in and out. She was burning and no one in this world could see those flames.

Ateet's behavior got worse and worse. Not a single day passed without some egregious expression of abuse. After a stressful day, in the middle of the night he had to quench his physical thirst—selfishly. With no feelings of intimacy remained in her, she surrendered her body to him several times just to avoid the cussing bitter words from his mouth. At times she made an excuse,

"I am very tired today."

"You are tired all the time. When are you not tired?" Same demanding tone, same attitude, same taunting.

Mahima stayed unresponsive.

"Okay, rest for half an hour and then we will see."

Those words of Ateet's, night after night pierced her heart like a sharp sword. She was being used for his selfish fulfillment. Why did he have to schedule a time for it, 30 minutes, 60 minutes or later.

Thirty minutes later what was going to take place? She pretended as if she was resting, but the fear of thirty minutes later caused her to lie awake. She stayed in one position without moving an inch in a fear that a tiny movement may wake him up and then she will have to cope with his lustful desire. She endured the "thirty minute" episode night after night.

After the family trip to India, Ateet's behavior became crueler and he acted totally belligerently. She hoped that his flirting with Ana would end soon, but once again her hopes were dashed. She blamed herself; it was a mistake to go to India with him, she should not have taken him along with her to visit her family knowing that he never cared for them; always spoke ill of them, never respected them. She underestimated her husband's capabilities of lowness that he would not even care that the girl he was flirting with and fooling around with was his wife's niece, essentially his own niece, young, half his age, and close to his own daughter's age. Through the phone conversations and the emails Ateet gave Ana high hopes along with the promise that he would leave his wife for her. Her intentions were to come to U.S., somehow or the other and his intentions were to fool her and use her.

The house environment during that time remained tense and volatile. The communication between husband and wife was almost non existent until the beginning of October when Ateet came to her and announced,

"I am going to India in December."

For the last so many years, he had been traveling to India alone without his wife or children. Just a few months ago they traveled as a family. That plan of his was a surprise to her.

"Why? Twice in one year? We just visited India. Why do you have to go again during the Christmas season?" She was blunt and straightforward.

"My brother is thinking of buying a house in India and I am going to look around."

His brother who was fully settled in the U.S., thinking of buying a house in India, and he needing to make a special trip to find a house for him—did not connect.

"You are going to find a house for your brother. Shouldn't he go himself?"

"No, I have to go." With no explanation, no justification, his travel plans were announced in a loud, threatening and dominant tone of voice.

All through her journey, each and every moment of the day, each and every day of the year she lived in a hope of a better tomorrow. That tomorrow never came. The uncertainty of her future and the battle to conquer the uncertainty exhausted her both physically and mentally. She was tired of begging for her own rights as a wife, but nothing in the world could move Ateet. His ego, his dictatorship, his dominance, his ignorance, his cruelty stayed with him, and got worse. The reasoning behind making another trip to India was transparent; to see Ana, to exploit the girl, to take advantage of her. Mahima kept silent—for her children and not to expose them with the ugliness of the game being played on her by their father, not to create an ugly environment in the house with two growing up children.

The month of December was not too far away. Ateet started his shopping. The bottles of perfumes, lipsticks, purses, clothes started appearing in the house. She saw her world burning in front of her, in front of her own eyes and could not do anything. She felt like a major failure, a neglected woman, a slave, a woman with no woman inside, a dead person living forcefully on this earth, helpless and broken, burning inside and swallowing her pain.

"These perfumes, lipsticks…Wow! So many nice things, you shopped for. Who are you taking them for?"

"Well, for my mother and also my aunt will be there for Christmas, for them only."

"Are you planning to go to Delhi?"

"Yes, upon my arrival. I have made my reservation in a hotel. I will stay there for a few days." He paused for a minute and continued the justification of his stay in Delhi.

"My real estate agent will pick me up from my hotel and take me around to show the houses in the suburbs of Delhi." He avoided any eye contact with her.

"Delhi is such a big and crowded place. For three days where will you be going to see the houses?" Mahima was prepared to listening to his phony stories.

"That is the agent's job, not mine." He clarified immediately.

The conversation paused for a few moments.

"Are you planing to visit Ana?" She came to the point.

"I was thinking about that. As she lives in Delhi, I will go to her house, see her as well as your sister and family."

In the past, whenever he visited India, he never showed any interests to visit any of Mahima's family. A few months ago in May was his first time to visit them.

"Ateet, I don't want you to go to Ana's house." She requested very humbly and rightfully.

"Oh, yes, I will. Whatever you say, it does not matter, I certainly will go to her house and visit her."

He simply ignored her request without a thought. His rigid response left Mahima stunned, as if a lightning struck her. She was out of words. She could not believe what she heard from her husband's mouth. With no shame, no reservations he threateningly announced to his wife that he was going to visit some other woman and would not honor her request.

All her efforts to keep that marriage alive, to keep the family together seemed to end in failure; nothing was in her control. She regretted that she pleaded to him in all humility knowing that he never cared for her or her needs. His selfishness, dirty acts, games kept on multiplying day after day. Once again, he had the same motive; to hurt her, to kill her inner self, to make her look like the dirt of his feet, and a useless human being. Perhaps, doing all that gave him a sense of power and dominance.

The future journey with her husband now seemed impossible. For the sake of her kids she took a load of unbearable burden on her shoulders and stayed under the same roof with him, just like a prisoner in her own house. The month of December came and Ateet was gone on his trip to India for three weeks.

In those three weeks, Mahima reflected on her life. She was determined to discuss the issue in detail with him upon his return. She was determined to ask him without any fear or restrictions, "What did he want?" She had no strength to burn in that fire and endure it anymore. She had no intentions of seeing the drama of her husband's infidelity, and that also in front of her children. She had to make a decision either way.

It was the night of his return. He entered through the main door of the house late into the night. Mahima was in the kitchen. She looked at him and he ignored her, did not even look at her, and did not say a word. She immediately sensed that something was not right. He carried his suitcases upstairs, entered into the bedroom and then straight to the bathroom. He took a long shower and without saying a word to her or going to the kids' rooms, he went to bed. For two days, there was no communication between him and her. Both slept in their bedroom on one bed on their sides. Finally, she initiated the conversation.

"What do you want Ateet?"

For the first time, he was silent. He did not say a word, did not respond the question and he did not yell.

"Do you want a divorce?" She wanted to settle the issue once for all.

"Let Sarah turn eighteen and then I will think." He spoke.

He had been threatening her by saying the same thing over and over again. *'When Sarah turns eighteen, I will get rid of you, I will kick you out of the house, and I will make your life miserable.'* Mahima had heard all of it several times before.

"No, I am not going to take this stress from you any more." She was determined.

"What kind of stress do you have?" He tried to provoke her.

"Up until now, you don't even know what kind of stress I am talking about?"

She was consumed with anger, and exploded.

"Did you go to Ana's house?"

"Yes, just for a couple of hours." He tried to calm down.

"You didn't even care, what I told you before you left?"

"I went to her house just one night when her mother invited me for dinner."

"Did you take Ana out?"

"Just once, she shopped and I bought her fresh juice."

"Just once this and just once that. What do you think of me? Do you think I am stupid? And now you are asking me the reason of all my stress. You are the reason and the only reason of my stress. Not for once in these years of our married life you treated me like your wife. I was treated like nothing more than your sex partner, to satisfy your appetite, a slave—who took your abuses all day and shared your bed at night."

Mahima got totally out of control. Those last gone years made her a fierce lioness.

"Enough is enough Ateet. I will not be able to live with you any more."

He never expected that she would ever talk about leaving him. He did not want a divorce. He wanted very much to preserve his social and professional image. His desire was to keep Mahima trapped with him to meet the financial and social needs.

"Why don't you file a divorce? You will be free and then you can do whatever you want." She was blunt.

He was fearful of a divorce. The social circle and his friends were not aware of his true colors. He maintained a good image of himself outside the house.

"You are making a big fuss out of nothing. I met Ana just once and I know she is a big flirt." He calmed down and to please Mahima he started talking bad about Ana.

"I swear on you, I will keep no contact with her any more."

Just like before—after hitting Mahima, "I will chop off my hands." after getting caught, "I will never do that again." Those were his old dishonest words, she did not trust anymore.

"Ateet, have you ever thought what are you really doing? Have you ever thought or tried to save this marriage somehow or the other? Have you ever imagined—if I leave the house, would you be able to take care of the children? What kind of example are you setting for your children? Have you ever ever thought why I am taking all this bullshit from you? This Ana; the age of your own daughter; do you have any self respect or shame, what you have done and are still doing? Are you forcing me to take the first step for a divorce?"

A few days later, he forgot to sign off from his email page. Mahima needed to use the computer at home. She read all his conversations back and forth with Ana, continuously dated from the month of June. In December he had booked a hotel in Delhi for six days. He stayed with Ana, bought her gold jewelry, promised her to visit her again for a longer time in the upcoming June, talked bad about Mahima and promised her that he will leave his wife within next two years.

Not only Ana, there was another ongoing romance with another married woman from his home town, who was a mother of two grown up kids. That woman was the reason for his solo trips, every December for the last several years. Mahima had no clue about that other woman until she read all his emails. Two women at the same time! Both were tempted by him that he could get them to the States without any problems. Mahima was portrayed as a bad wife and a bad mother too. The married woman was playing the same games telling Ateet bad things about her husband. The phoning times were being scheduled via email conversation at the time her husband was away from home and that was the time Ateet called her from his work to chat with her.

The matter was slipping out of Mahima's hands. Her efforts to keep the family together in all circumstances were going down the drain. One thing after another was unfolding. She did not have a moment of peace in her life, a hatred for him, his dirty body, and his touch. There was no trust left in him any more. Those were the two affairs caught by her, and maybe there were more. In the past, she tried to resolve all the issues by herself or with some help from her counselor. It was time for her to seek some help from her close friends.

She read all the email conversation without reservations. She took a deep breath and did not rush to confront Ateet. She drove to her friend's Shama's house, who she trusted very much. Shama was shocked to see her at the door at that late hour of night.

"Come on in Mahima, please come inside."

She held Mahima by her hand and took her in the living room of her house. Nadir, her husband heard the noise and came out of the bedroom, half asleep, rubbing his eyes. Shama turned some lights on. Mahima could not hide her burning red face, swollen and puffy eyes, as if she had not slept in ages. Shama ran to the kitchen, filled a glass with cold water and offered it to her.

"Sit comfortably, put your feet up. Did you eat?"

Shama was concerned. She sat by Mahima's side on the couch, held her hands in between hers, in her best efforts to comfort her. Mahima's sobbing, gushing tears were enough to explain her humility Shama was puzzled, confused, unable to start any conversation with her, and also considerate.

"Did Ateet hit you?" She asked after a few moments.

In the midst of her sobbing Mahima told them the story of Ateet's infidelity.

"Mahima, you are not going back home. This is your house. You stay here and bring both the children." Shama was firm.

Nadir kept his usual silence. There was an absolute silence in the room for several minutes.

"You should go back home and I will talk to Ateet tomorrow morning."

After spending some time with Nadir and Shama she returned home. She had nothing to talk about—nothing to say to Ateet. She had come so far in her journey. She could not even think how far she would be able to go. She accepted deep down in her heart that her marriage was nearing an end.

The very next evening Ateet came home from work. She cooked dinner and all four sat together at the dinner table. After her daily routine of washing the dishes, tucking the children in their beds, whispering a little prayer into their ears, she stepped into her bedroom and shut the door tight behind her. Ateet was laying comfortably in the bed and watching TV. She walked around the bed and sat on the other side resting her head against the pillows. Perhaps, she wanted to test him one more time.

"What are you watching?" She asked politely.

"The news."

"I hope, you are not keeping any contact with Ana any more."

"No... no... not at all." He tried to be convincing.

That was a blunt denial with no shame, no guilt, no changing of face expression and no reflection of any guilt!

"Any email? Did she write to you or you?"

"No, Mahima, I said no! Stop being suspicious now. Didn't I give you a promise?" How tactfully he lied again.

And then, she failed. She failed to keep control on herself. She blasted, exploded again.

"So, six days in Delhi were spent with Ana. The only thing you did was treated her with a glass of juice."

"Mahima! I told you the truth. Those six days, I was with the agent looking for the houses for my brother. I took Ana out just once. Don't you trust me?"

He downplayed again. What a liar and player her own husband was. Not only that time, he may have been dishonest, may be all the time, always. She felt the most dumb, inferior, and stupid woman on this earth, being taken advantage of at each and every step of her married life, for so long.

"Who is this woman Asha?"

Ateet's innocent face expressions turned into a panic. Asha's name from Mahima's mouth shocked him. He was unprepared, unable to defend himself. She threw all the printed emails in front of him.

"Lies after lies… You are such a big liar, a player, worst I have ever seen in my life… I don't understand why you don't file a divorce."

"And listen to me for the last time. Never ever again… try to even touch me. For God's sake leave me alone…for ever." She blasted loud to be heard and got out of the room.

She had no strength to cope with her abusive, unfaithful, and infidel husband anymore. Private confrontations with her husband for years and years did not bring any resolution. She involved the family friends. Shama, Nadir with another elderly couple came to her house. The traditional Indian culture was not to even bring the word 'divorce' on your lips. Take the beatings from your husband, take his abuses, swallow the nasty foul language, keep tolerating whatever he does, keep watching him sleeping with the other women, but don't bring the word of 'divorce' on your lips.

Chapter 33
JUSTICE FOR MAHIMA

*H*er house appeared to be a court room with elders and close friends. She failed to hide the smoke coming from her burning heart. After so many years of marriage, that day, Ateet sat amongst them and the reality of his true color was about to be displayed. The face, which was only visible inside the closed door of their house, the face which crushed Mahima's soul, paralyzing her body was about to be shown. The real him who was responsible for making her body into a walking dead was about to be unveiled.

Mahima broke the hidden silence within her. She spoke and spoke firmly about how she was mistreated by her husband in the past several years and also about his adultery. She declared that she was ready to end that marriage. Ateet never in his dreams had assumed that Mahima could be courageous enough to consider the split and a divorce so seriously. He never had attended to her and her needs. He took her for granted and treated her like a piece of furniture in the house. He presumed that like other Indian traditional women, she would keep taking his abuses, and to preserve her integrity, she would not speak up or involve other people, especially the people in the circle of their close friends. Perhaps he speculated that under all circumstances, she would stay with him like the dirt of his feet and he will keep using her, torturing her to the point that she would suffocate and die.

Up until that day, Ateet had played the game of asking for forgiveness from Mahima only when he felt the need of it and only when he was caught, but that day the same game was played out in front of all the people surrounding him to convince them that he would never repeat those acts of vulgarity and he seemed ashamed. She was totally sick and tired of the games played by him over and over, again and again, and the dramas played to reconcile. An old friend of her Mamma was also among the people visiting that day. She and Mamma knew each other for a long time from the time of their youth. She held Mahima by her hand and took her in the privacy of her bedroom. The people sitting in the living room had one and only one intention and that was to save that marriage. In reality the institution of that marriage was broken and there was nothing left in that marriage to save.

"Beta, please sit here." The elderly friend of her Mamma, Mahima called 'aunty' requested her to sit on the bed and she also sat with her holding her hand in hers.

"Think about it. Would you be able to survive if you separate from him?"

A complex question with a fear of unknown was posed to her in a few simple words in such a critical phase of her journey. Mahima had no idea, no clue how to answer that question. Truly she did not have an answer to that question. She spoke with her shattered heart and sobbing voice.

"Aunty, I am very tired, very tired of my life. Ateet never treated me like a woman, a wife. He never considered me a part of him. What do you want aunty? Do you want me to keep watching him sleeping with other women and remain quiet." Mahima was unable to stop sobbing. She was broken into pieces.

"Listen to me very carefully, I am also a woman and understand your pain." Aunty continued.

"When your Mamma visited last time, she told me everything about you and Ateet. She was grieved. She saw your suffering with her own eyes. She saw his attitude towards you with her own eyes."

Aunty was talking and Mahima was listening. The room was filled up with Aunty's talking in her soft voice and Mahima's sobbing.

"Remember Mahima! Your Mamma spent a weekend with me before she left for India. That's when she shared a lot and she urged me to take care of you. She was hopeful. I am just like your mother, so listen to me my dear."

"Aunty! You are asking me to stay in this hell, knowing everything. I was thinking that you will pull me out of it."

"Your Mamma also urged me and asked me not to let your family fall apart. Her biggest concern was you and Sarah and Aaron." Aunty was firm.

"But Mamma only knew about his abuses, she had no idea of his unfaithfulness and adultery."

"I know Mahima, but didn't you see him? How remorseful was he? He was in tears and asking for forgiveness in front of all of us."

Ateet was successful in melting Aunty's and other peoples' hearts also.

"Oh! This act of this kind of forgiveness was played by him many many times before."

"But don't you see that this time he admitted his mistake and asked for forgiveness in front of so many. Beta all I am asking is to give him just one more chance." Aunty appealed and she could not stop her tears.

The fear of breaking up her family, the fear of uncertain future, the fear of unknown, and to top them all she had pressure from all the people sitting in her house. How unbearable! She felt like she was going mad.

Chapter 34
MAMMA'S SOLEMN DEPARTURE

*F*rom the very beginning Mahima was a person who could find pearls in a pile of rubbish. She always hoped for the best and kept a very positive attitude. Once more, Ateet was successful in convincing her that he did not have any sexual relations with any of those women and she was fooled again. Time kept creeping and fleeting simultaneously. In the beginning of January, she received a letter from her Mamma. About two months ago in November Mamma fell down and broke her hip bone. She tried to convince Mahima that it was a minor fracture and would heal in no time as the doctor said. The truth of the matter was that it was not minor, and it was a worrisome episode to have taken place at that stage of her Mamma's life. Mahima sensed that her Mamma was sicker than what she had reflected through her letter.*'I hope, Mamma is okay. I should immediately go and visit Mamma.'*

She arrived at her work in the morning, restless and unable to concentrate on anything. She must go home to see her Mamma—that was the only thought in her mind. With no uncertainty in her mind, she was convinced that her Mamma desired to see her youngest daughter. Without wasting any time she phoned her travel agent and made a reservation to travel a week later.

One week was too long to wait to see her mother and too short to shop a little bit and pack and prepare for an overseas trip. She made all the arrangements for her children and also called her brother to pick her up from the airport in Delhi. The preparations went smoothly and her flight arrived in the middle of the night at the New Delhi airport. Her brother drove five hours in the middle of the night to pick her up from the airport. It was obvious that he was exhausted. It was a cold and foggy night. The visibility on the road was very poor. Her Bhaiya had no heat in his car. Thoughtfully he carried a nice, thick, woolen blanket for her. She wrapped herself up from head to toe in that blanket with a little opening at the face to look around and to breathe.

Her brother always traveled well prepared. He had an empty thermos of consumed tea sitting on the back seat of the car.

"Would you like some hot tea Mahima?"

"Oh, Yes!" That's what she was probing for in that empty thermos.

He stopped the car at a *dhaba* (tea stall) by the road side, got a refill of hot *chai* in that thermos and carried it back to her. She sat nice and cozy wrapped into that thick woolen blanket. He handed the thermos to her. She barely and reluctantly pulled her hands out of the warm blanket and took the thermos.

"Great! Nice and hot."

She held the thermos tight in between her hands to get some warmth. Bhaiya started driving on the bumpy roads of New Delhi. She managed to pour the hot, steaming tea into the cups; handed one to her brother and poured one for her. The fresh brewed cup of hot tea and the wrapped around blanket were plenty to give her some relief and warmth against the chilling cold. The roads were quiet with no traffic whatsoever. Only the sleeping cows and goats were crowding the road sides of the villages they passed through and occasionally they were in the middle of the road. Some stray dogs also chased their car perhaps in a hope of getting some food. They drove through the night to the dawn. The rays of the sun started peeping through the dense fog little by little as they got closer to their home town. She kept chatting with Bhaiya to keep him awake while driving. Just a little more distance to arrive at their destination was left.

"Look, Mahima! Your friend's Pop's sugar mill." Bhaiya pointed to the right side of the street.

The bullock carts, the tractors with trolleys overfilled with sugar canes were lined up to enter into the main gate of the sugar mill. The workers on their bikes wrapped in their blankets with the monkey face mufflers on their heads were entering the gate at that time of the early dawn. The smoke coming out of the chimney of the mill mixed with the fog was spreading a distinct pungent aroma into the environment. That was the same sugar mill, Mahima toured on the inauguration ceremony thirty years ago with her best friend Anita, the daughter of a rich industrialist who was the owner of the sugar mill. Anita's house was right behind her college and she enjoyed several lunches of *daal-chaaval* (lentil with rice) or *roti-sabzi* (Indian bread with curried vegetables) at her house during their lunch hour. That brought back all the wonderful memories, when both the friends cooked their lunches together during the mid day break, skipped the classes and enjoyed watching movies in the local theater not too far from Anita's house. Mahima was aware that her friend Anita was also married and lived with her husband and children away from the city, but her parents lived in the same house in which they lived thirty years ago. That long time ago memory gave her an incentive to visit Anita's parents some time during her stay.

Mahima was in her dreams of those good old times and Bhaiya was focused on his driving. He could barely keep his eyes open to see the roads after a long day and night of driving and tiredness. The car came upon an old bridge made over the Ganges canal; only ten more miles to go. The village right after crossing the bridge seemed to be wide awake at that early hour of the day. The bullock carts were all loaded with *gur* (the patties and balls of brown condensed juice from sugar canes), spreading a sweet aroma, causing Mahima's salivary glands to water. The drivers of the bullock carts and the bullocks were all ready to go to the market place to sell the '*gur*' to the merchants. Inside of the small mud huts of the village, some families were still asleep or perhaps getting ready to start their day. The hens and the roosters were roaming around those huts to find some breakfast food and the street dogs were chasing them.

The last ten miles of the journey were the longest ten miles. Mahima was anxious to see her Mamma, to be in her arms. Two years ago, when she visited home with Ateet, Sarah and Aaron, Mamma was on her own, independent. At that time she walked with her *laathi* (stick) in the house and outside the house in the whole neighborhood. She kept a close eye on everybody, mending the house cleaning lady, noting if she swept and mopped the floors properly or not. She never did forget to count the clothes given to the laundry man and also when they were delivered back. She checked that they were properly washed, starched, ironed, and folded, and the laundry man did not damage or lose any of those. If her count did not match, that was not good news for the poor laundry man; he would not be able to escape. The same Mamma was now stuck to her bed. She was totally bed ridden, unable to move on her own and so dependent on others. How could that be?

They were driving through the military compound; the outskirts of the city. She was deep in the dreamland of her childhood. Just two streets to the right side of the road was her middle school. She recalled the beautiful view of her school from the main road, the building of the school surrounded by blooming green Asoka trees and the boundary wall, but not anymore. Those trees were replaced by shops and buildings; a drastic change, she observed.

The sun rays cutting through the fog, falling upon the beautiful trees and flowers, enhancing the glory of the morning, and the glistening droplets of the dew on the shrubs defined a beautiful dawn. The city began to awaken. The day to day routine activities started picking up. Just like years ago, the milkman was trying to awake the families by ringing his bicycle bell.

"Hurry up memsahib; I have so many houses to deliver the milk."

The same old newspaper man, appeared just a bit older with his face covered in a monkey cap, the newspapers hung on both sides of the handle bar was enjoying his morning bike ride and throwing the newspapers at his customer's houses. For the last several years he was the only designated newspaper distributor in that area of the town. Mahima's Pappa was his once upon a time faithful customer. The poor guy did not show any sign of tiredness even in that tender old age.

Before entering the compound where her Bhaiya and his family lived, they passed a little neighborhood almost like a little village. Mahima's enjoyed each and every glimpse of the land of her birth. She observed no changes in people's day to day activities. The women were pumping the water into their buckets from the public hand pumps, the owner of the corner 'thela' (portable store on wheels) was busy re-arranging his cigarettes, 'bidis' and 'paans' for his daily customers.

The car arrived at the gate of Bhaiya's house. His pet dog recognized Mahima and welcomed her by his friendly bark, wagging his tail and jumping on her. Without losing a moment, Mahima ran to her Mamma's bedroom. Mamma was partially asleep and trying to wake up.

"Come Beta, come to me."

Mamma's voice had no power like before, no command like before though it was sweet and gentle and soft. Mahima bent towards her Mamma, gave her a kiss and got a kiss from her. Mamma looked like a powerless lioness. She could not even sit up to hold her daughter in her arms. Mahima felt broken by looking at her Mamma and her fragile condition. Mamma rolled her fingers in her hair and lifted the blanket on one side inviting her to lay by her side. Just like before, in her childhood she always loved to sleep with her Mamma. Slowly and carefully she entered into the bed, under the warm blankets on Mamma's side and covered her up all the way to her face. Just like a long time ago she wrapped her right arm around her chest, but was unable to rest her leg on her legs. Mamma had a fractured hip. Her body heat and the warm thick blanket gave Mahima enough warmth to fall asleep after a long exhausting journey. Bhaiya and Bhaabi retreated to their room and Mahima slept like a baby with her mother.

When she woke up, the room was filled with shimmering sunlight coming through the open curtains and windows, warming up the cold room. Bhaabi was in the kitchen making breakfast tea and waiting to serve it to the family. Bhaiya, dead tired from his back and forth journey and losing a night's sleep was still in his room tucked in his comforter, asleep.

Mahima felt privileged to be with her mother, help her, and support her. Nothing was hidden from her Mamma. In her youth, her Mamma was her adviser. Mahima was determined to tell everything to her Mamma about Ateet and his other relationships, and the tension that was created in her house because of those. Both mother and daughter talked lying under the warm blankets. Mamma's eye sight was also weakening, but her other senses were sharp. She could sense her daughter's emotions by her voice.

"Beta, you worry too much. I am just fine and it is just a matter of days, my hip will be just fine and I will start walking again."

"Yes, Mamma, I know you will."

"How are the kids and Ateet?"

"They are well, very well."

"I know my dear, you are very strong. I know everything. You just be a good wife and all things will be just fine with you." Her voice was weak, but full of confidence and support.

"Maa, last time when you came to visit me in U.S., you said the same thing. Tell me Mamma—when? When will every thing be fine? Why do you keep giving me this false hope?" She failed to keep her emotions inside her. Tears started gushing from her both eyes.

"No, Beta, never lose hope. Have faith. Think about your two beautiful children. These other women business does not last for long, and don't even utter the word 'divorce'"

Mahima came prepared to tell her mother that her hopes were dead and deep inside her she knew that her marriage was ending. After hearing her mother's advice, she had no courage left in her to share the pain with her own mother knowing that her condition was deteriorating moment by moment. Two days later her Mamma was burning with a high fever and was rushed to a private clinic. She had to go through several poking of needles for several blood tests and was diagnosed with a serious infection in her body. Immediately she was admitted to the clinic and with no delay the antibiotics started infusing through her intravenous line to kill the infection. Mahima decided to stay with her in the clinic. She slept in her mamma's hospital room on a bench by the window. She gave her mother a nice hot oil massage in the mornings to strengthen her muscles and a sponge bath before breakfast, combed her hair into a bun, and made her up with some face creme and powder, and some shimmering lipstick on her thin naturally pinkish lips. Her mother was a beautiful eighty nine year old woman with a beautiful heart within her. Mahima sat in front of her mother, gazed upon her glorious face, and admired it. Every morning she read a chapter from the Bible for her Mamma and Mamma repeated her favorite verse,

"For I am the Lord your God, who upholds your right hand, who says to you, 'do not fear, I will help you.'"

Mamma repeated the verse over and over again and said a prayer. In her prayers, she asked,

"My Lord, please take me home or make me stand on my feet."

Her voice did not tremble. Her faith did not shake. There was no doubt that she was in excruciating and unbearable pain.

After her prayers, she sang hymns. How could she? How could she possibly sing in the midst of that pain and not shed a tear? The answer to the question was not easy for Mahima or any one else. Her mother in her ripe age came to that point of her life after a long journey, strong faith, everlasting hope, blessed by beautiful children, grand children and great-grand children. Fourteen years ago she was separated from her love, the love of her life, the man who loved her and supported her and never let her fall, always held her hand, never left her alone—not even for one night. She spent those fourteen years without her love and not even sighed once. Yes, if she could do that, she could also sing in the midst of her pain.

Mamma—all dressed up in a fresh gown, sat upright with her back resting on the head board of the hospital bed, waited for her breakfast. Bhaabi brought freshly cooked blended breakfast with a thermos full of hot tea, fed Mamma with her own hands and stayed with her all morning. During that time Mahima went home, took a bath, ate her breakfast, and then came back to the clinic. That was her routine for ten days during her stay in India. After spending ten days in the hospital, Mamma was discharged to go home. The doctor wrote her prescriptions with an advice to keep her at home and to give her a lot of love and attention. The advice was quite indicative of her state. Even on the medications, her condition kept deteriorating rapidly. Most of the time she appeared to be half asleep or in a deep dream. She was not alert any more. Mahima had to return back to her home in the United States.

Two weeks passed since Mahima returned from India. It was a Monday morning, a national holiday in the U.S. She did not have to get up early to go to work. Around 7 o'clock in the morning, she met her Mamma in her dream. Mamma came to her house. She was wearing a pure white soft sari. Her face was glorious reflecting an angelic glory. There were no signs of pain, worries or sadness. It appeared to be a healthy, happy, and a peaceful face.

"Mamma! You did not even inform me. What a surprise!" In her dream, Mahima was shocked to see her mother came to her house.

"Oh dear, I came to see you." Mamma replied in her sweetest, melodious voice.

"But, Maa, just two weeks ago, when I left you, you could not even get up from your bed. How did you fly such a long distance?" The conversation was taking place as if it was real, not in her dreams.

"Oh, dear Beta, the air-hostess was very nice. She helped me all the way." Mamma replied.

In her dream Mahima lifted up her Mamma's white sari.

"The swelling in your legs is also completely gone, all gone!"

"Isn't that a miracle Beta? Now I am absolutely fine, but very tired my dear, I just need some rest and don't you worry about anything."

And she walked to the guest room by herself, the room she stayed in before. She was not limping. She had no walking stick in her hand. She seemed to be absolutely independent. She needed rest after a long journey. As soon as she entered into her room, Mahima woke up from her dream.

Her body was trembling, perspiring; she was panting and was bemused. She rubbed her eyes and tried to open them wide to make sure that that was a dream, a real dream. She pulled her pillow and placed it up behind her back, sat there for a while and got herself together. *'I hope Mamma is fine, nothing happened to her.'* She was restless, anxious, overwhelmed.

Not before long, she picked up the phone and called her sister's house in India, where her Mamma was staying.

"Mamma left us about an hour ago."

Her Mamma died that morning. She had departed from this world leaving her memories alive forever. She affirmed to her youngest daughter Mahima that the world she went to was far away from pain and worries, the world of peace and rest where she will live forever.

A small piece of land just next to her father's grave was bought by Mamma after his death. Both her Mamma and Pappa are laying side by side and resting together in peace forever.

Chapter 35
DEATH OF A MARRIAGE

"*Never ever bring the word divorce on your lips...*"
"*Think about your beautiful children and their future...*"
"*Never let your family split...*"
"*Stay strong in all circumstances...*"

Those statements of strength, integrity, morality and courage by Mamma followed Mahima like a shadow day and night. Mamma's death was nothing to grieve about, not even mourning. It was not dying, but a beautiful occasion in the celebration of her life, a celebration of her eighty nine years on this earth. She was a successful woman, a warrior, a loved wife and a blessed mother of seven, with many, many grand children and great grand children. Her prayers during the last period of her journey were very indicative that she was ready for eternity and she was happy. Mahima was not able to be a part of her funeral, but she did not worry about that either as her Mamma herself came to say goodbye to her.

Mahima started working harder by putting some overtime hours including Saturdays. Half of all the house expenses were on her shoulders and the kids' school expenses with tuition payment was her responsibility too. Providing the best education for her children within her capacity became her priority. At that time Ateet and Ana's flirting was over or that's what she thought. Perhaps involving the family friends in their personal life helped them. Perhaps, he came to his senses and would remain so for the future, and that was her hope.

"Beta, Ateet will never do that again. He knows that all of us are involved now." Perhaps, her aunty was right.

Ateet kept his earned money in a separate account. He was still addicted to the stock market and did not have any savings for the kids' future and their college expenses. She must take some step to keep him away from that habit of day trading.

"I was thinking that both of us should merge our accounts and take care of the budget together."

She intimated her plans to him. He did not respond immediately, but showed his willingness that he would give the plan some more thought and he needed some time. She waited for a week and asked him again to start a joint account in his and her name together.

"I don't have much savings in my bank account." He conveyed his situation in all honesty though it was not a surprise to Mahima. She was prepared for that answer. She suspected it before but was very happy to see his honesty.

"That is okay, whatever you and I have in our accounts, we will keep in one bank and run our expenses together." She was firm. He seemed to resist the idea and Mahima understood the reasons of his hesitation.

"I do have some debt on my credit card also." He again declared in all honesty.

That was also expected and was not a surprise to her either. All she desired in all fairness was to have knowledge of his money, so he would not lose that in the stock market.

"Well! Whatever is done is done. We will get rid of that debt slowly but surely." She had no intentions of giving up.

He was in debt, a huge debt of several thousand dollars. That took a while to get rid off. The money lost in the stock market was lost and burnt, so it was better to forget about that. Both of them ran the budget together and the plan seemed to be successful. He stopped gambling in the stock market. A wave of happiness was felt in the house; a ray of hope was awakened in her heart.

Aaron finished his High School and gained admission into a local college. Mahima tried her best to erase all the bad memories of the past and started dreaming of a happy and new future again. Both of them started going to Church and other places together, playing tennis together and also going for the evening walks together like any other happy couple. The desires inside her started rejuvenating. A hope, a hope and the promise given by her Mamma "every thing will be just fine in time." seemed to be coming true. Perhaps that time did arrive and for a few months she felt like she was a wife.

A few months later, suddenly his behavior started changing again. His body language and attitude became brutal. Something was not right again and she sensed it. At times, when they were together in the car or at home, his cellular phone rang. He saw the incoming number and did not answer. He ignored it and that act of his was obvious that he was trying to hide something from her. She stayed silent and did not express her concerns.

The good days did not last for long. Ateet started avoiding eating dinner with the family. Every evening after coming back from his work, he went into the kitchen to make tea, took his cup upstairs in the bedroom and watched television. After a few minutes of rest, he freshened himself up, changed his clothes and without saying a word to her he exited the house. Every single day his return time was at 10PM. Without even changing his clothes or going upstairs, he entered into the home office and stayed on the computer with the doors shut until very late at night. If he saw Aaron on the computer at the time he entered in the house, he stepped out of the house with his mobile phone and did not return until midnight. And that was his set routine.

"The foundation of any relationship is trust."

That trust was broken several times in the past; nonetheless, for the last few months Mahima tried her best to bring that trust back and live a normal family life. She was at the stage of denial and was fooling herself by hoping that her husband's acts were only her suspicion—not reality. The fact of the matter was that her suspicion was nothing but a reality. The online statement of his mobile phone bill revealed his secrets. There were several pages of incoming and outgoing calls from his phone with two prominent numbers, long conversation times, day and night, non stop. She recognized one of the numbers, a woman's number who she knew, who was recently separated from her husband. The woman had two young children, who lived with their father as she did not want their custody and did not want to take any responsibilities associated with her children.

Taunting, threatening, scaring, dictating behavior took the toll again. He separated his bank account again without even telling Mahima, bought a new mobile plan with a different phone number in his name and withdrew from the family plan. He stopped talking with Mahima and strictly kept the pattern to leave the house after the evening cup of tea, staying out of the house until ten, on the computer afterward with the door closed until twelve midnight, and then quietly sneaking into the room to sleep. Mahima knew where the local woman lived. She drove to the parking lot of her house. His car was parked across the street and he was inside. Again, she had no choice but to face another bitter reality. She swallowed the anger and drove back home. She was frightened to talk to him about the matter. She was frightened that any confrontation may very well create a scene in the house in front of their young growing son.

It was a Friday in August. Every Friday Ateet worked from home. She came back from her work in the evening and he was not at home. Aaron relayed to her the message that his father went away for the weekend and will return on Sunday evening.

"I have found a doctor woman and now I will kick you out of the house." Those were his spoken words just a few days ago in the middle of the night.

He returned from his weekend trip late on Sunday evening. His face was blood red; the expressions of guilt were quite evident. He avoided any eye contact with her, ignored her as if she did not exist and walked to the fridge, took some food out, ate and left home immediately. Every evening of that week he stayed home. He did not go out and did not even go in the computer room.

Aaron was not at home. She found a perfect opportunity to talk to him. She took a deep breath, stayed strong, stayed bold and with no fear what-so-ever she spoke.

"Do you have to go somewhere today?" She had firmness in her voice.

"No." His eyes were glued on the TV.

She walked to the TV and turned it off. He did not protest. He prepared himself to face her that day.

"Where did you go last weekend?"

"Don't ever ask me that again." He raised his voice immediately; just like always, to suppress her, to put her down, to scare her, to threaten her, to make her keep quiet—his old tricks.

"I am talking to you and there is no need to raise your voice." No power or threat in this world could stop her talking to her husband.

"I flew to Florida with a friend from my work."

"You flew to Florida with a friend and you did not feel a need to tell Aaron or me?"

"To have fun or was it work related?" She continued.

"Oh no, not work related."

"Not work related, with a friend, you must have planned, must have made flight reservations, which takes time, and you never bothered to telling either the kids or me?"

Ateet had no answer to her questions.

"Why do you lie so much Ateet? If you want to maintain the marriage and stay together, at least tell the truth and try to save this marriage. Why do you treat me like I am stupid and assume that I will believe whatever story you come up with?" She suspected that he went away with the local woman with whom he had been spending every evening.

"You want to know the truth? I went to Florida to see this woman, I met online." He said it in a very simple way to his wife.

She took a deep breath, maintained her self-control. She was burning inside, but remained balanced.

"Really! So, did you get to meet with her?"

"This world is full of fake and deceitful people." He immediately tried to twist that sensitive issue into a joke, giggling and smiling.

She was eager to hear the rest of the story.

"Alas! The biggest deceitful person is standing right in front of my eyes." She spoke to herself and with her empty eyes, she waited to hear the next twist in his story and he continued.

"She emailed me the picture of her youth taken years and years ago. In reality, she was so fat and ugly looking. She met me for the dinner on Friday night. I felt obligated to dine with her, but nothing clicked. After the dinner she was on her way and I came back to my motel, end of the story."

How painful! How painful was the whole story for Mahima, to hear a story of a lustful affair of her husband with some other woman, which started on-line at some match making site! How easily he made a story and tried to fool her by saying that he did not get a chance to sleep with the other woman because she was fat and ugly! Mahima got out of control. Her face turned red like a mad woman. She pulled those phone statements and threw them in front of him.

"Did you have sex with these women?" She screamed on the top of her lungs.

He was not ready for that kind of question. He was shocked and gazed at her thinking how dare did she ask that question from him. After a deafening silence for several seconds, she screamed louder.

"I am asking you again. Did you have sex with these women?"

He had no words to speak. He shook his head and the answer to the question was 'yes'. Then he came closer to Mahima and grabbed her hand.

"I have committed this sin."

And she pulled her hand out of his.

Every evening, he had been going to that local woman, had been picking her up from her house to go to the pubs to dance with her and take her out for dinner, drinking with her at her house, sleeping with her. After ten at night, his routine was to talk to the woman in Florida by phone or on line. He stayed three nights with that woman in Florida and slept with her. No one knew how many more women he was involved with. After years of hoping in a state of feeling hopeless; try to believe despite her disbelief, she finally became void of both hope and belief…and with that, a marriage of twenty four years was dissolved. For Mahima there was no turning back.

Epilogue

"And a marriage of twenty four years was dissolved." Thus ended this phase of Mahima's journey. One could change the number of years and this statement is repeated *ad infinitum* in our society as thousands of marriages dissolve daily. Marriages end, but why they end and the circumstances that lead to the ending are what form the narrative of pain and brokenness. Mahima's story invites the reader to ponder on the nature and meaning of marriage and indeed relationships. When is a marriage not a marriage? Is it the case that the ceremony and rituals constitute a marriage? Is love the essential foundation of marriage? Trust? Commitment? Promise of fidelity? Mutuality? Companionship and partnership? Loyalty?

Societal conventions dictate that marriage is an institution whereby a man and a woman are joined in a special kind of social and legal dependence for the purpose of maintaining a family, an intimate union, and a nurturing of each other in mutual affection and love. With this general template, were Ateet and Mahima united in marriage? Was their marriage structured around the word 'institution'? Was their family maintained? Was there any true intimacy between them? The answers to these questions in general is 'no', and given this how could one speak of the end of a 'marriage'? In truth what Ateet and Mahima had was but a shell without the substance of a marriage. For twenty four years they resided under the same roof and for a major portion of that time, Mahima simply survived.

Even though the term "marriage" might have something of a universal usage, nonetheless the manner in which it is understood and embraced ranges widely. So when the narrative concludes with the dissolution of a marriage, the word "marriage" itself has refused to leave me. I am left with a state of persistent wondering about the meaning of the word. One of the many challenges in seeking to ascertain a deep and lasting meaning has to do with the very common and casual use of the word. The word is used with the fundamental presupposition that everyone knows what it means and has shared, and common beliefs about it. But of course that is simply not the case. Mahima's story surely will resonate with many, across religion, culture, race, nationality and ethnicity.

Longevity in marriage is a noble ideal, even as two persons make commitments to spend their lives together united as one until death parts them, but longevity in marriage at all cost is neither noble nor desirable. Mahima's twenty four years of angst, pain and abuse in the context of marriage attests to this.

Mahima's dreams, her hopes and aspirations from early childhood were pursued with singular determination, and she traveled a long journey in reaching the goals she set for herself. With all of the hills and valleys, straightaways and blind corners of every journey, she persisted. She never believed in traditional arranged marriages as was customary in her family and the larger society of her birth. Instead she dreamed of a 'Raja', who would take her away. That was a dream, not a Prince Charming, with whom she would mystically live happily ever after, but a 'Raja', who would believe in mutual love, respect, honesty, one who would embrace the uniqueness of who she was. This particular dream was never realized; indeed it died before it had a chance to blossom.

The reality is that those twenty four years of life, her identity was crushed and in the process lost herself; she found herself in the wilderness. As was the case in biblical times, even the wilderness was a refuge, a source of blessing and promise, a place of new beginnings; so also it was for Mahima. The greatest blessings of her wilderness experience were her two beautiful children, whom she loves with the deepest maternal love. It was that wilderness, where she experienced rejection that also helped define for her the meaning of acceptance and belonging. Certainly there were many moments of despair, hopelessness and anguish, and yet, the very hope that she felt was borne out of these moments. In those times of uncertainty, she recalled the promise she read in her writing, "When you go through trials and pain in your life, you may think like your life is a mess. You may wonder why God is allowing such things to happen in your life. But remember, God is working in your life, to make you a blessing to others. You will be thrilled when He shows you the plan that He has been working for you and you will not cease thanking Him all your life."

Mahima's strength of character and her personal faith were truly remarkable. The rocky roads on her path failed to cause any permanent damage in her life. She lived each day of her life in a hope for a better tomorrow, a better future, both for her and her children. And today she lives a joyous life. Like Mahima, her children set their goals, travel wisely, and they too dare to dream dreams as their mother once did.

"Give light, and the darkness will disappear."

Glossary

Beta	Affectionate term for "my child"
Bhaabi	Brother's wife
Bhaiya	Brother
Chaaval	Rice
Chawkidar	Gate Keeper
Daal	Indian lentils
Dada	Paternal Grandfather
Dadi	Paternal Grandmother
Didi	Elder sister
Dupatta	Scarf
Gobhi	Cauliflower
Gudda	A little boy
Gulli-Dandaa	Authentic Indian game
Gur	Flat cakes and balls of brown sugar
Halva	A sweet dish
Jijaji	Sister's husband
Laathi	Walking stick
Nana	Maternal Grandfather
Nani	Maternal Grandmother
Paraatha	Fried flat bread
Poori	Deep fried bread
Roti	Indian bread
Sabzi	Vegetables
Salvaar-Kurtaa	Indian costume
Takhti	A wooden flat slab polished with clay

)